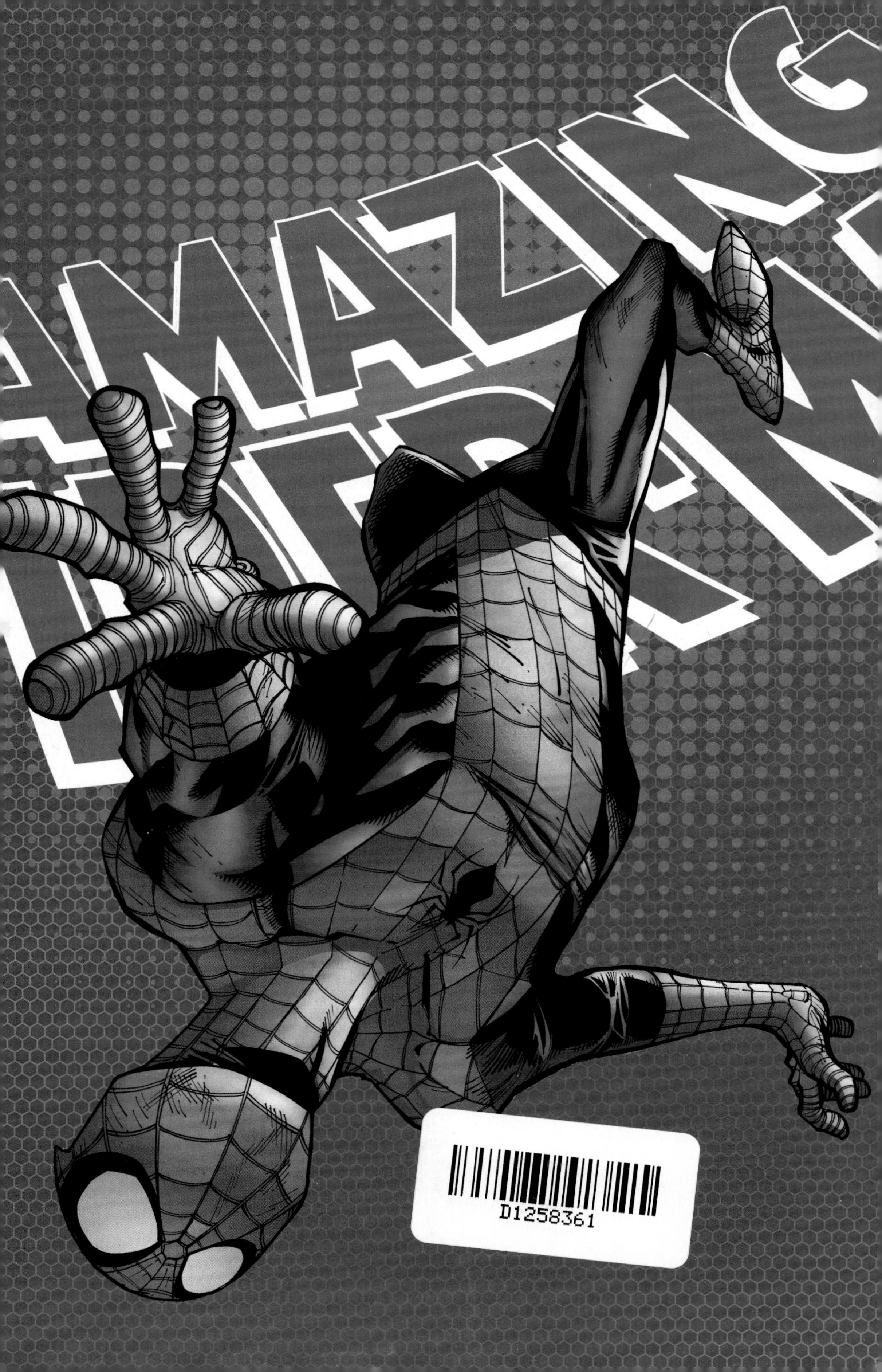
AMAZING

Did you hear? Everything is back to normal for Peter Parker. He's back together with Spider-Man after being split in a freak lab accident. He's also back together with Mary Jane (though not in the same way), and things are going great. He's even back together with former roommate Randy Robertson (in a different way from the previous two things), and it's going great...if you ignore their other roommate, Fred Myers, A.K.A. the criminal Boomerang. Come to think of it, I guess everything ISN'T normal, since the Kingpin is still mayor of New York City and Kraven the Hunter (with help from Black Ant and Taskmaster) is up to something strange that isn't just hunting Spider-Man. But apart from that, things are totally status quo, and Spider-Man's villains have all been dealt with and won't be a problem for the foreseeable future.

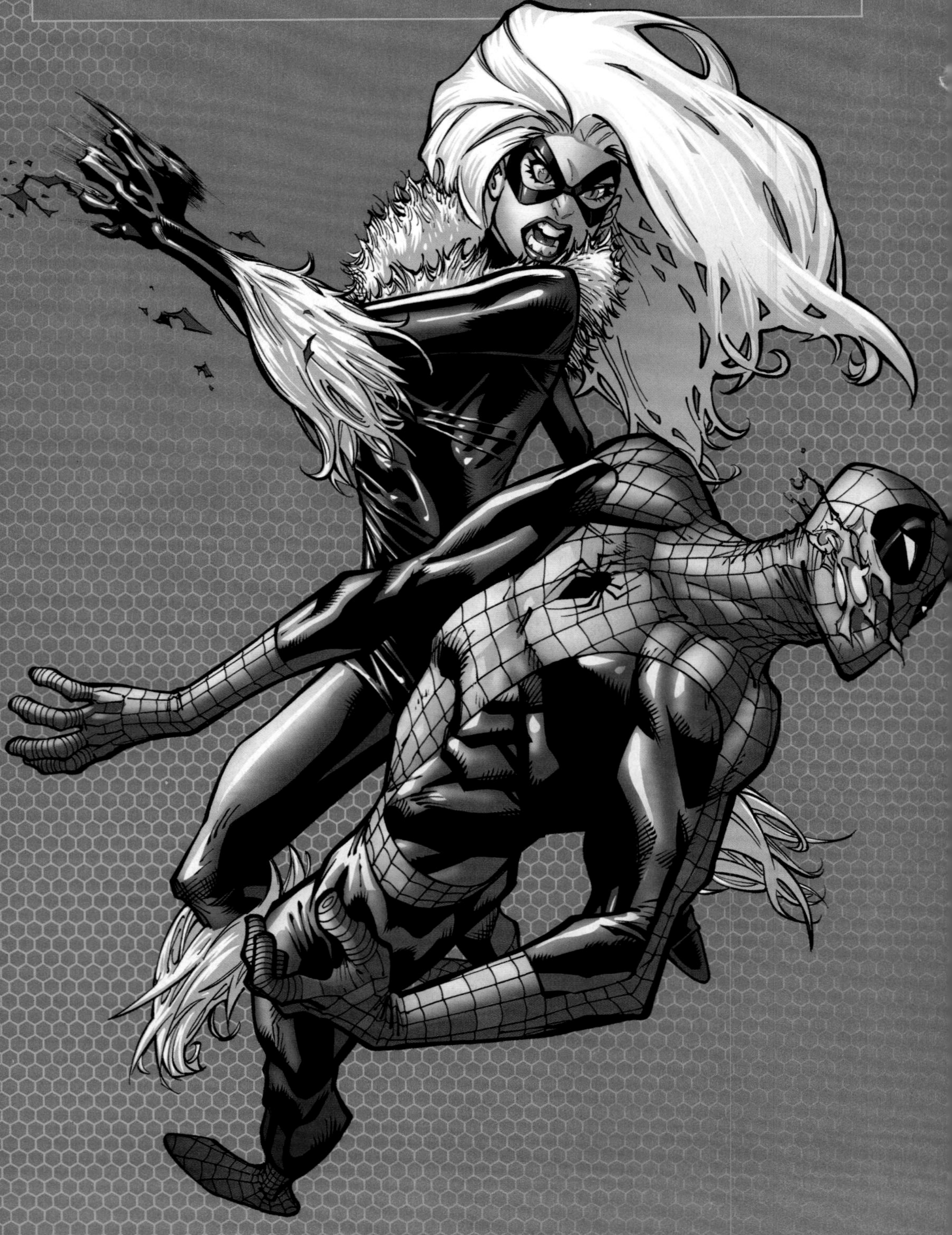

THE AMAZING SPIDER-MAN

FRIENDS AND FOES

WRITER **NICK SPENCER**

PENCILERS **HUMBERTO RAMOS**
WITH **STEVE LIEBER** (#6-7)
& **MICHELE BANDINI** (#9-10)

INKERS **VICTOR OLAZABA**
WITH **STEVE LIEBER** (#6-7)
& **MICHELE BANDINI** (#9-10)

COLORISTS **EDGAR DELGADO**
WITH **RACHELLE ROSENBERG** (#6-7)
& **ERICK ARCINIEGA** (#9-10)

LETTERER **VC's JOE CARAMAGNA**
COVER ART **HUMBERTO RAMOS & EDGAR DELGADO**
ASSISTANT EDITOR **KATHLEEN WISNESKI**
EDITOR **NICK LOWE**
SPECIAL THANKS **ANTONIO RUIZ**

SPIDER-MAN CREATED BY STAN LEE & STEVE DITKO

COLLECTION EDITOR **JENNIFER GRÜNWALD** • ASSISTANT EDITOR **CAITLIN O'CONNELL** • ASSOCIATE MANAGING EDITOR **KATERI WOODY**
EDITOR, SPECIAL PROJECTS **MARK D. BEAZLEY** • VP PRODUCTION & SPECIAL PROJECTS **JEFF YOUNGQUIST**
SVP PRINT, SALES & MARKETING **DAVID GABRIEL** • BOOK DESIGNER **JAY BOWEN**

EDITOR IN CHIEF **C.B. CEBULSKI** • CHIEF CREATIVE OFFICER **JOE QUESADA**
PRESIDENT **DAN BUCKLEY** • EXECUTIVE PRODUCER **ALAN FINE**

AMAZING SPIDER-MAN BY NICK SPENCER VOL. 2: FRIENDS AND FOES. Contains material originally published in magazine form as AMAZING SPIDER-MAN #6-10. First printing 2018. ISBN 978-1-302-91232-1. Published by MARVEL WORLDWIDE, INC., a subsidiary of MARVEL ENTERTAINMENT, LLC. OFFICE OF PUBLICATION: 135 West 50th Street, New York, NY 10020. **Printed in Canada.** DAN BUCKLEY, President, Marvel Entertainment; JOHN NEE, Publisher; JOE QUESADA, Chief Creative Officer; TOM BREVOORT, SVP of Publishing; DAVID BOGART, SVP of Business Affairs & Operations, Publishing & Partnership; DAVID GABRIEL, SVP of Sales & Marketing, Publishing; JEFF YOUNGQUIST, VP of Production & Special Projects; DAN CARR, Executive Director of Publishing Technology; ALEX MORALES, Director of Publishing Operations; DAN EDINGTON, Managing Editor; SUSAN CRESPI, Production Manager; STAN LEE, Chairman Emeritus. For information regarding advertising in Marvel Comics or on Marvel.com, please contact Vit DeBellis, Custom Solutions & Integrated Advertising Manager, at vdebellis@marvel.com. For Marvel subscription inquiries, please call 888-511-5480. **Manufactured between 12/14/2018 and 1/29/2019 by SOLISCO PRINTERS, SCOTT, QC, CANADA.**

10 9 8 7 6 5 4 3 2 1

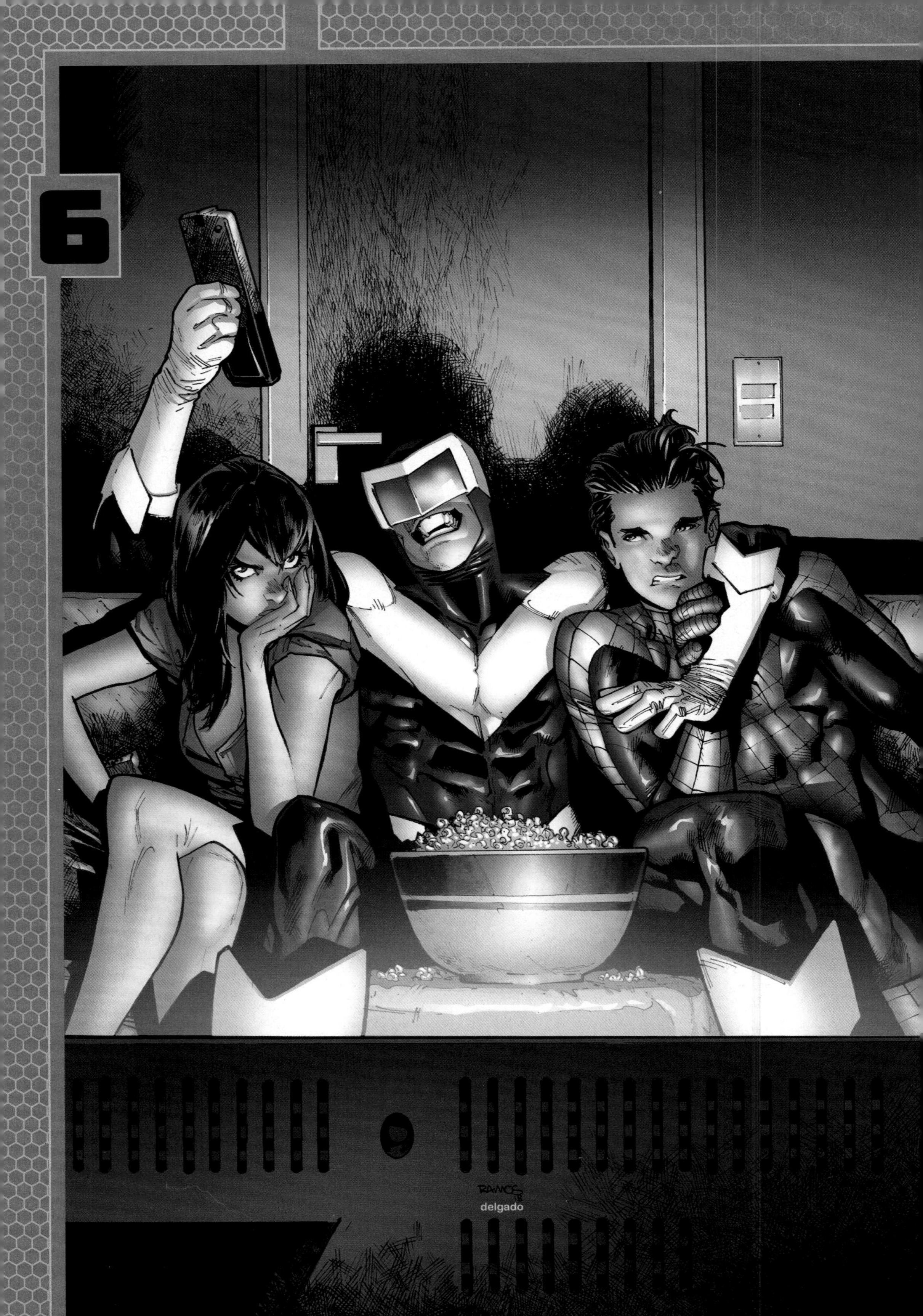
6
RAMOS '18
delgado

A TRIVIAL PURSUIT PART 1

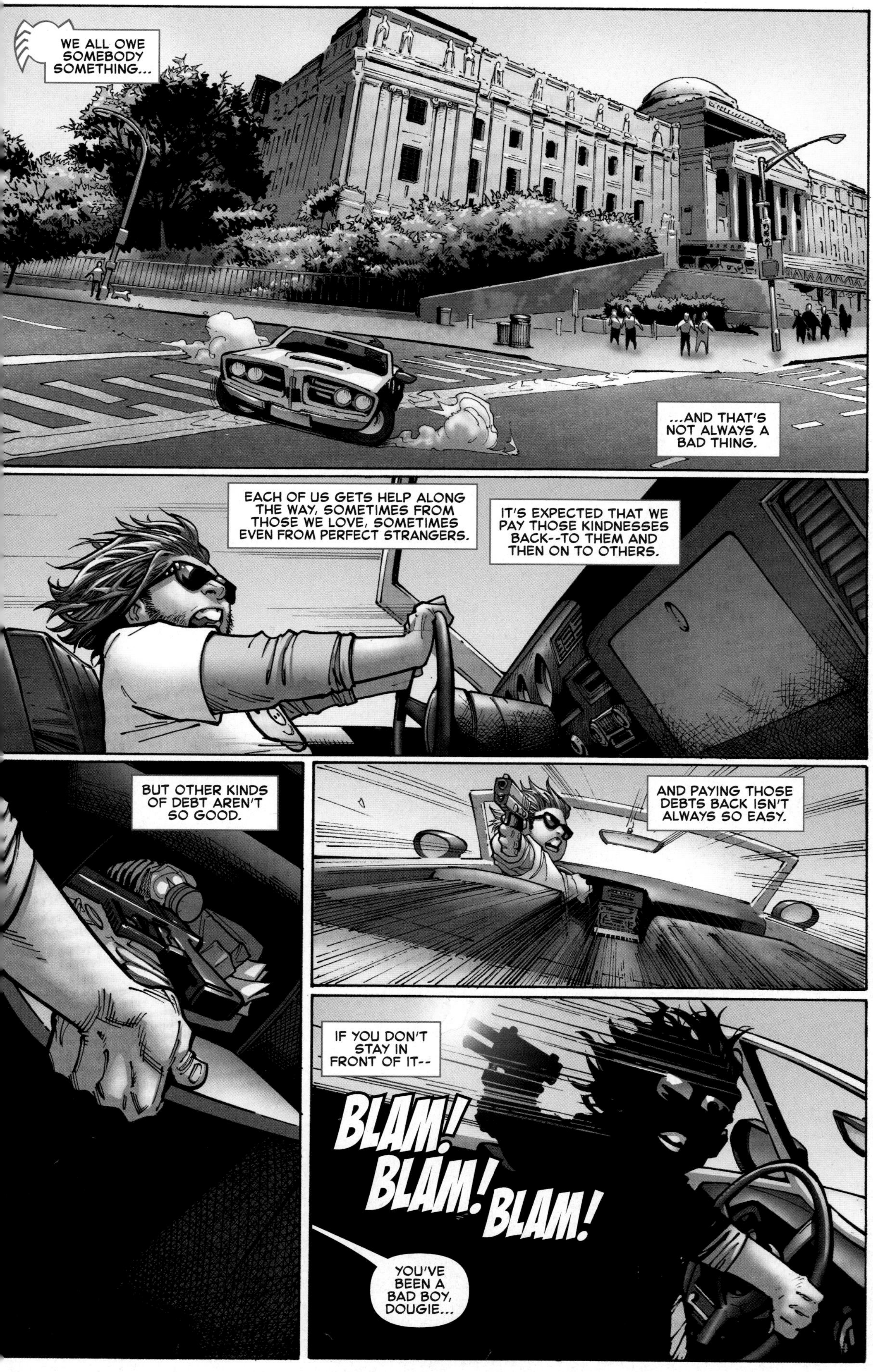
WE ALL OWE SOMEBODY SOMETHING...
...AND THAT'S NOT ALWAYS A BAD THING.
EACH OF US GETS HELP ALONG THE WAY, SOMETIMES FROM THOSE WE LOVE, SOMETIMES EVEN FROM PERFECT STRANGERS.
IT'S EXPECTED THAT WE PAY THOSE KINDNESSES BACK--TO THEM AND THEN ON TO OTHERS.
BUT OTHER KINDS OF DEBT AREN'T SO GOOD.
AND PAYING THOSE DEBTS BACK ISN'T ALWAYS SO EASY.
IF YOU DON'T STAY IN FRONT OF IT--
BLAM! BLAM! BLAM!
YOU'VE BEEN A BAD BOY, DOUGIE...

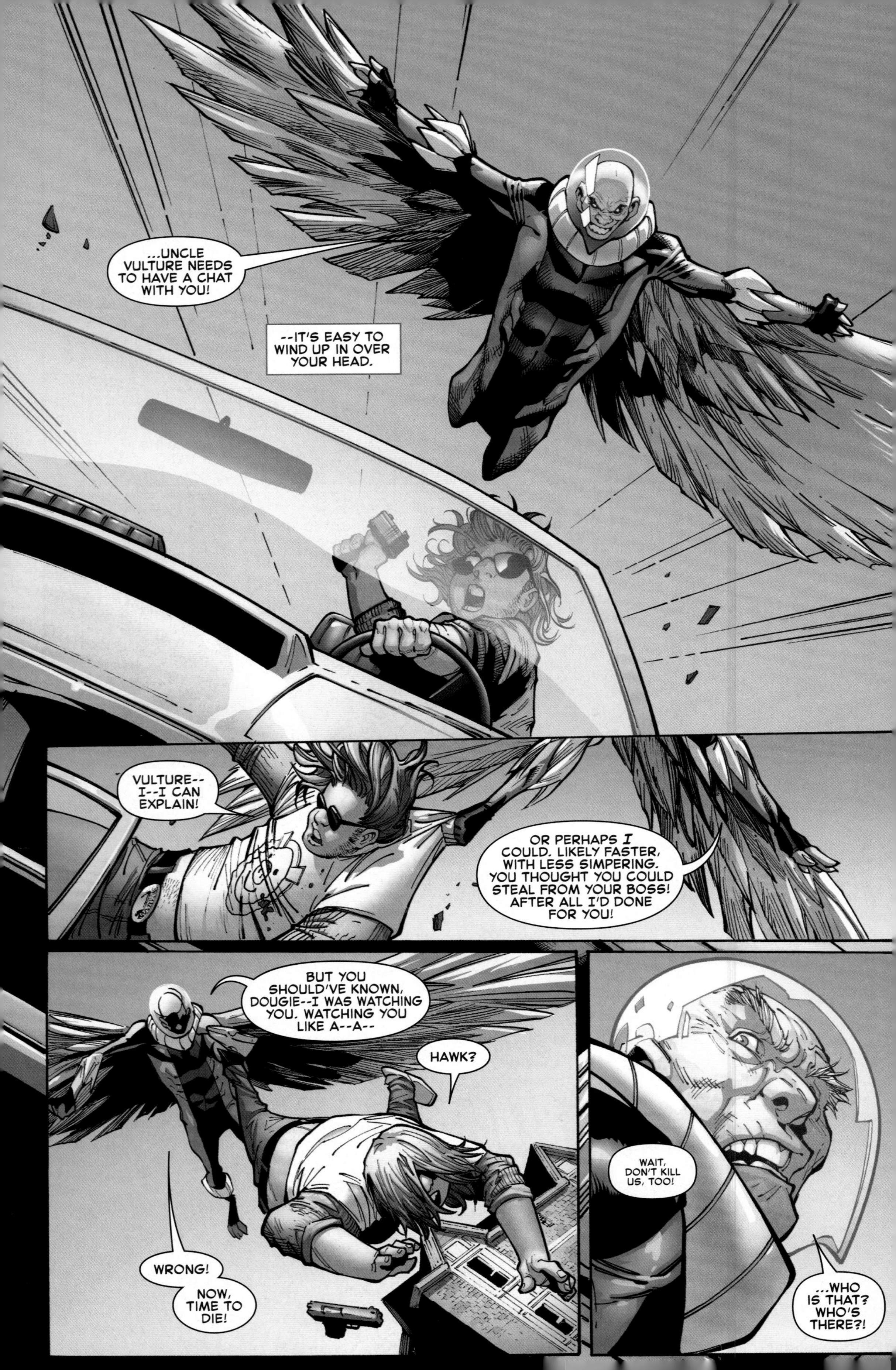
...UNCLE VULTURE NEEDS TO HAVE A CHAT WITH YOU!
--IT'S EASY TO WIND UP IN OVER YOUR HEAD.
VULTURE-- I--I CAN EXPLAIN!
OR PERHAPS I COULD. LIKELY FASTER, WITH LESS SIMPERING. YOU THOUGHT YOU COULD STEAL FROM YOUR BOSS! AFTER ALL I'D DONE FOR YOU!
BUT YOU SHOULD'VE KNOWN, DOUGIE--I WAS WATCHING YOU. WATCHING YOU LIKE A--A--
HAWK?
WRONG!
NOW, TIME TO DIE!
WAIT, DON'T KILL US, TOO!
...WHO IS THAT? WHO'S THERE?!

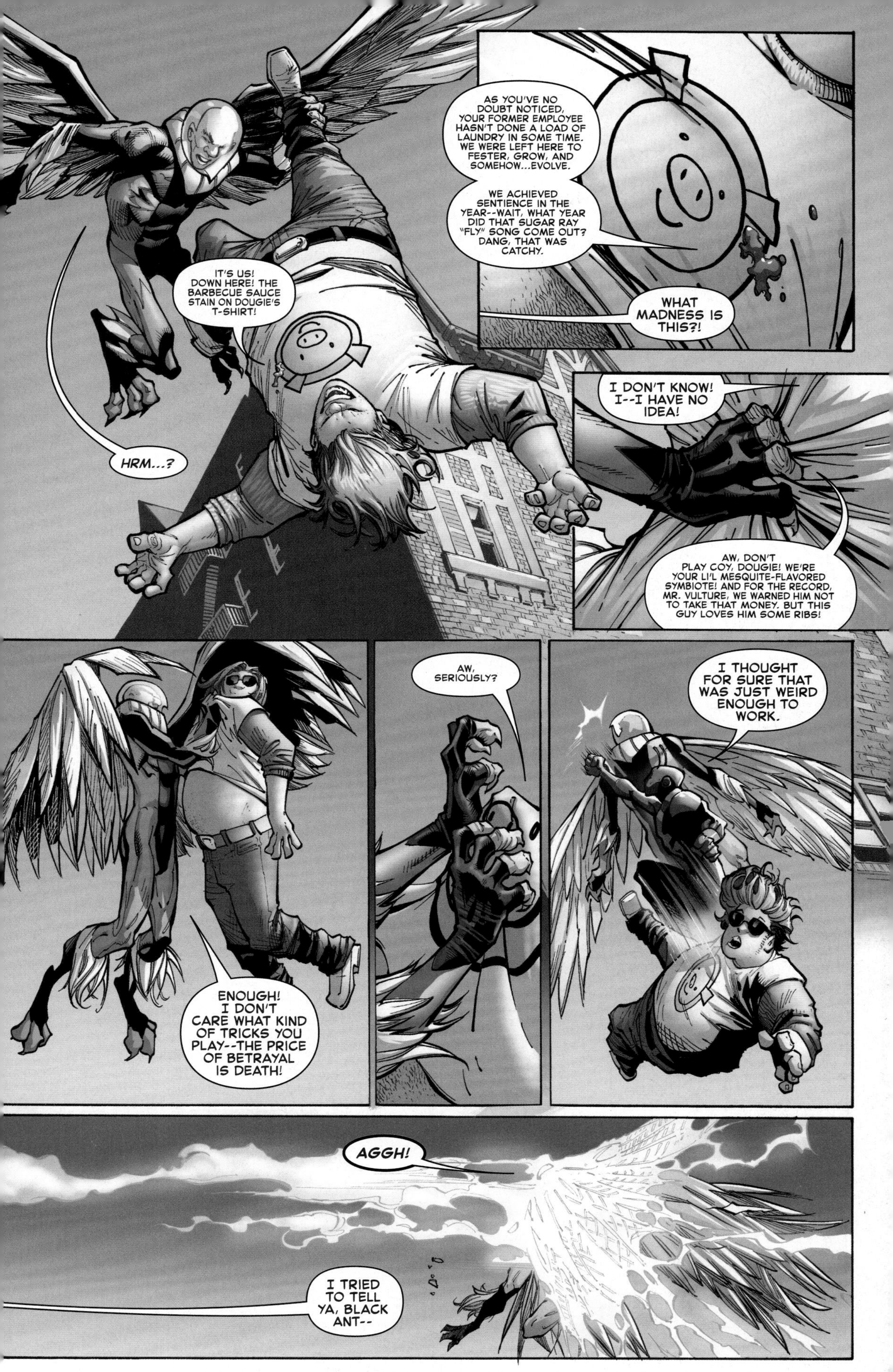
AS YOU'VE NO DOUBT NOTICED, YOUR FORMER EMPLOYEE HASN'T DONE A LOAD OF LAUNDRY IN SOME TIME. WE WERE LEFT HERE TO FESTER, GROW, AND SOMEHOW...EVOLVE.
WE ACHIEVED SENTIENCE IN THE YEAR--WAIT, WHAT YEAR DID THAT SUGAR RAY "FLY" SONG COME OUT? DANG, THAT WAS CATCHY.
IT'S US! DOWN HERE! THE BARBECUE SAUCE STAIN ON DOUGIE'S T-SHIRT!
WHAT MADNESS IS THIS?!
HRM...?
I DON'T KNOW! I--I HAVE NO IDEA!
AW, DON'T PLAY COY, DOUGIE! WE'RE YOUR LI'L MESQUITE-FLAVORED SYMBIOTE! AND FOR THE RECORD, MR. VULTURE, WE WARNED HIM NOT TO TAKE THAT MONEY. BUT THIS GUY LOVES HIM SOME RIBS!
ENOUGH! I DON'T CARE WHAT KIND OF TRICKS YOU PLAY--THE PRICE OF BETRAYAL IS DEATH!
AW, SERIOUSLY?
I THOUGHT FOR SURE THAT WAS JUST WEIRD ENOUGH TO WORK.
AGGH!
I TRIED TO TELL YA, BLACK ANT--

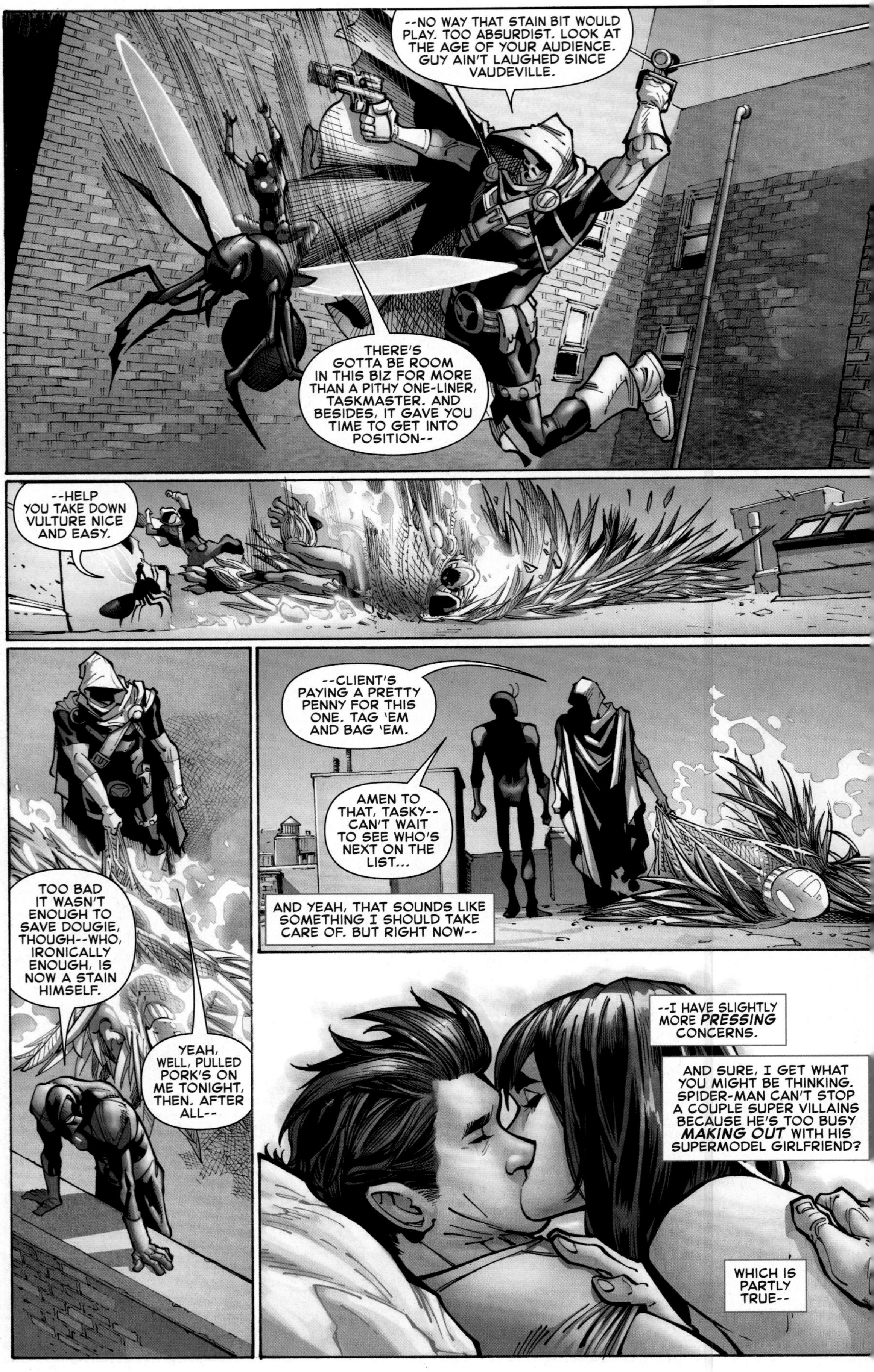
--NO WAY THAT STAIN BIT WOULD PLAY. TOO ABSURDIST. LOOK AT THE AGE OF YOUR AUDIENCE. GUY AIN'T LAUGHED SINCE VAUDEVILLE.
THERE'S GOTTA BE ROOM IN THIS BIZ FOR MORE THAN A PITHY ONE-LINER, TASKMASTER. AND BESIDES, IT GAVE YOU TIME TO GET INTO POSITION--
--HELP YOU TAKE DOWN VULTURE NICE AND EASY.
--CLIENT'S PAYING A PRETTY PENNY FOR THIS ONE. TAG 'EM AND BAG 'EM.
AMEN TO THAT, TASKY--CAN'T WAIT TO SEE WHO'S NEXT ON THE LIST...
AND YEAH, THAT SOUNDS LIKE SOMETHING I SHOULD TAKE CARE OF. BUT RIGHT NOW--
TOO BAD IT WASN'T ENOUGH TO SAVE DOUGIE, THOUGH--WHO, IRONICALLY ENOUGH, IS NOW A STAIN HIMSELF.
YEAH, WELL, PULLED PORK'S ON ME TONIGHT, THEN. AFTER ALL--
--I HAVE SLIGHTLY MORE PRESSING CONCERNS.
AND SURE, I GET WHAT YOU MIGHT BE THINKING. SPIDER-MAN CAN'T STOP A COUPLE SUPER VILLAINS BECAUSE HE'S TOO BUSY MAKING OUT WITH HIS SUPERMODEL GIRLFRIEND?
WHICH IS PARTLY TRUE--

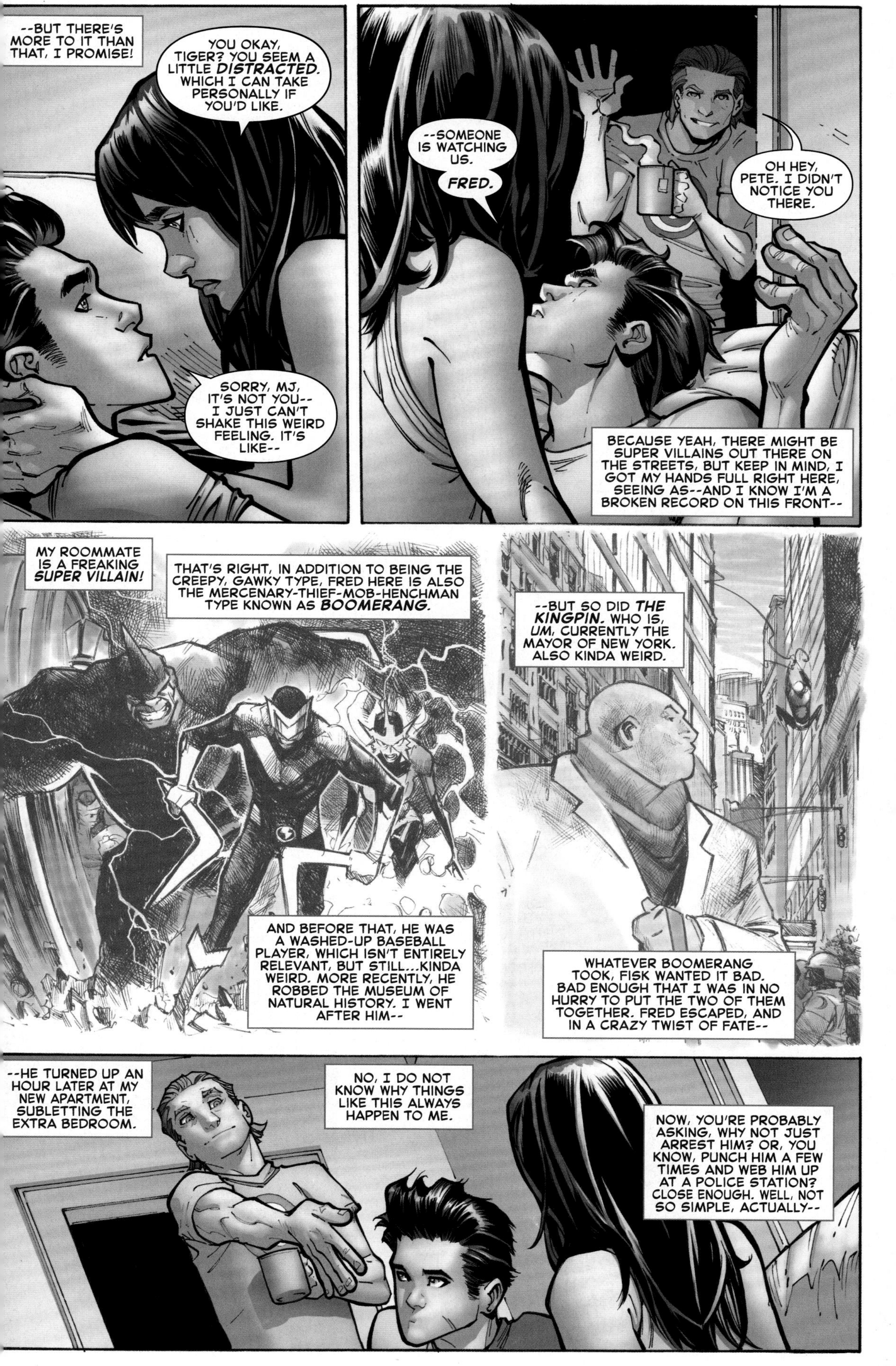
--BUT THERE'S MORE TO IT THAN THAT, I PROMISE!
YOU OKAY, TIGER? YOU SEEM A LITTLE DISTRACTED. WHICH I CAN TAKE PERSONALLY IF YOU'D LIKE.
SORRY, MJ, IT'S NOT YOU-- I JUST CAN'T SHAKE THIS WEIRD FEELING. IT'S LIKE--
--SOMEONE IS WATCHING US.
FRED.
OH HEY, PETE. I DIDN'T NOTICE YOU THERE.
BECAUSE YEAH, THERE MIGHT BE SUPER VILLAINS OUT THERE ON THE STREETS, BUT KEEP IN MIND, I GOT MY HANDS FULL RIGHT HERE, SEEING AS--AND I KNOW I'M A BROKEN RECORD ON THIS FRONT--
MY ROOMMATE IS A FREAKING SUPER VILLAIN!
THAT'S RIGHT, IN ADDITION TO BEING THE CREEPY, GAWKY TYPE, FRED HERE IS ALSO THE MERCENARY-THIEF-MOB-HENCHMAN TYPE KNOWN AS BOOMERANG.
AND BEFORE THAT, HE WAS A WASHED-UP BASEBALL PLAYER, WHICH ISN'T ENTIRELY RELEVANT, BUT STILL...KINDA WEIRD. MORE RECENTLY, HE ROBBED THE MUSEUM OF NATURAL HISTORY. I WENT AFTER HIM--
--BUT SO DID THE KINGPIN. WHO IS, UM, CURRENTLY THE MAYOR OF NEW YORK. ALSO KINDA WEIRD.
WHATEVER BOOMERANG TOOK, FISK WANTED IT BAD. BAD ENOUGH THAT I WAS IN NO HURRY TO PUT THE TWO OF THEM TOGETHER. FRED ESCAPED, AND IN A CRAZY TWIST OF FATE--
--HE TURNED UP AN HOUR LATER AT MY NEW APARTMENT, SUBLETTING THE EXTRA BEDROOM.
NO, I DO NOT KNOW WHY THINGS LIKE THIS ALWAYS HAPPEN TO ME.
NOW, YOU'RE PROBABLY ASKING, WHY NOT JUST ARREST HIM? OR, YOU KNOW, PUNCH HIM A FEW TIMES AND WEB HIM UP AT A POLICE STATION? CLOSE ENOUGH. WELL, NOT SO SIMPLE, ACTUALLY--

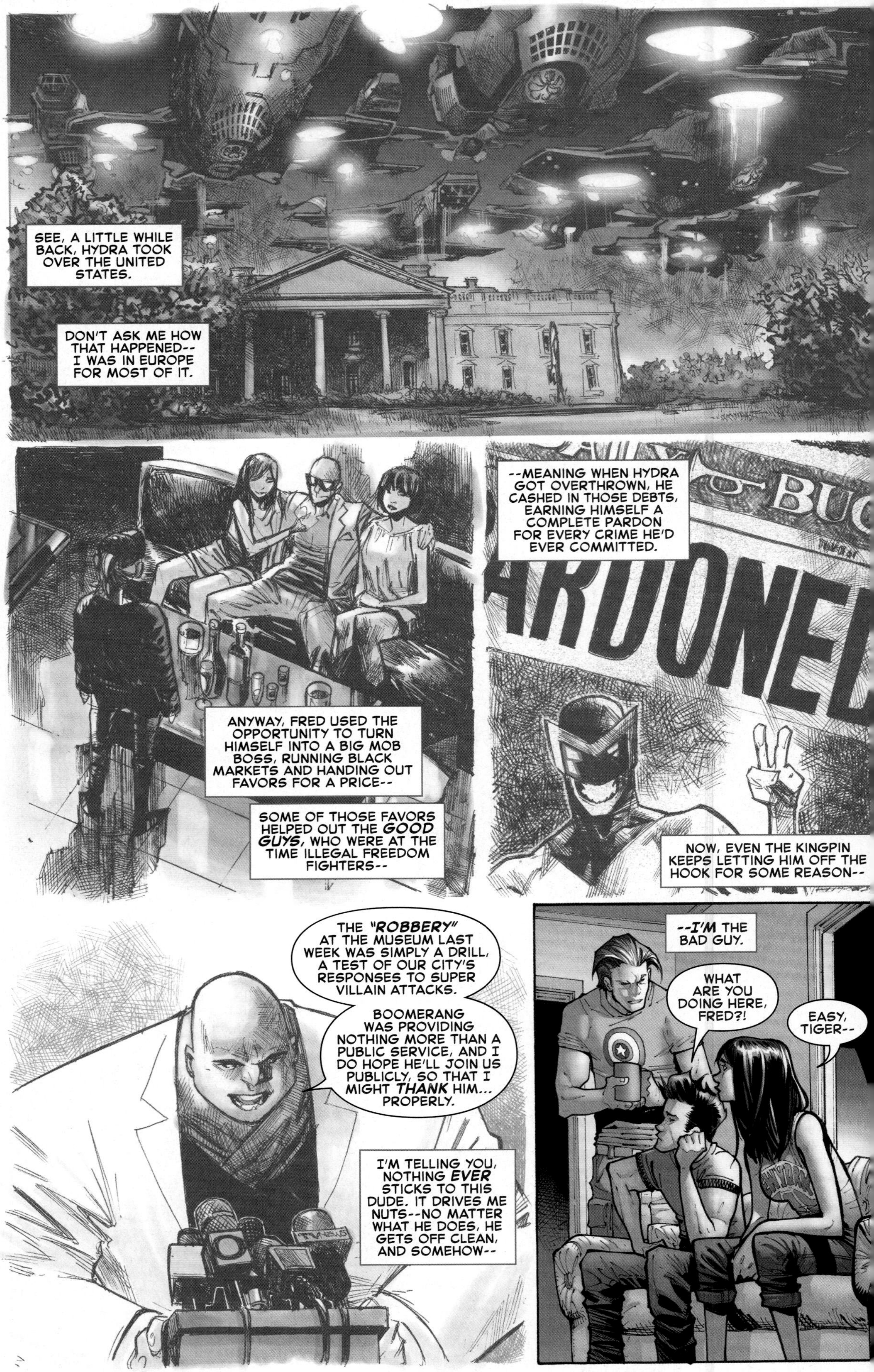
SEE, A LITTLE WHILE BACK, HYDRA TOOK OVER THE UNITED STATES.
DON'T ASK ME HOW THAT HAPPENED-- I WAS IN EUROPE FOR MOST OF IT.
ANYWAY, FRED USED THE OPPORTUNITY TO TURN HIMSELF INTO A BIG MOB BOSS, RUNNING BLACK MARKETS AND HANDING OUT FAVORS FOR A PRICE--
SOME OF THOSE FAVORS HELPED OUT THE GOOD GUYS, WHO WERE AT THE TIME ILLEGAL FREEDOM FIGHTERS--
--MEANING WHEN HYDRA GOT OVERTHROWN, HE CASHED IN THOSE DEBTS, EARNING HIMSELF A COMPLETE PARDON FOR EVERY CRIME HE'D EVER COMMITTED.
BUG
ARDONED
NOW, EVEN THE KINGPIN KEEPS LETTING HIM OFF THE HOOK FOR SOME REASON--
THE "ROBBERY" AT THE MUSEUM LAST WEEK WAS SIMPLY A DRILL, A TEST OF OUR CITY'S RESPONSES TO SUPER VILLAIN ATTACKS.
BOOMERANG WAS PROVIDING NOTHING MORE THAN A PUBLIC SERVICE, AND I DO HOPE HE'LL JOIN US PUBLICLY, SO THAT I MIGHT THANK HIM... PROPERLY.
I'M TELLING YOU, NOTHING EVER STICKS TO THIS DUDE. IT DRIVES ME NUTS--NO MATTER WHAT HE DOES, HE GETS OFF CLEAN, AND SOMEHOW--
--I'M THE BAD GUY.
WHAT ARE YOU DOING HERE, FRED?!
EASY, TIGER--

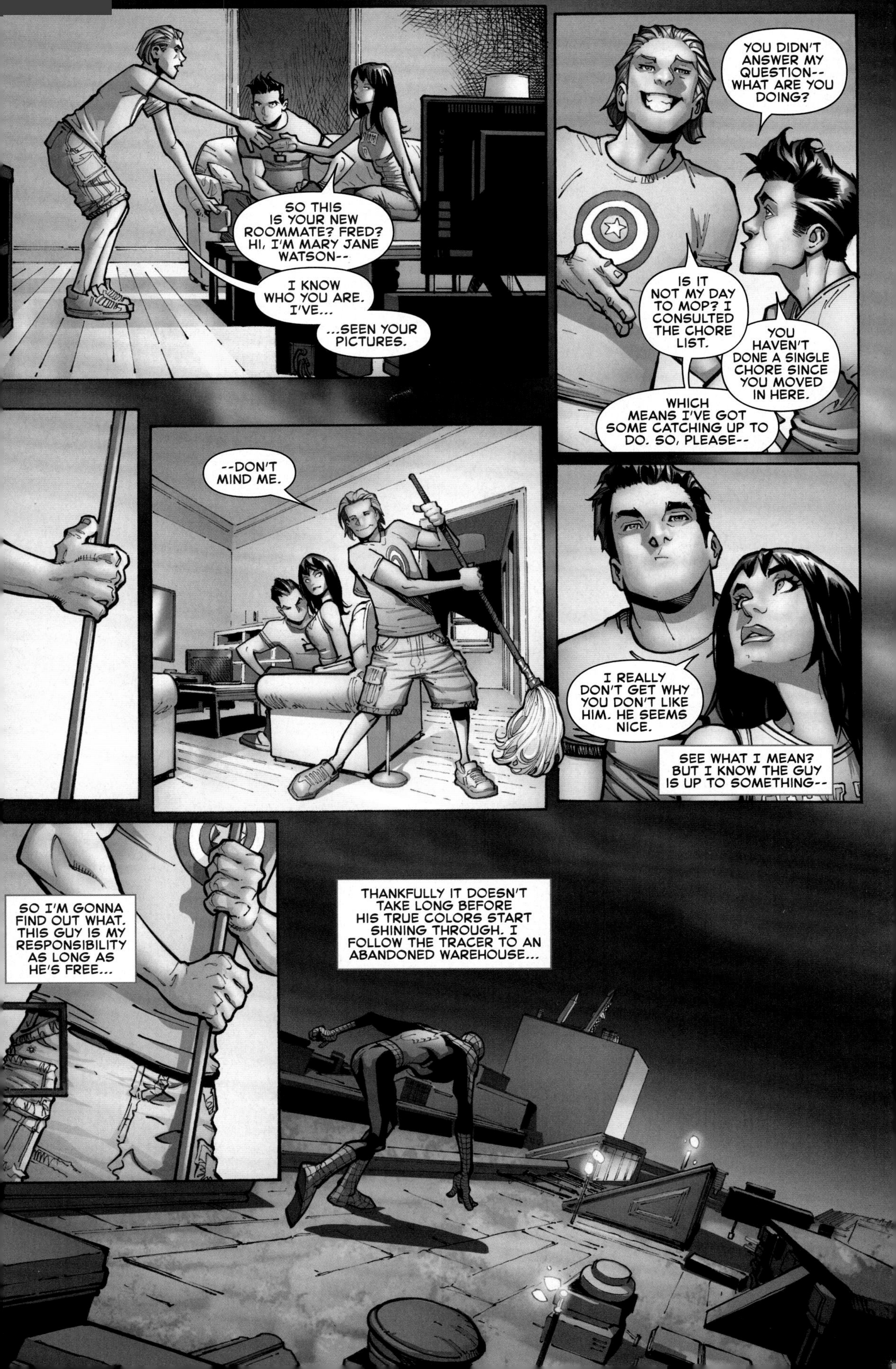
SO THIS IS YOUR NEW ROOMMATE? FRED? HI, I'M MARY JANE WATSON--
I KNOW WHO YOU ARE. I'VE...
...SEEN YOUR PICTURES.
YOU DIDN'T ANSWER MY QUESTION-- WHAT ARE YOU DOING?
IS IT NOT MY DAY TO MOP? I CONSULTED THE CHORE LIST.
YOU HAVEN'T DONE A SINGLE CHORE SINCE YOU MOVED IN HERE.
WHICH MEANS I'VE GOT SOME CATCHING UP TO DO. SO, PLEASE--
--DON'T MIND ME.
I REALLY DON'T GET WHY YOU DON'T LIKE HIM. HE SEEMS NICE.
SEE WHAT I MEAN? BUT I KNOW THE GUY IS UP TO SOMETHING--
SO I'M GONNA FIND OUT WHAT. THIS GUY IS MY RESPONSIBILITY AS LONG AS HE'S FREE...
THANKFULLY IT DOESN'T TAKE LONG BEFORE HIS TRUE COLORS START SHINING THROUGH. I FOLLOW THE TRACER TO AN ABANDONED WAREHOUSE...

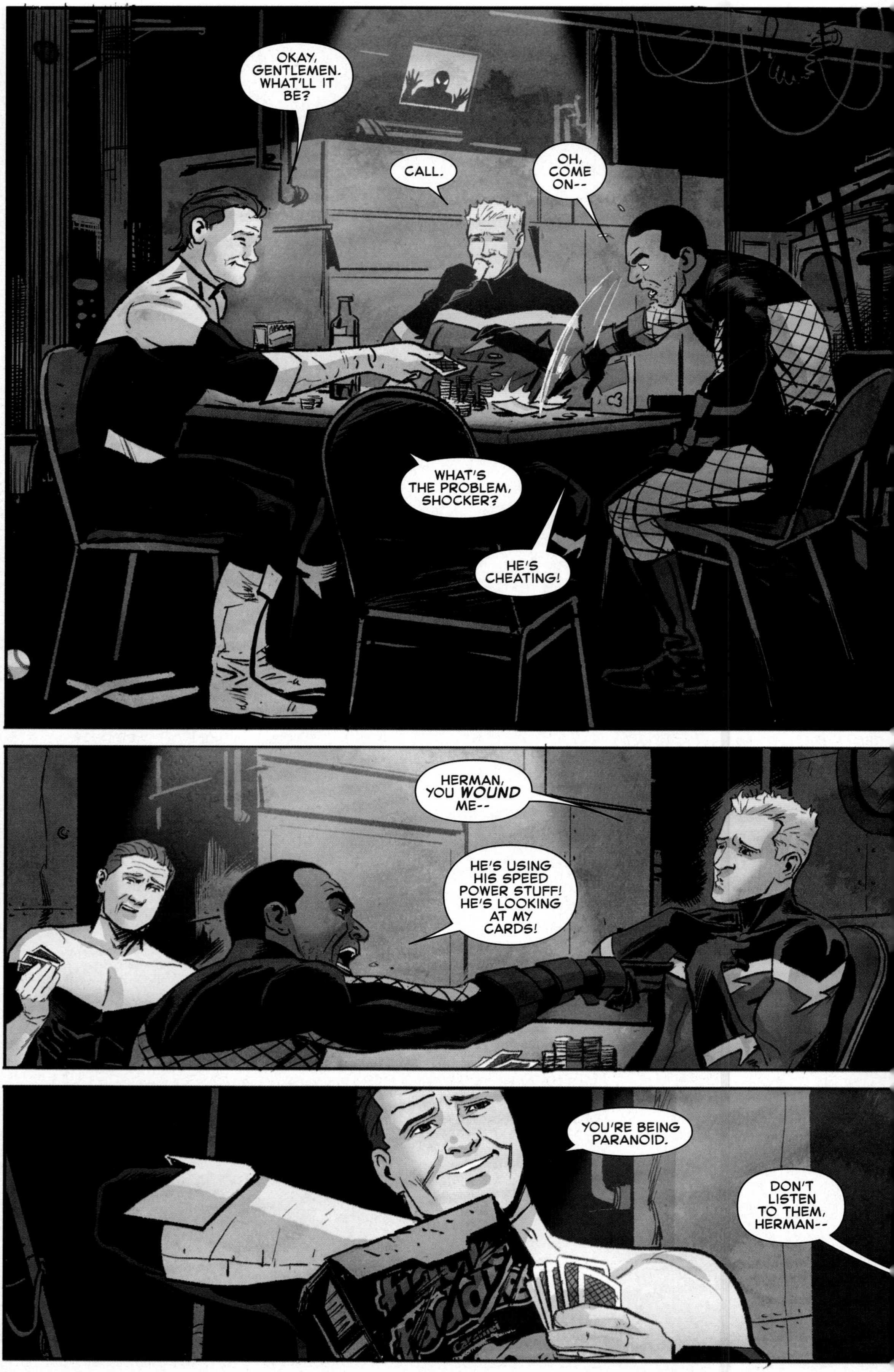
OKAY, GENTLEMEN. WHAT'LL IT BE?
CALL.
OH, COME ON--
WHAT'S THE PROBLEM, SHOCKER?
HE'S CHEATING!
HERMAN, YOU *WOUND* ME--
HE'S USING HIS SPEED POWER STUFF! HE'S LOOKING AT MY CARDS!
YOU'RE BEING PARANOID.
DON'T LISTEN TO THEM, HERMAN--

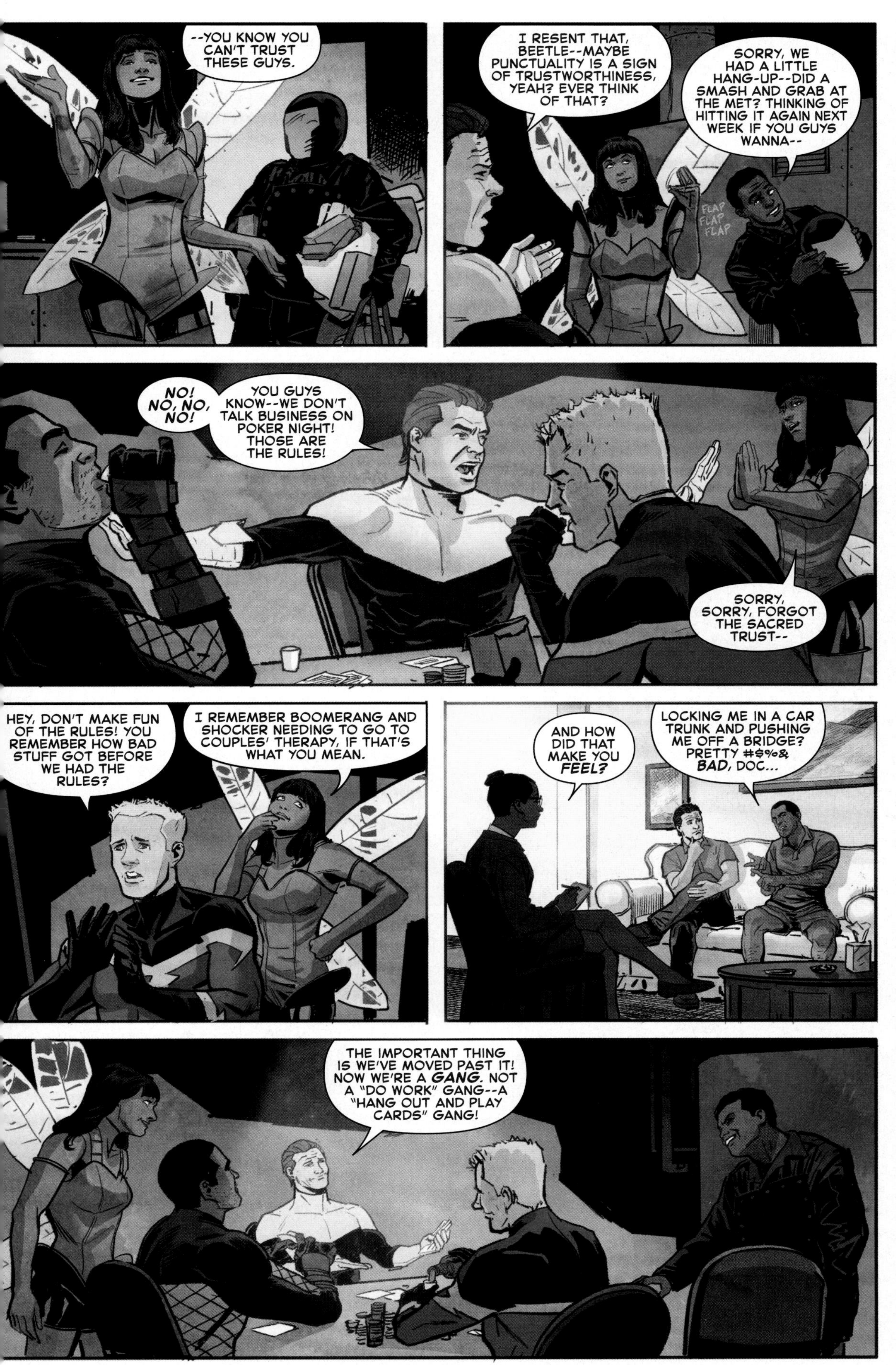
--YOU KNOW YOU CAN'T TRUST THESE GUYS.
I RESENT THAT, BEETLE--MAYBE PUNCTUALITY IS A SIGN OF TRUSTWORTHINESS, YEAH? EVER THINK OF THAT?
SORRY, WE HAD A LITTLE HANG-UP--DID A SMASH AND GRAB AT THE MET? THINKING OF HITTING IT AGAIN NEXT WEEK IF YOU GUYS WANNA--
FLAP FLAP FLAP
NO! NO, NO, NO!
YOU GUYS KNOW--WE DON'T TALK BUSINESS ON POKER NIGHT! THOSE ARE THE RULES!
SORRY, SORRY, FORGOT THE SACRED TRUST--
HEY, DON'T MAKE FUN OF THE RULES! YOU REMEMBER HOW BAD STUFF GOT BEFORE WE HAD THE RULES?
I REMEMBER BOOMERANG AND SHOCKER NEEDING TO GO TO COUPLES' THERAPY, IF THAT'S WHAT YOU MEAN.
AND HOW DID THAT MAKE YOU FEEL?
LOCKING ME IN A CAR TRUNK AND PUSHING ME OFF A BRIDGE? PRETTY #$%& BAD, DOC...
THE IMPORTANT THING IS WE'VE MOVED PAST IT! NOW WE'RE A GANG. NOT A "DO WORK" GANG--A "HANG OUT AND PLAY CARDS" GANG!

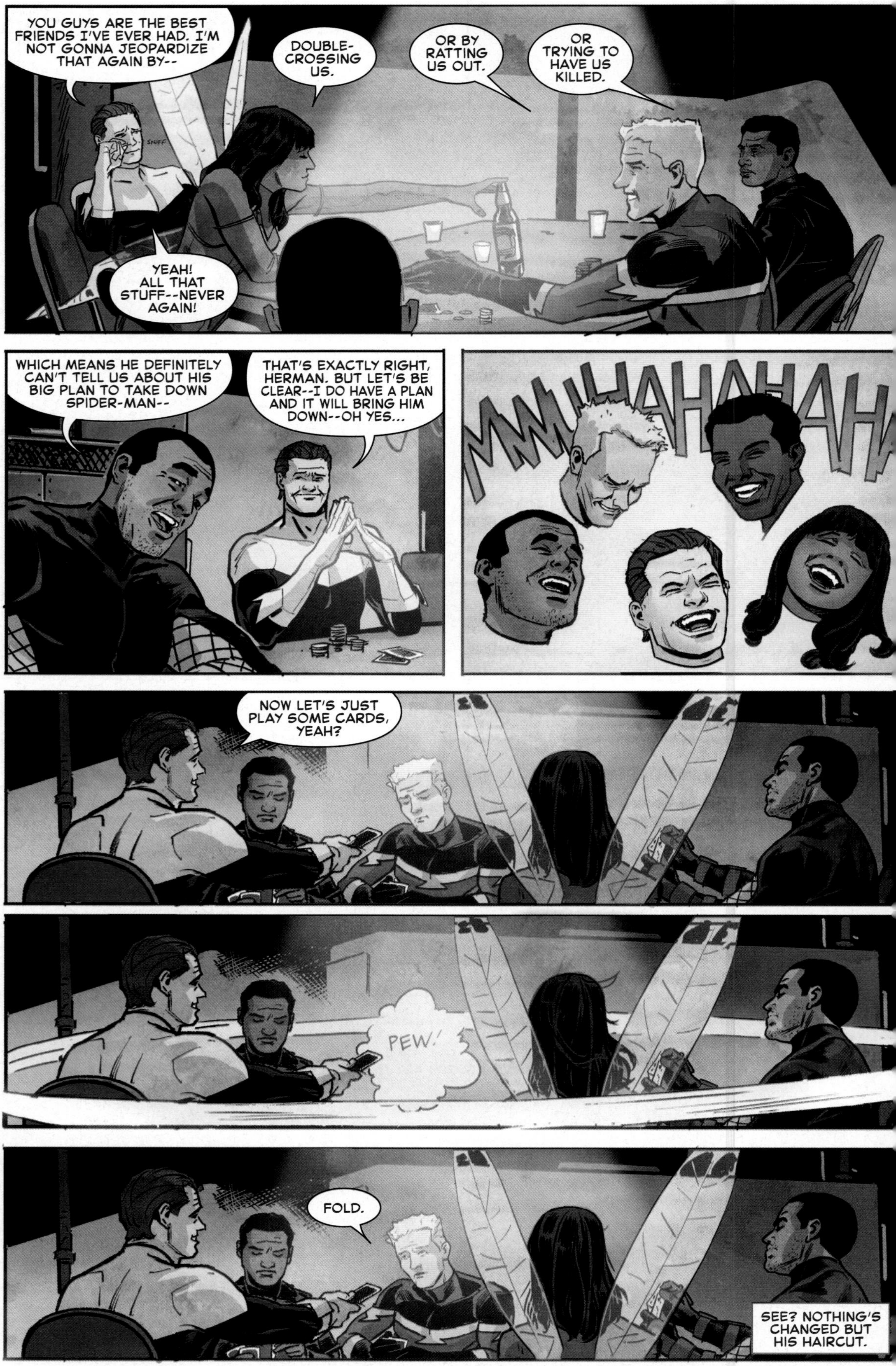
YOU GUYS ARE THE BEST FRIENDS I'VE EVER HAD. I'M NOT GONNA JEOPARDIZE THAT AGAIN BY--
DOUBLE-CROSSING US.
OR BY RATTING US OUT.
OR TRYING TO HAVE US KILLED.
SNIFF
YEAH! ALL THAT STUFF--NEVER AGAIN!
WHICH MEANS HE DEFINITELY CAN'T TELL US ABOUT HIS BIG PLAN TO TAKE DOWN SPIDER-MAN--
THAT'S EXACTLY RIGHT, HERMAN. BUT LET'S BE CLEAR--I DO HAVE A PLAN AND IT WILL BRING HIM DOWN--OH YES...
MWHAHAHAHAH
NOW LET'S JUST PLAY SOME CARDS, YEAH?
PEW!
FOLD.
SEE? NOTHING'S CHANGED BUT HIS HAIRCUT.

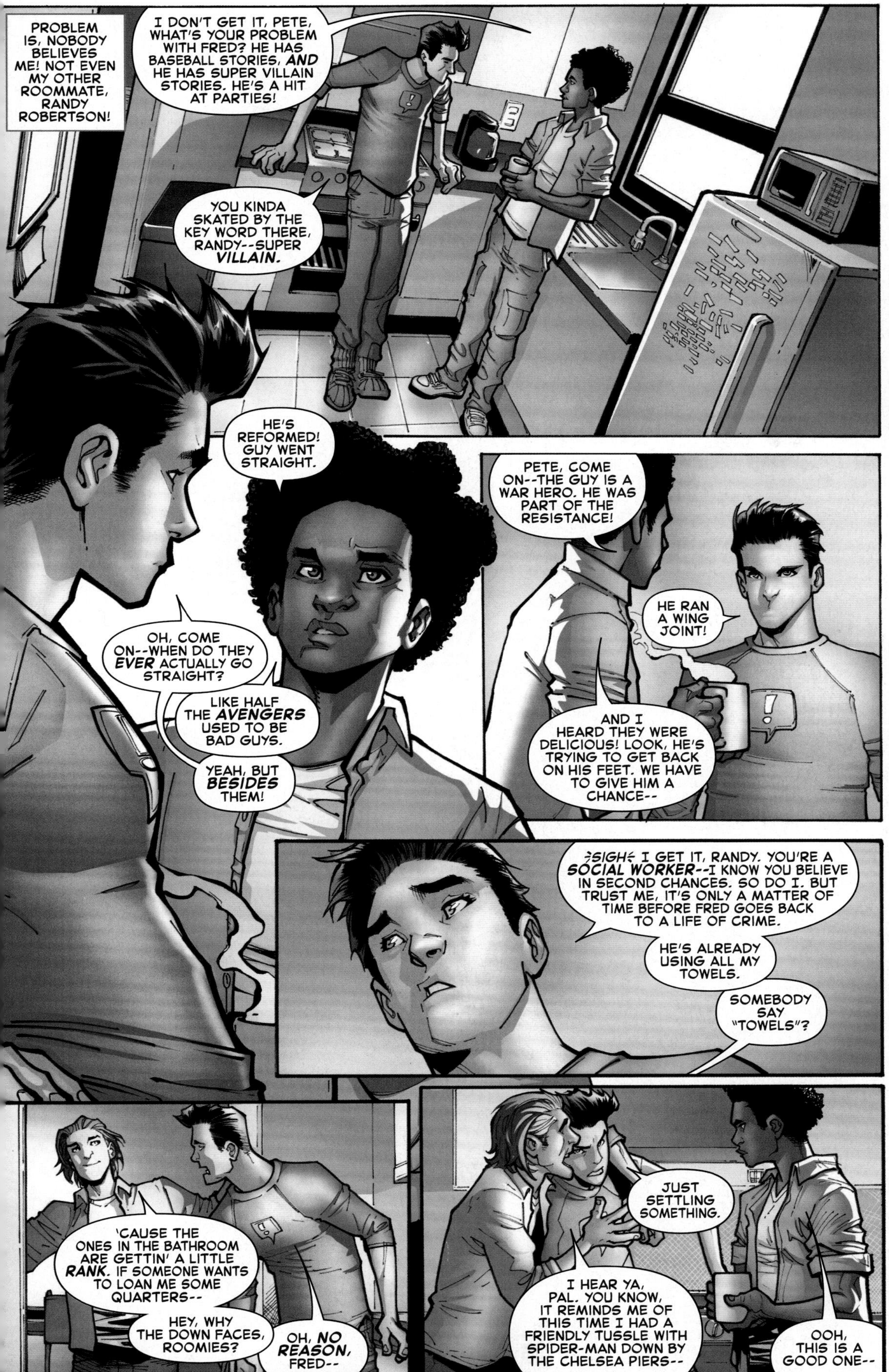
PROBLEM IS, NOBODY BELIEVES ME! NOT EVEN MY OTHER ROOMMATE, RANDY ROBERTSON!
I DON'T GET IT, PETE, WHAT'S YOUR PROBLEM WITH FRED? HE HAS BASEBALL STORIES, AND HE HAS SUPER VILLAIN STORIES. HE'S A HIT AT PARTIES!
YOU KINDA SKATED BY THE KEY WORD THERE, RANDY--SUPER VILLAIN.
HE'S REFORMED! GUY WENT STRAIGHT.
OH, COME ON--WHEN DO THEY EVER ACTUALLY GO STRAIGHT?
LIKE HALF THE AVENGERS USED TO BE BAD GUYS.
YEAH, BUT BESIDES THEM!
PETE, COME ON--THE GUY IS A WAR HERO. HE WAS PART OF THE RESISTANCE!
HE RAN A WING JOINT!
AND I HEARD THEY WERE DELICIOUS! LOOK, HE'S TRYING TO GET BACK ON HIS FEET. WE HAVE TO GIVE HIM A CHANCE--
SIGH I GET IT, RANDY. YOU'RE A SOCIAL WORKER--I KNOW YOU BELIEVE IN SECOND CHANCES. SO DO I. BUT TRUST ME, IT'S ONLY A MATTER OF TIME BEFORE FRED GOES BACK TO A LIFE OF CRIME.
HE'S ALREADY USING ALL MY TOWELS.
SOMEBODY SAY "TOWELS"?
'CAUSE THE ONES IN THE BATHROOM ARE GETTIN' A LITTLE RANK. IF SOMEONE WANTS TO LOAN ME SOME QUARTERS--
HEY, WHY THE DOWN FACES, ROOMIES?
OH, NO REASON, FRED--
JUST SETTLING SOMETHING.
I HEAR YA, PAL. YOU KNOW, IT REMINDS ME OF THIS TIME I HAD A FRIENDLY TUSSLE WITH SPIDER-MAN DOWN BY THE CHELSEA PIERS--
OOH, THIS IS A GOOD ONE--

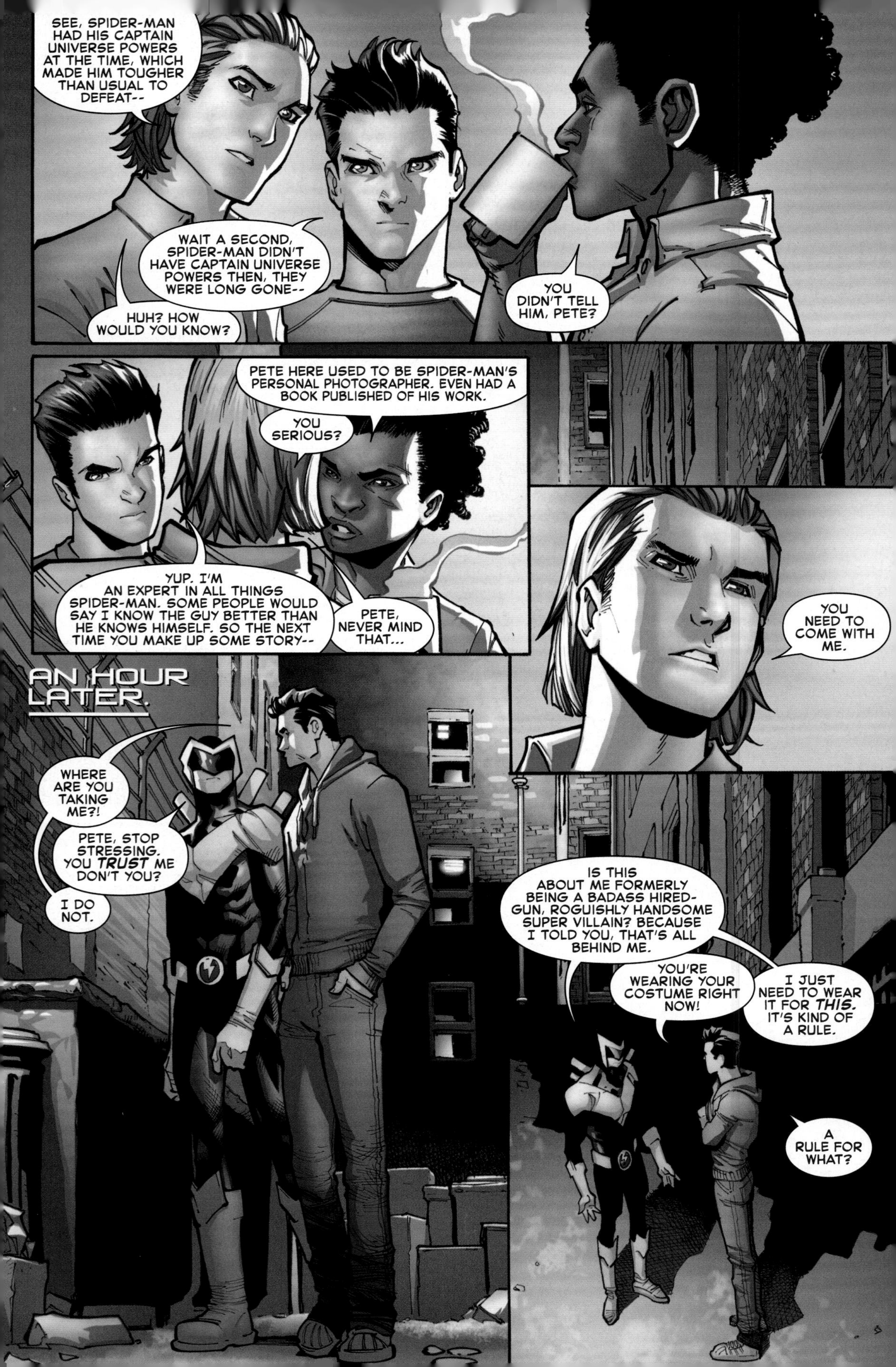

SEE, SPIDER-MAN HAD HIS CAPTAIN UNIVERSE POWERS AT THE TIME, WHICH MADE HIM TOUGHER THAN USUAL TO DEFEAT--
WAIT A SECOND, SPIDER-MAN DIDN'T HAVE CAPTAIN UNIVERSE POWERS THEN, THEY WERE LONG GONE--
HUH? HOW WOULD YOU KNOW?
YOU DIDN'T TELL HIM, PETE?
PETE HERE USED TO BE SPIDER-MAN'S PERSONAL PHOTOGRAPHER. EVEN HAD A BOOK PUBLISHED OF HIS WORK.
YOU SERIOUS?
YUP. I'M AN EXPERT IN ALL THINGS SPIDER-MAN. SOME PEOPLE WOULD SAY I KNOW THE GUY BETTER THAN HE KNOWS HIMSELF. SO THE NEXT TIME YOU MAKE UP SOME STORY--
PETE, NEVER MIND THAT...
YOU NEED TO COME WITH ME.
AN HOUR LATER.
WHERE ARE YOU TAKING ME?!
PETE, STOP STRESSING. YOU TRUST ME DON'T YOU?
I DO NOT.
IS THIS ABOUT ME FORMERLY BEING A BADASS HIRED-GUN, ROGUISHLY HANDSOME SUPER VILLAIN? BECAUSE I TOLD YOU, THAT'S ALL BEHIND ME.
YOU'RE WEARING YOUR COSTUME RIGHT NOW!
I JUST NEED TO WEAR IT FOR THIS. IT'S KIND OF A RULE.
A RULE FOR WHAT?

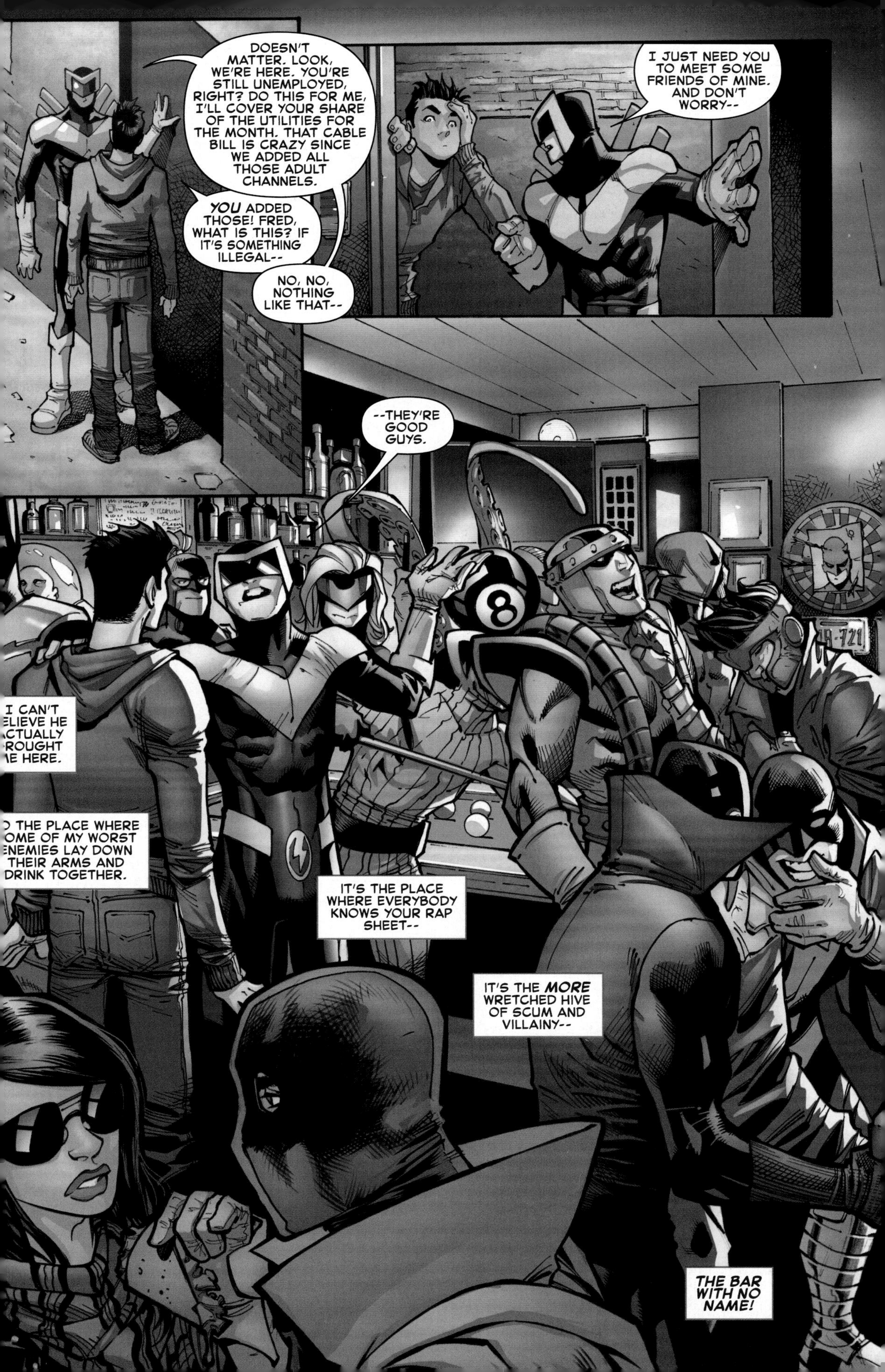
DOESN'T MATTER. LOOK, WE'RE HERE. YOU'RE STILL UNEMPLOYED, RIGHT? DO THIS FOR ME, I'LL COVER YOUR SHARE OF THE UTILITIES FOR THE MONTH. THAT CABLE BILL IS CRAZY SINCE WE ADDED ALL THOSE ADULT CHANNELS.
YOU ADDED THOSE! FRED, WHAT IS THIS? IF IT'S SOMETHING ILLEGAL--
NO, NO, NOTHING LIKE THAT--
I JUST NEED YOU TO MEET SOME FRIENDS OF MINE. AND DON'T WORRY--
--THEY'RE GOOD GUYS.
I CAN'T ELIEVE HE CTUALLY ROUGHT E HERE.
THE PLACE WHERE OME OF MY WORST ENEMIES LAY DOWN THEIR ARMS AND DRINK TOGETHER.
IT'S THE PLACE WHERE EVERYBODY KNOWS YOUR RAP SHEET--
IT'S THE *MORE* WRETCHED HIVE OF SCUM AND VILLAINY--
THE BAR WITH NO NAME!

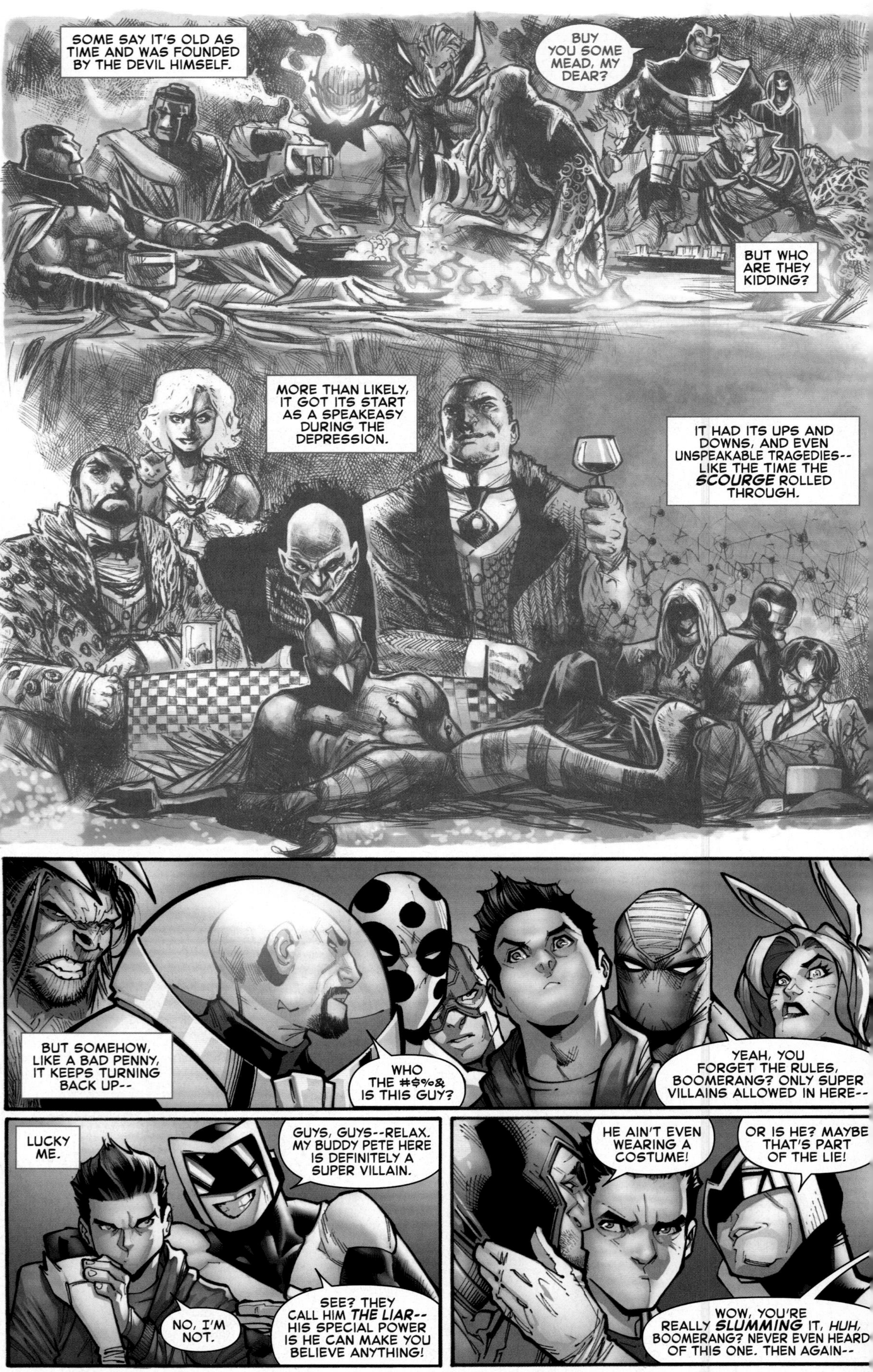
SOME SAY IT'S OLD AS TIME AND WAS FOUNDED BY THE DEVIL HIMSELF.
BUY YOU SOME MEAD, MY DEAR?
BUT WHO ARE THEY KIDDING?
MORE THAN LIKELY, IT GOT ITS START AS A SPEAKEASY DURING THE DEPRESSION.
IT HAD ITS UPS AND DOWNS, AND EVEN UNSPEAKABLE TRAGEDIES-- LIKE THE TIME THE SCOURGE ROLLED THROUGH.
BUT SOMEHOW, LIKE A BAD PENNY, IT KEEPS TURNING BACK UP--
WHO THE #$%& IS THIS GUY?
YEAH, YOU FORGET THE RULES, BOOMERANG? ONLY SUPER VILLAINS ALLOWED IN HERE--
LUCKY ME.
GUYS, GUYS--RELAX. MY BUDDY PETE HERE IS DEFINITELY A SUPER VILLAIN.
NO, I'M NOT.
SEE? THEY CALL HIM THE LIAR-- HIS SPECIAL POWER IS HE CAN MAKE YOU BELIEVE ANYTHING!
HE AIN'T EVEN WEARING A COSTUME!
OR IS HE? MAYBE THAT'S PART OF THE LIE!
WOW, YOU'RE REALLY SLUMMING IT, HUH, BOOMERANG? NEVER EVEN HEARD OF THIS ONE. THEN AGAIN--

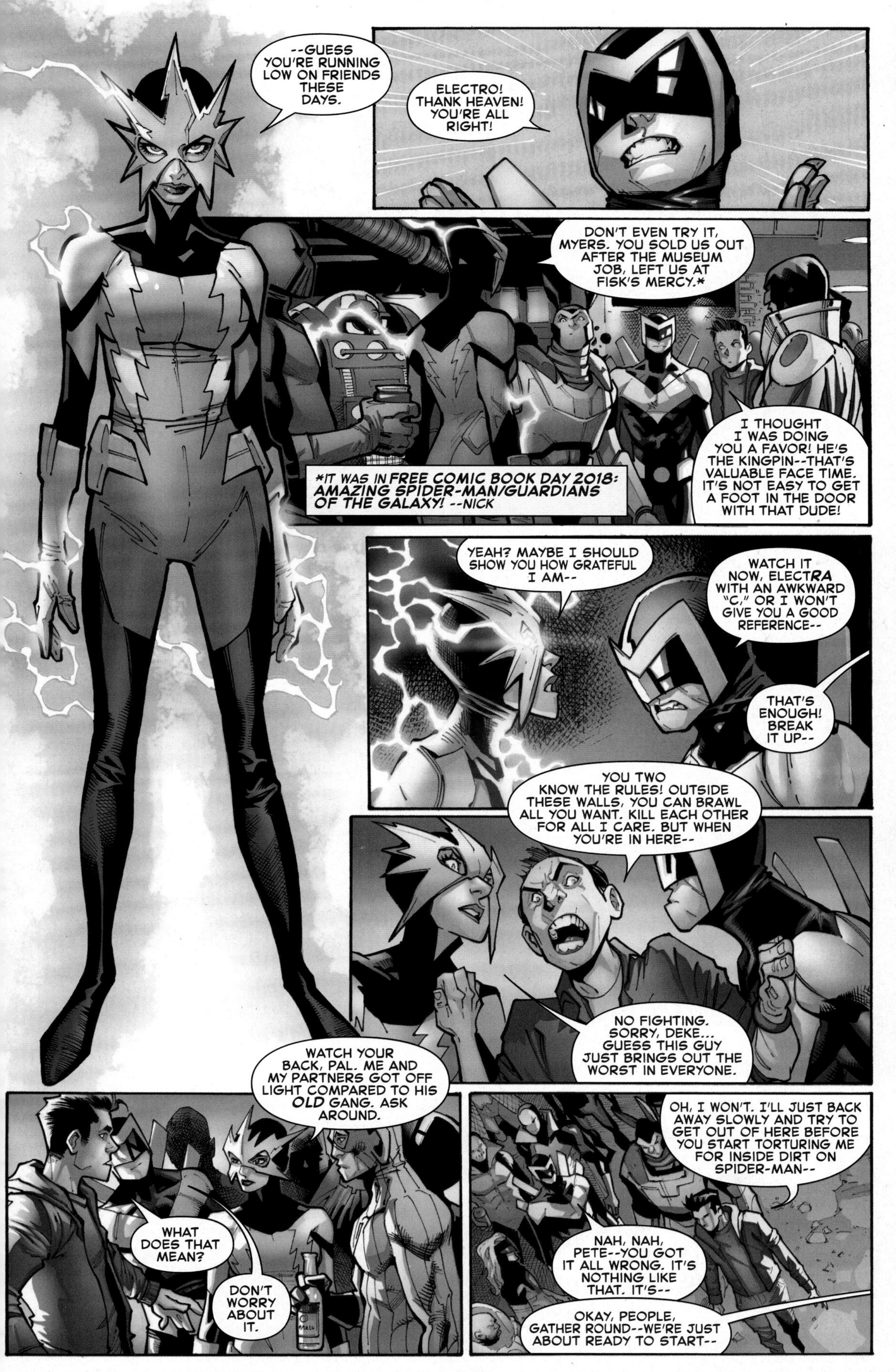
--GUESS YOU'RE RUNNING LOW ON FRIENDS THESE DAYS.
ELECTRO! THANK HEAVEN! YOU'RE ALL RIGHT!
DON'T EVEN TRY IT, MYERS. YOU SOLD US OUT AFTER THE MUSEUM JOB, LEFT US AT FISK'S MERCY.*
*IT WAS IN FREE COMIC BOOK DAY 2018: AMAZING SPIDER-MAN/GUARDIANS OF THE GALAXY! --NICK
I THOUGHT I WAS DOING YOU A FAVOR! HE'S THE KINGPIN--THAT'S VALUABLE FACE TIME. IT'S NOT EASY TO GET A FOOT IN THE DOOR WITH THAT DUDE!
YEAH? MAYBE I SHOULD SHOW YOU HOW GRATEFUL I AM--
WATCH IT NOW, ELECTRA WITH AN AWKWARD "C," OR I WON'T GIVE YOU A GOOD REFERENCE--
THAT'S ENOUGH! BREAK IT UP--
YOU TWO KNOW THE RULES! OUTSIDE THESE WALLS, YOU CAN BRAWL ALL YOU WANT. KILL EACH OTHER FOR ALL I CARE. BUT WHEN YOU'RE IN HERE--
NO FIGHTING. SORRY, DEKE... GUESS THIS GUY JUST BRINGS OUT THE WORST IN EVERYONE.
WATCH YOUR BACK, PAL. ME AND MY PARTNERS GOT OFF LIGHT COMPARED TO HIS OLD GANG. ASK AROUND.
WHAT DOES THAT MEAN?
DON'T WORRY ABOUT IT.
OH, I WON'T. I'LL JUST BACK AWAY SLOWLY AND TRY TO GET OUT OF HERE BEFORE YOU START TORTURING ME FOR INSIDE DIRT ON SPIDER-MAN--
NAH, NAH, PETE--YOU GOT IT ALL WRONG. IT'S NOTHING LIKE THAT. IT'S--
OKAY, PEOPLE, GATHER ROUND--WE'RE JUST ABOUT READY TO START--

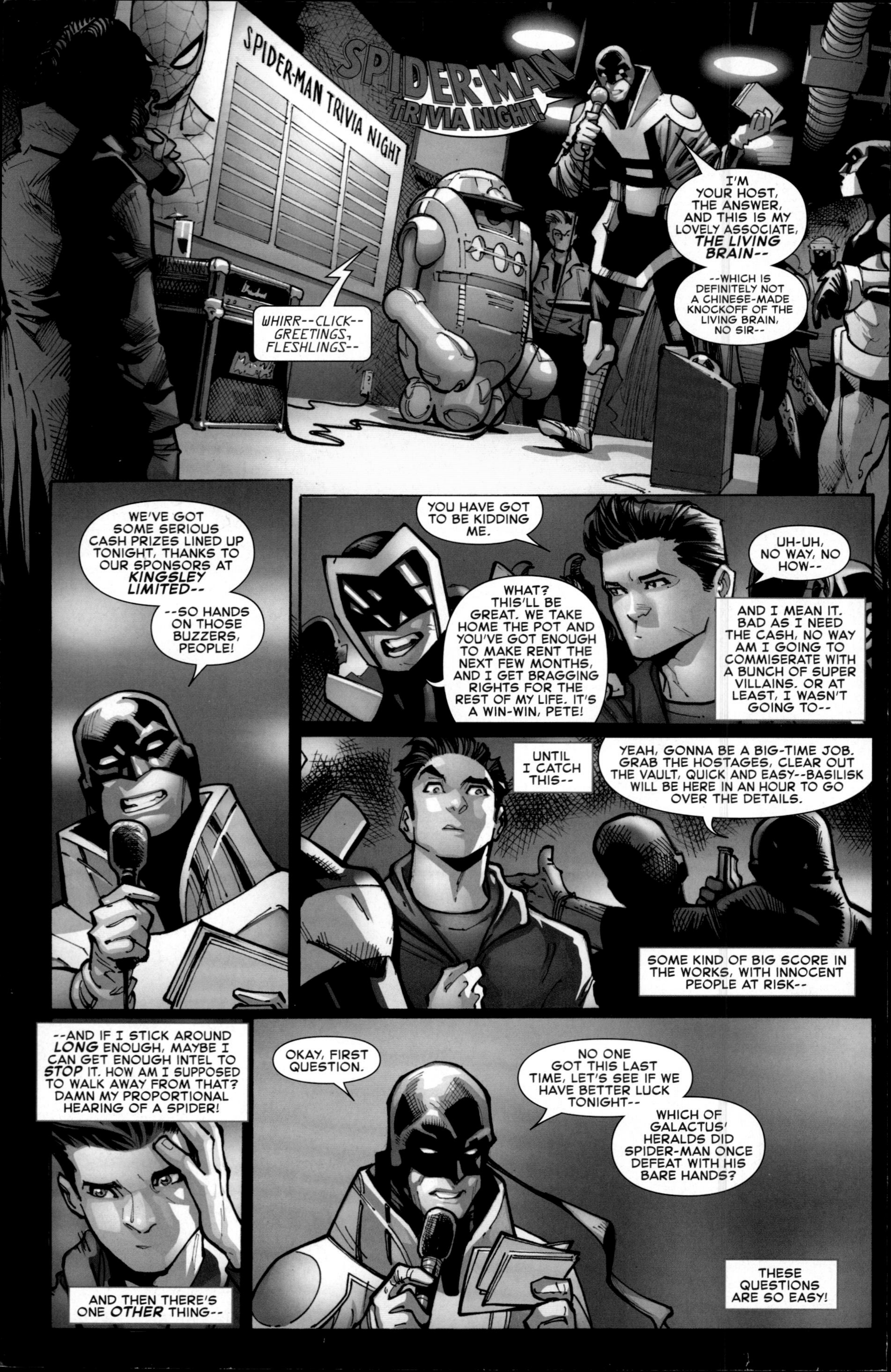
SPIDER-MAN TRIVIA NIGHT
SPIDER-MAN TRIVIA NIGHT!
WHIRR--CLICK--GREETINGS, FLESHLINGS--
I'M YOUR HOST, THE ANSWER, AND THIS IS MY LOVELY ASSOCIATE, THE LIVING BRAIN--
--WHICH IS DEFINITELY NOT A CHINESE-MADE KNOCKOFF OF THE LIVING BRAIN, NO SIR--
WE'VE GOT SOME SERIOUS CASH PRIZES LINED UP TONIGHT, THANKS TO OUR SPONSORS AT KINGSLEY LIMITED--
--SO HANDS ON THOSE BUZZERS, PEOPLE!
YOU HAVE GOT TO BE KIDDING ME.
WHAT? THIS'LL BE GREAT. WE TAKE HOME THE POT AND YOU'VE GOT ENOUGH TO MAKE RENT THE NEXT FEW MONTHS, AND I GET BRAGGING RIGHTS FOR THE REST OF MY LIFE. IT'S A WIN-WIN, PETE!
UH-UH, NO WAY, NO HOW--
AND I MEAN IT. BAD AS I NEED THE CASH, NO WAY AM I GOING TO COMMISERATE WITH A BUNCH OF SUPER VILLAINS. OR AT LEAST, I WASN'T GOING TO--
UNTIL I CATCH THIS--
YEAH, GONNA BE A BIG-TIME JOB. GRAB THE HOSTAGES, CLEAR OUT THE VAULT, QUICK AND EASY--BASILISK WILL BE HERE IN AN HOUR TO GO OVER THE DETAILS.
SOME KIND OF BIG SCORE IN THE WORKS, WITH INNOCENT PEOPLE AT RISK--
--AND IF I STICK AROUND LONG ENOUGH, MAYBE I CAN GET ENOUGH INTEL TO STOP IT. HOW AM I SUPPOSED TO WALK AWAY FROM THAT? DAMN MY PROPORTIONAL HEARING OF A SPIDER!
AND THEN THERE'S ONE OTHER THING--
OKAY, FIRST QUESTION.
NO ONE GOT THIS LAST TIME, LET'S SEE IF WE HAVE BETTER LUCK TONIGHT--
WHICH OF GALACTUS' HERALDS DID SPIDER-MAN ONCE DEFEAT WITH HIS BARE HANDS?
THESE QUESTIONS ARE SO EASY!

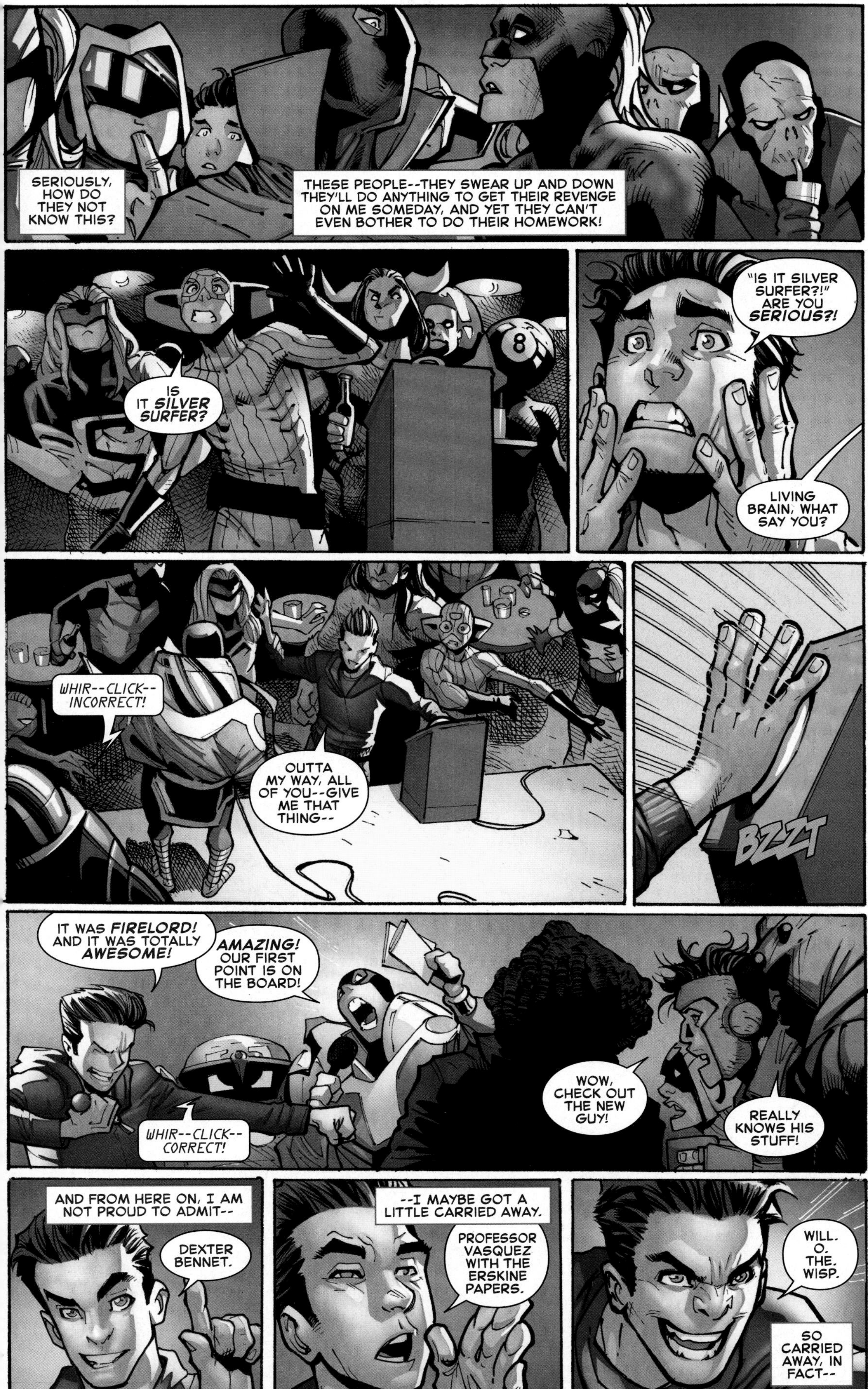

SERIOUSLY, HOW DO THEY NOT KNOW THIS?
THESE PEOPLE--THEY SWEAR UP AND DOWN THEY'LL DO ANYTHING TO GET THEIR REVENGE ON ME SOMEDAY, AND YET THEY CAN'T EVEN BOTHER TO DO THEIR HOMEWORK!
IS IT SILVER SURFER?
"IS IT SILVER SURFER?!" ARE YOU SERIOUS?!
LIVING BRAIN, WHAT SAY YOU?
WHIR--CLICK--INCORRECT!
OUTTA MY WAY, ALL OF YOU--GIVE ME THAT THING--
BZZT
IT WAS FIRELORD! AND IT WAS TOTALLY AWESOME!
AMAZING! OUR FIRST POINT IS ON THE BOARD!
WHIR--CLICK--CORRECT!
WOW, CHECK OUT THE NEW GUY!
REALLY KNOWS HIS STUFF!
AND FROM HERE ON, I AM NOT PROUD TO ADMIT--
DEXTER BENNET.
--I MAYBE GOT A LITTLE CARRIED AWAY.
PROFESSOR VASQUEZ WITH THE ERSKINE PAPERS.
WILL. O. THE. WISP.
SO CARRIED AWAY, IN FACT--

--I DON'T EVEN NOTICE FRED LEAVE.
STOLEN PHONE, WHO DIS?
THIS IS THE OFFICE OF MAYOR FISK, MR. MYERS--THIS LINE WAS SPECIFICALLY SET UP TO ALLOW YOU TO CONTACT US WHEN YOU WERE READY TO SEND US YOUR TERMS...
OH YEAH?
WELL, I'LL GIVE YOU CREDIT FOR KNOWING HOW TO FIND ME.
BOOMERANG FOR A GOOD TIME CALL
THE MAYOR FEELS HE'S BEEN MORE THAN PATIENT WITH YOU, MR. MYERS. WE COULD HUNT YOU DOWN, HAVE YOU ARRESTED, INTERROGATE YOU, BUT INSTEAD, WE CHOSE TO ENGAGE YOU AS A PROFESSIONAL--
YEAH, BAD CALL.
EXCUSE ME?
NOW, IF YOU'D TRIED TO HAVE ME *KILLED*, *THAT* I'D RESPECT. BUT THIS NICE-GUY ACT, CALLING ME A HERO AT YOUR FANCY PRESS CONFERENCE--PEOPLE ARE REALLY STARTING TO BELIEVE I'M *LEGIT.* IT'S INFURIATING!
'SIDES, YOU PLAYING IT THIS WAY ONLY TELLS ME HOW DESPERATE FISK REALLY IS. I GOT THE CARDS HERE, SO YOU TELL THE MAYOR I JUST DOUBLED MY PRICE!
AND SOON I'LL GET TO A CALCULATOR SO I CAN FIGURE OUT HOW MUCH THAT IS!
MR. MYERS, WAIT--
I SAID GOOD DAY, SIR!
I ALSO DON'T NOTICE MY PHONE HAS GONE MISSING.

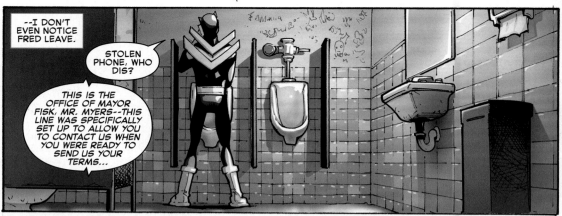

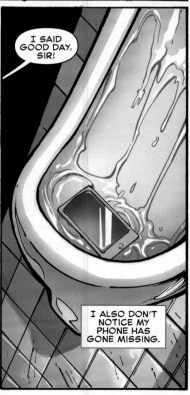

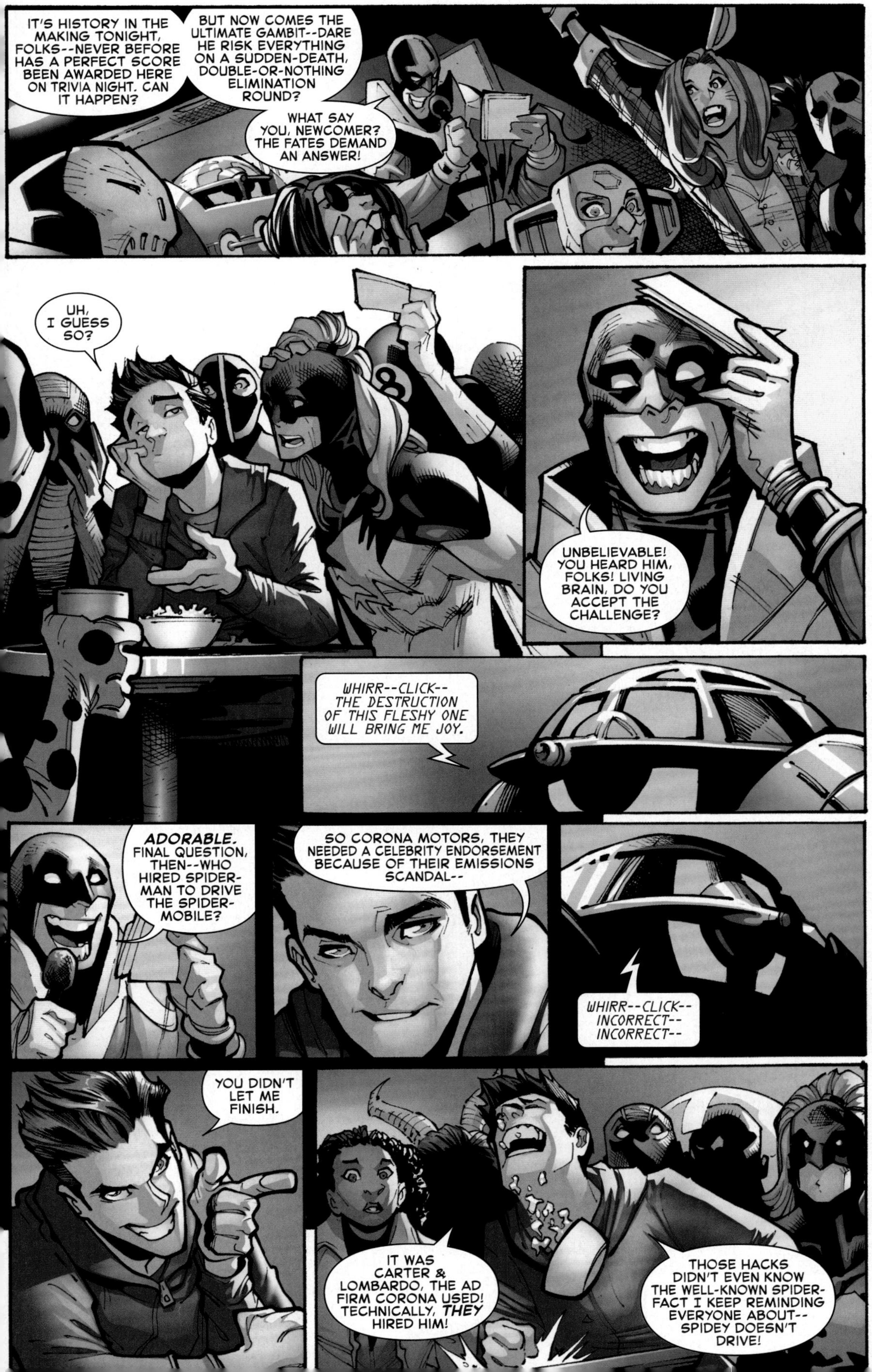
IT'S HISTORY IN THE MAKING TONIGHT, FOLKS--NEVER BEFORE HAS A PERFECT SCORE BEEN AWARDED HERE ON TRIVIA NIGHT. CAN IT HAPPEN?
BUT NOW COMES THE ULTIMATE GAMBIT--DARE HE RISK EVERYTHING ON A SUDDEN-DEATH, DOUBLE-OR-NOTHING ELIMINATION ROUND?
WHAT SAY YOU, NEWCOMER? THE FATES DEMAND AN ANSWER!
UH, I GUESS SO?
UNBELIEVABLE! YOU HEARD HIM, FOLKS! LIVING BRAIN, DO YOU ACCEPT THE CHALLENGE?
WHIRR--CLICK-- THE DESTRUCTION OF THIS FLESHY ONE WILL BRING ME JOY.
ADORABLE. FINAL QUESTION, THEN--WHO HIRED SPIDER-MAN TO DRIVE THE SPIDER-MOBILE?
SO CORONA MOTORS, THEY NEEDED A CELEBRITY ENDORSEMENT BECAUSE OF THEIR EMISSIONS SCANDAL--
WHIRR--CLICK-- INCORRECT-- INCORRECT--
YOU DIDN'T LET ME FINISH.
IT WAS CARTER & LOMBARDO, THE AD FIRM CORONA USED! TECHNICALLY, THEY HIRED HIM!
THOSE HACKS DIDN'T EVEN KNOW THE WELL-KNOWN SPIDER-FACT I KEEP REMINDING EVERYONE ABOUT-- SPIDEY DOESN'T DRIVE!

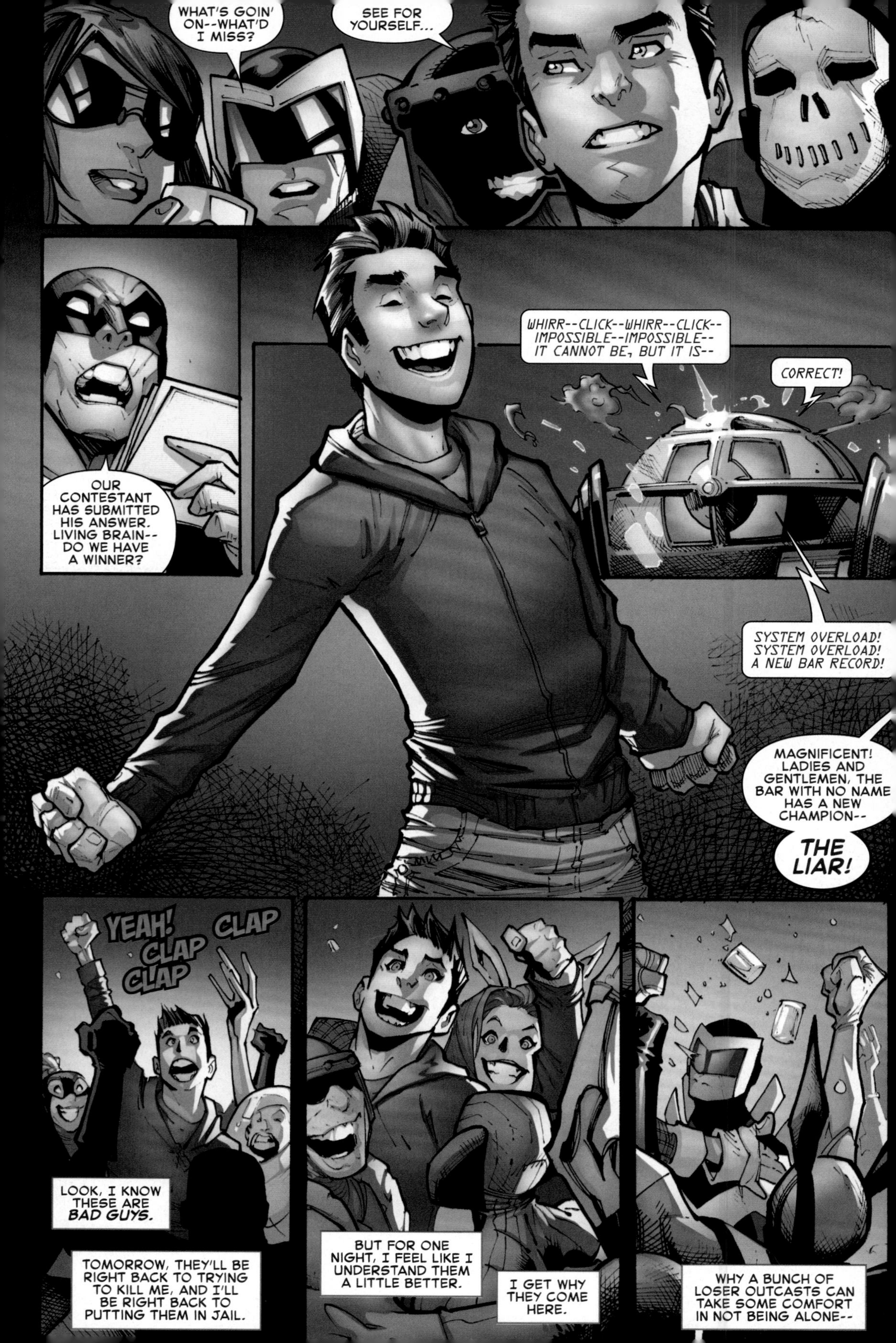
WHAT'S GOIN' ON--WHAT'D I MISS?
SEE FOR YOURSELF...
OUR CONTESTANT HAS SUBMITTED HIS ANSWER. LIVING BRAIN--DO WE HAVE A WINNER?
WHIRR--CLICK--WHIRR--CLICK--IMPOSSIBLE--IMPOSSIBLE--IT CANNOT BE, BUT IT IS--
CORRECT!
SYSTEM OVERLOAD! SYSTEM OVERLOAD! A NEW BAR RECORD!
MAGNIFICENT! LADIES AND GENTLEMEN, THE BAR WITH NO NAME HAS A NEW CHAMPION--
THE LIAR!
YEAH! CLAP CLAP CLAP
LOOK, I KNOW THESE ARE BAD GUYS.
TOMORROW, THEY'LL BE RIGHT BACK TO TRYING TO KILL ME, AND I'LL BE RIGHT BACK TO PUTTING THEM IN JAIL.
BUT FOR ONE NIGHT, I FEEL LIKE I UNDERSTAND THEM A LITTLE BETTER.
I GET WHY THEY COME HERE.
WHY A BUNCH OF LOSER OUTCASTS CAN TAKE SOME COMFORT IN NOT BEING ALONE--

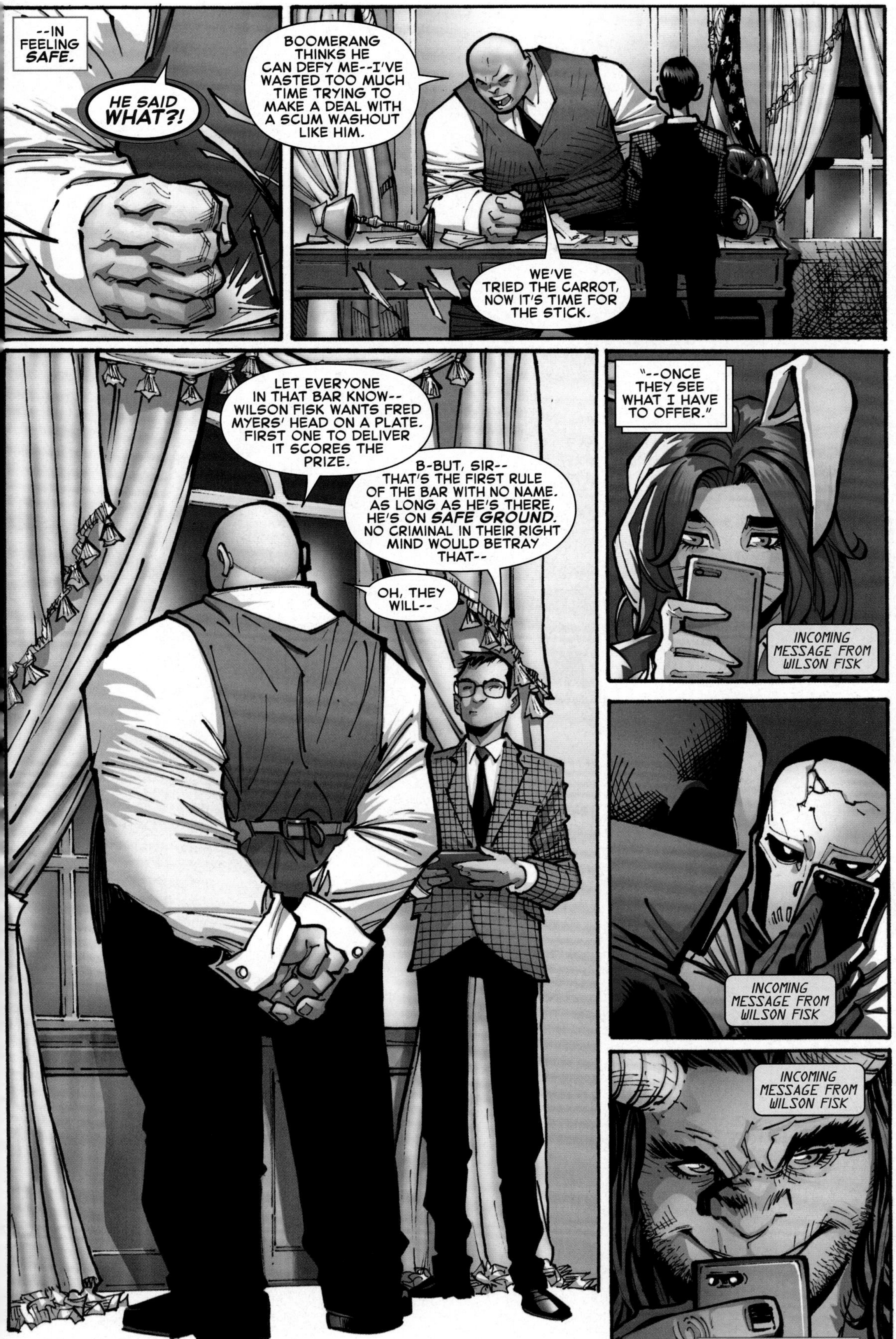
--IN FEELING SAFE.
HE SAID WHAT?!
BOOMERANG THINKS HE CAN DEFY ME--I'VE WASTED TOO MUCH TIME TRYING TO MAKE A DEAL WITH A SCUM WASHOUT LIKE HIM.
WE'VE TRIED THE CARROT, NOW IT'S TIME FOR THE STICK.
LET EVERYONE IN THAT BAR KNOW--WILSON FISK WANTS FRED MYERS' HEAD ON A PLATE. FIRST ONE TO DELIVER IT SCORES THE PRIZE.
B-BUT, SIR--THAT'S THE FIRST RULE OF THE BAR WITH NO NAME. AS LONG AS HE'S THERE, HE'S ON SAFE GROUND. NO CRIMINAL IN THEIR RIGHT MIND WOULD BETRAY THAT--
OH, THEY WILL--
"--ONCE THEY SEE WHAT I HAVE TO OFFER."
INCOMING MESSAGE FROM WILSON FISK
INCOMING MESSAGE FROM WILSON FISK
INCOMING MESSAGE FROM WILSON FISK
YEAH, THIS WHOLE EXPERIENCE KINDA HAS ME THINKING--

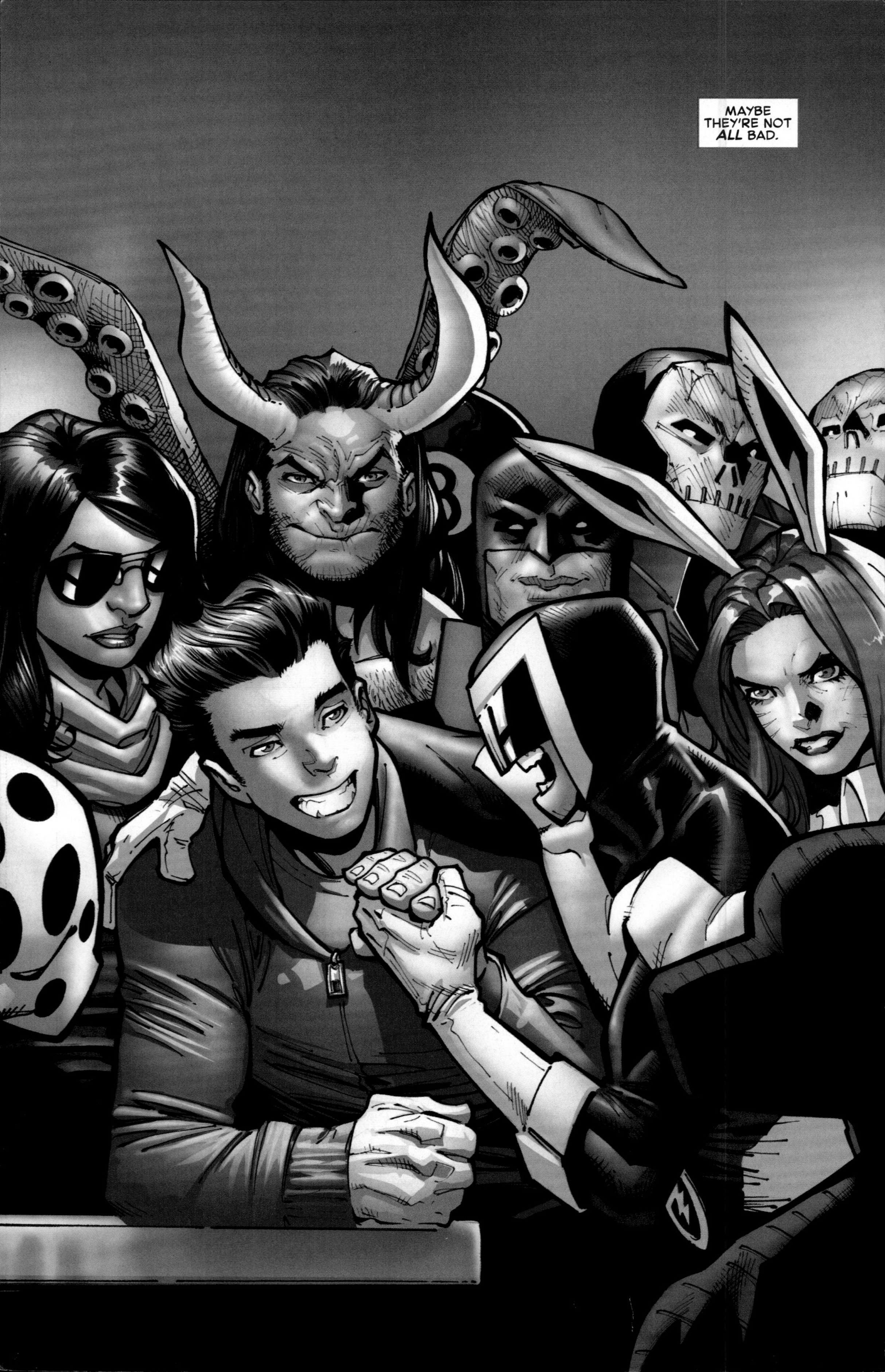
MAYBE THEY'RE NOT ALL BAD.

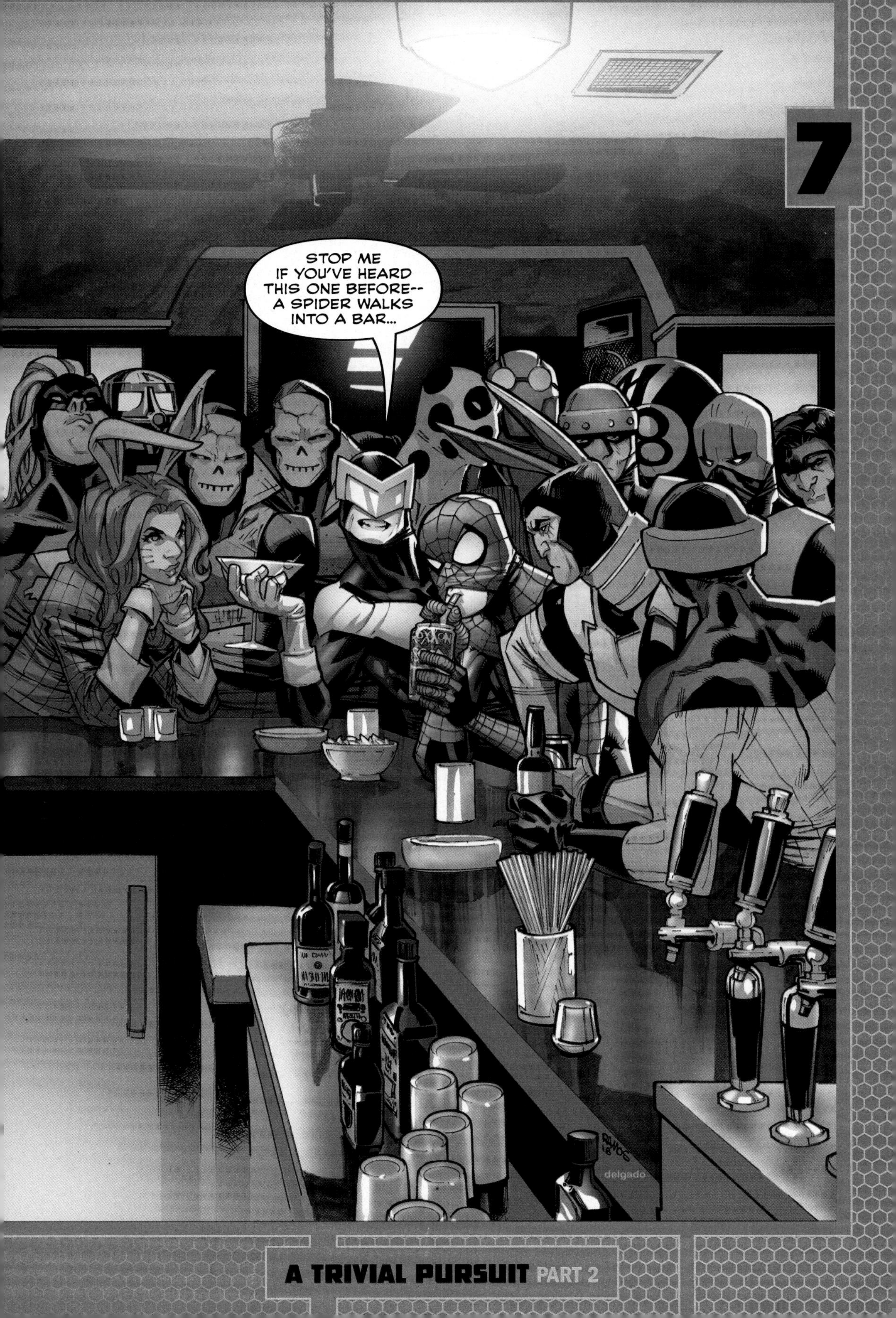
STOP ME IF YOU'VE HEARD THIS ONE BEFORE-- A SPIDER WALKS INTO A BAR...
delgado

7

A TRIVIAL PURSUIT PART 2

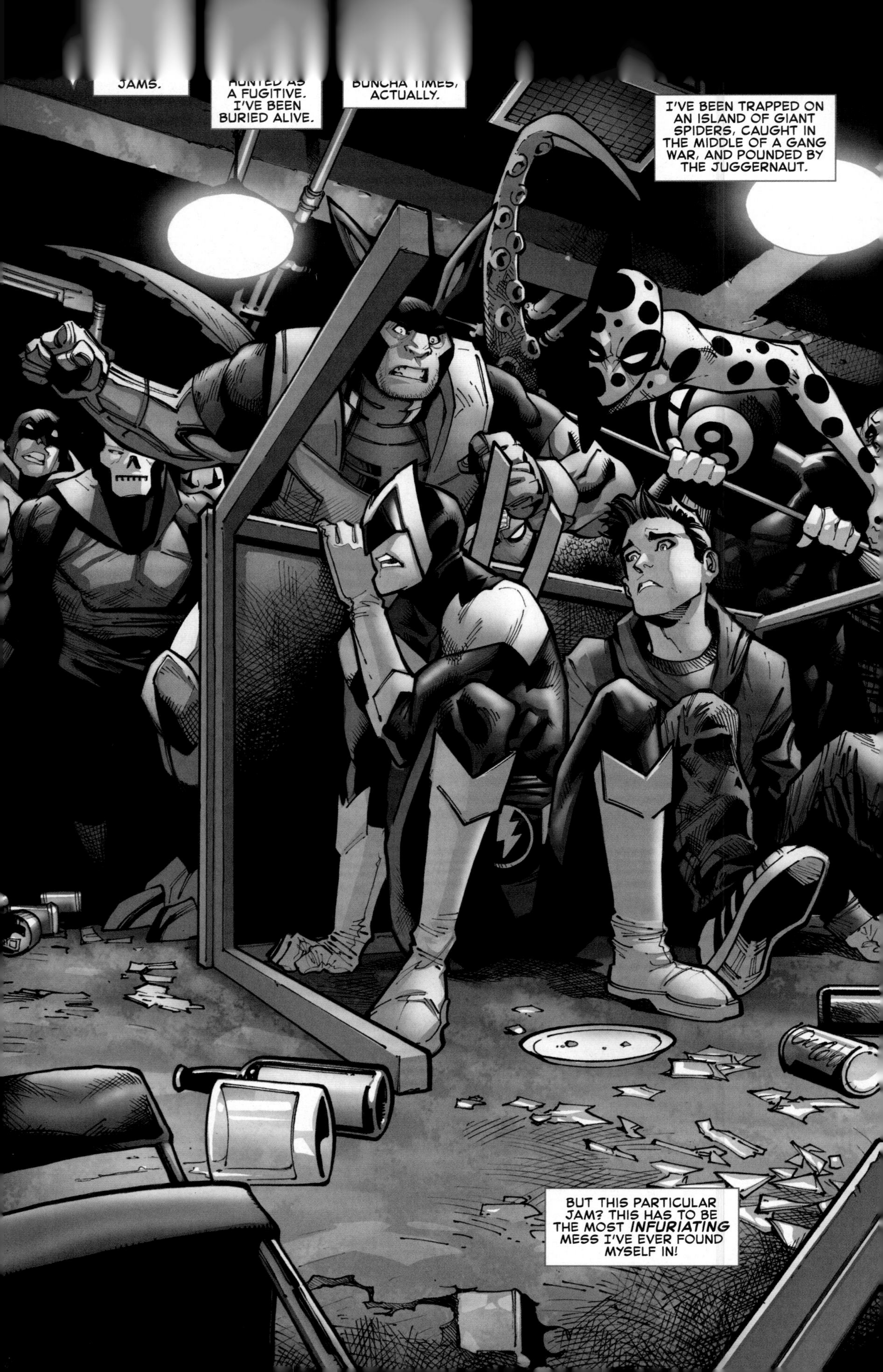
JAMS.
A FUGITIVE. I'VE BEEN BURIED ALIVE.
ACTUALLY.
I'VE BEEN TRAPPED ON AN ISLAND OF GIANT SPIDERS, CAUGHT IN THE MIDDLE OF A GANG WAR, AND POUNDED BY THE JUGGERNAUT.
BUT THIS PARTICULAR JAM? THIS HAS TO BE THE MOST *INFURIATING* MESS I'VE EVER FOUND MYSELF IN!

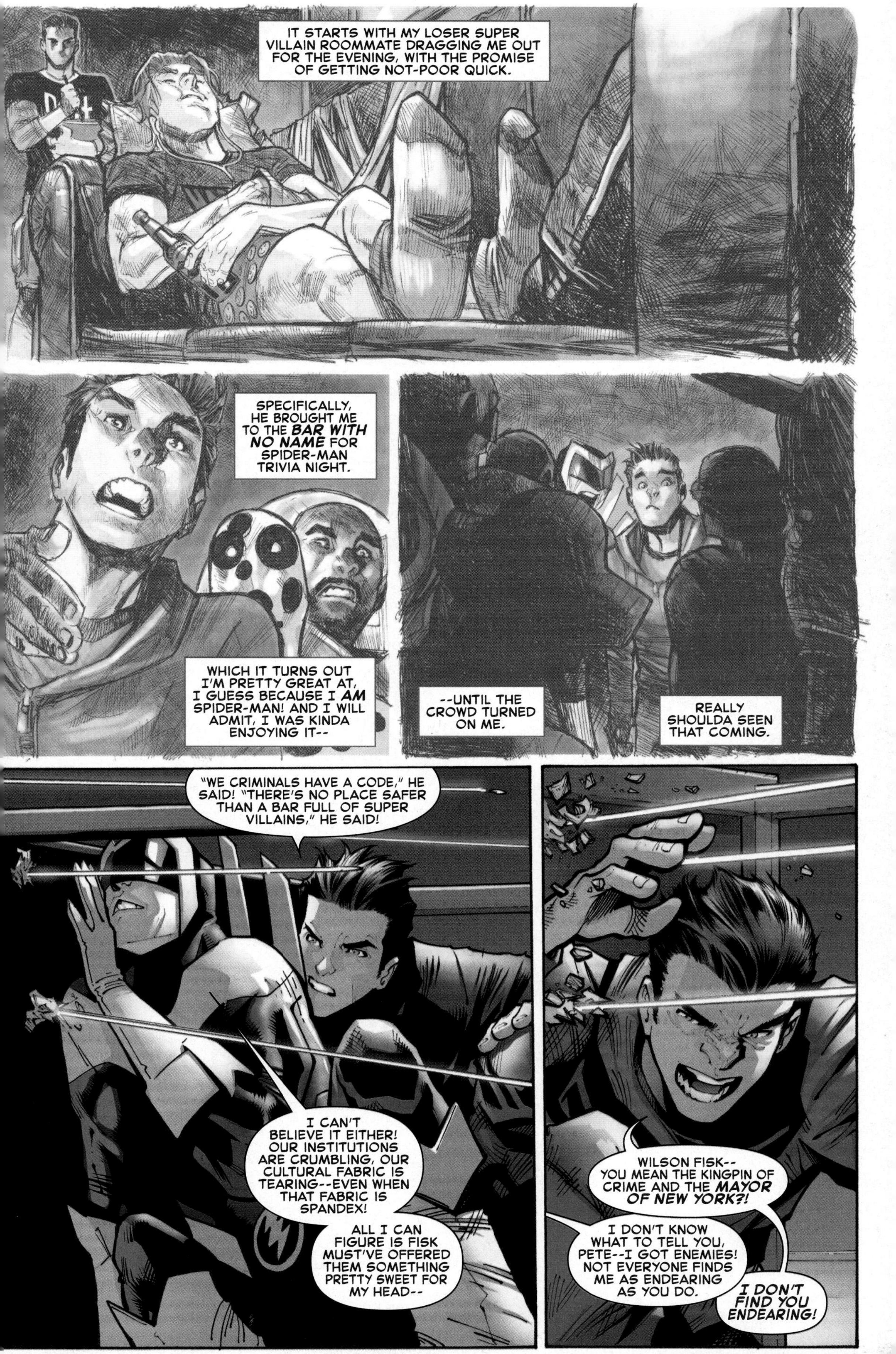
IT STARTS WITH MY LOSER SUPER VILLAIN ROOMMATE DRAGGING ME OUT FOR THE EVENING, WITH THE PROMISE OF GETTING NOT-POOR QUICK.
SPECIFICALLY, HE BROUGHT ME TO THE BAR WITH NO NAME FOR SPIDER-MAN TRIVIA NIGHT.
WHICH IT TURNS OUT I'M PRETTY GREAT AT, I GUESS BECAUSE I AM SPIDER-MAN! AND I WILL ADMIT, I WAS KINDA ENJOYING IT--
--UNTIL THE CROWD TURNED ON ME.
REALLY SHOULDA SEEN THAT COMING.
"WE CRIMINALS HAVE A CODE," HE SAID! "THERE'S NO PLACE SAFER THAN A BAR FULL OF SUPER VILLAINS," HE SAID!
I CAN'T BELIEVE IT EITHER! OUR INSTITUTIONS ARE CRUMBLING, OUR CULTURAL FABRIC IS TEARING--EVEN WHEN THAT FABRIC IS SPANDEX!
ALL I CAN FIGURE IS FISK MUST'VE OFFERED THEM SOMETHING PRETTY SWEET FOR MY HEAD--
WILSON FISK-- YOU MEAN THE KINGPIN OF CRIME AND THE MAYOR OF NEW YORK?!
I DON'T KNOW WHAT TO TELL YOU, PETE--I GOT ENEMIES! NOT EVERYONE FINDS ME AS ENDEARING AS YOU DO.
I DON'T FIND YOU ENDEARING!

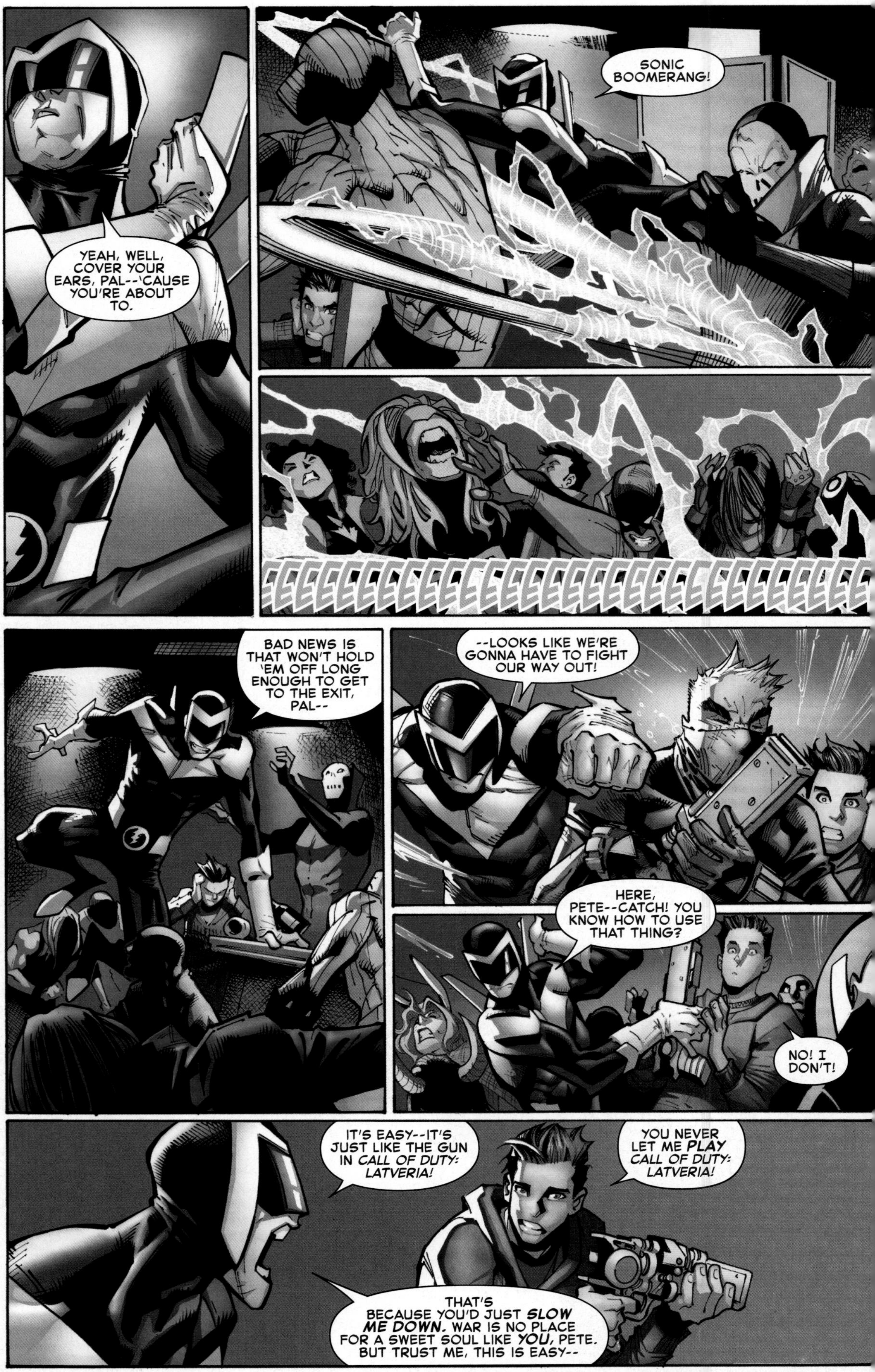
YEAH, WELL, COVER YOUR EARS, PAL--'CAUSE YOU'RE ABOUT TO.
SONIC BOOMERANG!
EEEEEEEEEEEEEEEEEEEEEEEEEEEEEEEE
BAD NEWS IS THAT WON'T HOLD 'EM OFF LONG ENOUGH TO GET TO THE EXIT, PAL--
--LOOKS LIKE WE'RE GONNA HAVE TO FIGHT OUR WAY OUT!
HERE, PETE--CATCH! YOU KNOW HOW TO USE THAT THING?
NO! I DON'T!
IT'S EASY--IT'S JUST LIKE THE GUN IN CALL OF DUTY: LATVERIA!
YOU NEVER LET ME PLAY CALL OF DUTY: LATVERIA!
THAT'S BECAUSE YOU'D JUST SLOW ME DOWN. WAR IS NO PLACE FOR A SWEET SOUL LIKE YOU, PETE. BUT TRUST ME, THIS IS EASY--

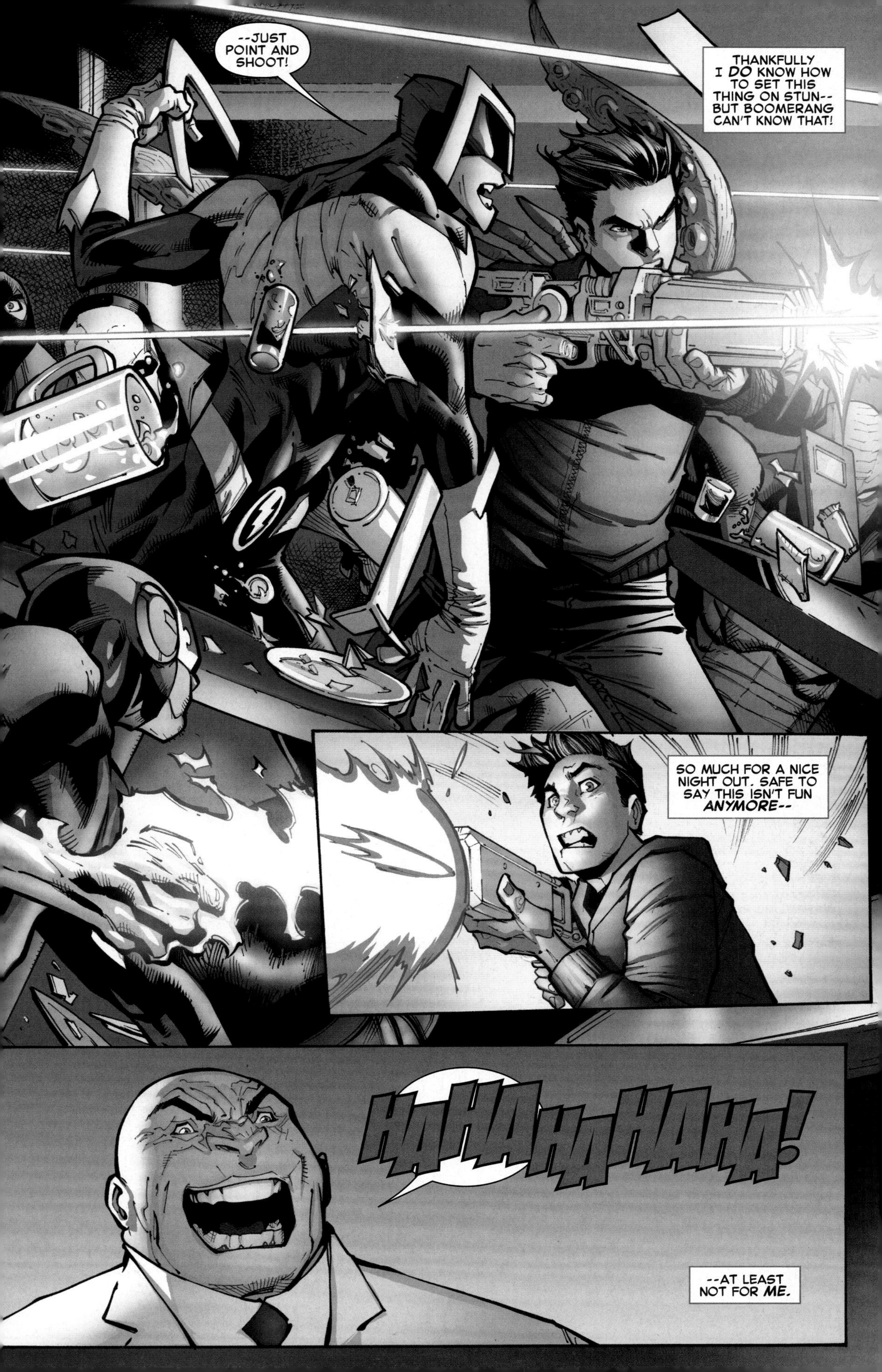
--JUST POINT AND SHOOT!
THANKFULLY I *DO* KNOW HOW TO SET THIS THING ON STUN-- BUT BOOMERANG CAN'T KNOW THAT!
SO MUCH FOR A NICE NIGHT OUT. SAFE TO SAY THIS ISN'T FUN ***ANYMORE--***
HAHAHAHAHA!
--AT LEAST NOT FOR ***ME.***

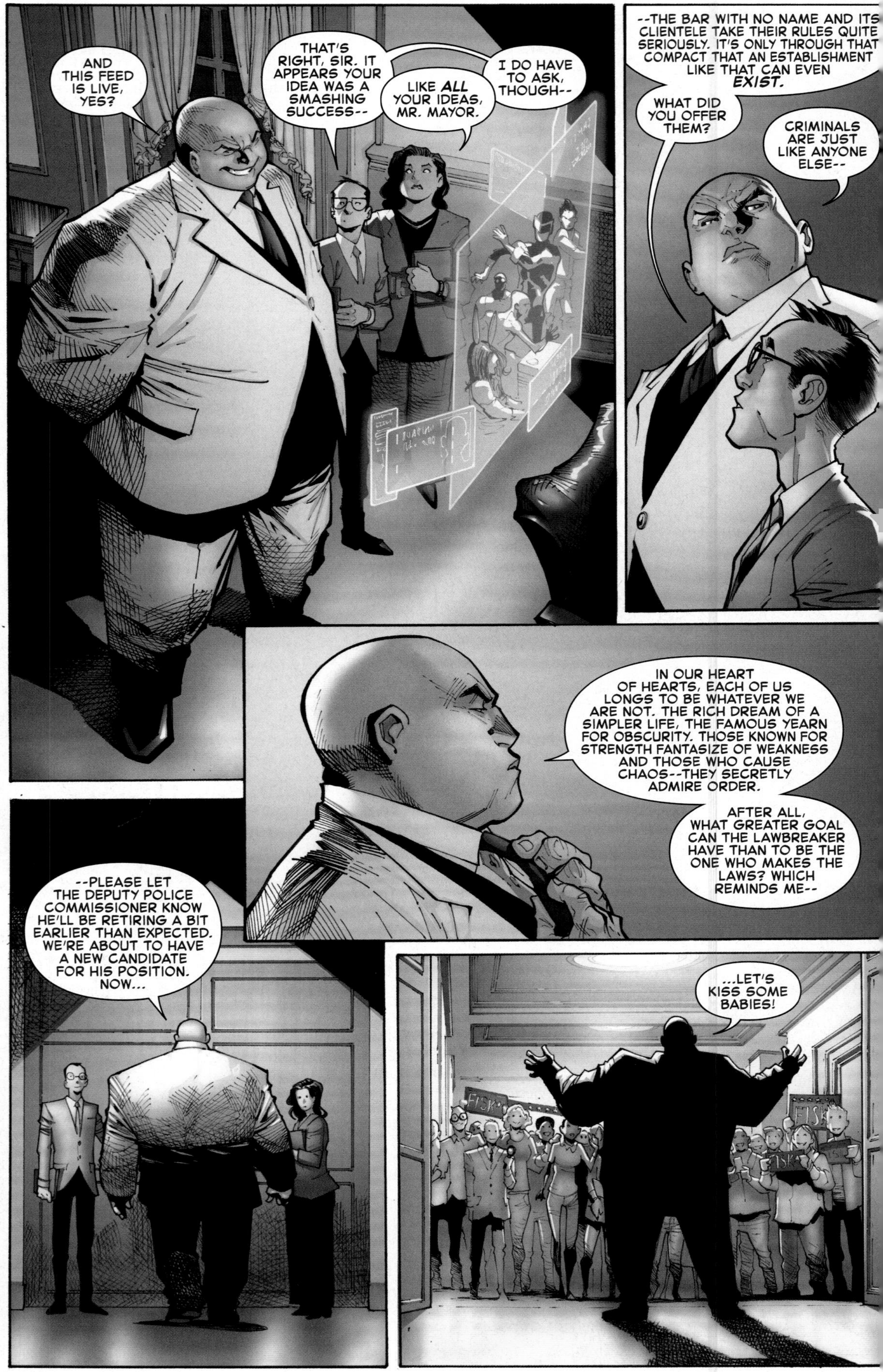
AND THIS FEED IS LIVE, YES?
THAT'S RIGHT, SIR. IT APPEARS YOUR IDEA WAS A SMASHING SUCCESS--
LIKE ALL YOUR IDEAS, MR. MAYOR.
I DO HAVE TO ASK, THOUGH--
--THE BAR WITH NO NAME AND ITS CLIENTELE TAKE THEIR RULES QUITE SERIOUSLY. IT'S ONLY THROUGH THAT COMPACT THAT AN ESTABLISHMENT LIKE THAT CAN EVEN EXIST.
WHAT DID YOU OFFER THEM?
CRIMINALS ARE JUST LIKE ANYONE ELSE--
IN OUR HEART OF HEARTS, EACH OF US LONGS TO BE WHATEVER WE ARE NOT. THE RICH DREAM OF A SIMPLER LIFE, THE FAMOUS YEARN FOR OBSCURITY. THOSE KNOWN FOR STRENGTH FANTASIZE OF WEAKNESS AND THOSE WHO CAUSE CHAOS--THEY SECRETLY ADMIRE ORDER.
AFTER ALL, WHAT GREATER GOAL CAN THE LAWBREAKER HAVE THAN TO BE THE ONE WHO MAKES THE LAWS? WHICH REMINDS ME--
--PLEASE LET THE DEPUTY POLICE COMMISSIONER KNOW HE'LL BE RETIRING A BIT EARLIER THAN EXPECTED. WE'RE ABOUT TO HAVE A NEW CANDIDATE FOR HIS POSITION. NOW...
...LET'S KISS SOME BABIES!
FISK
FISK
FISK

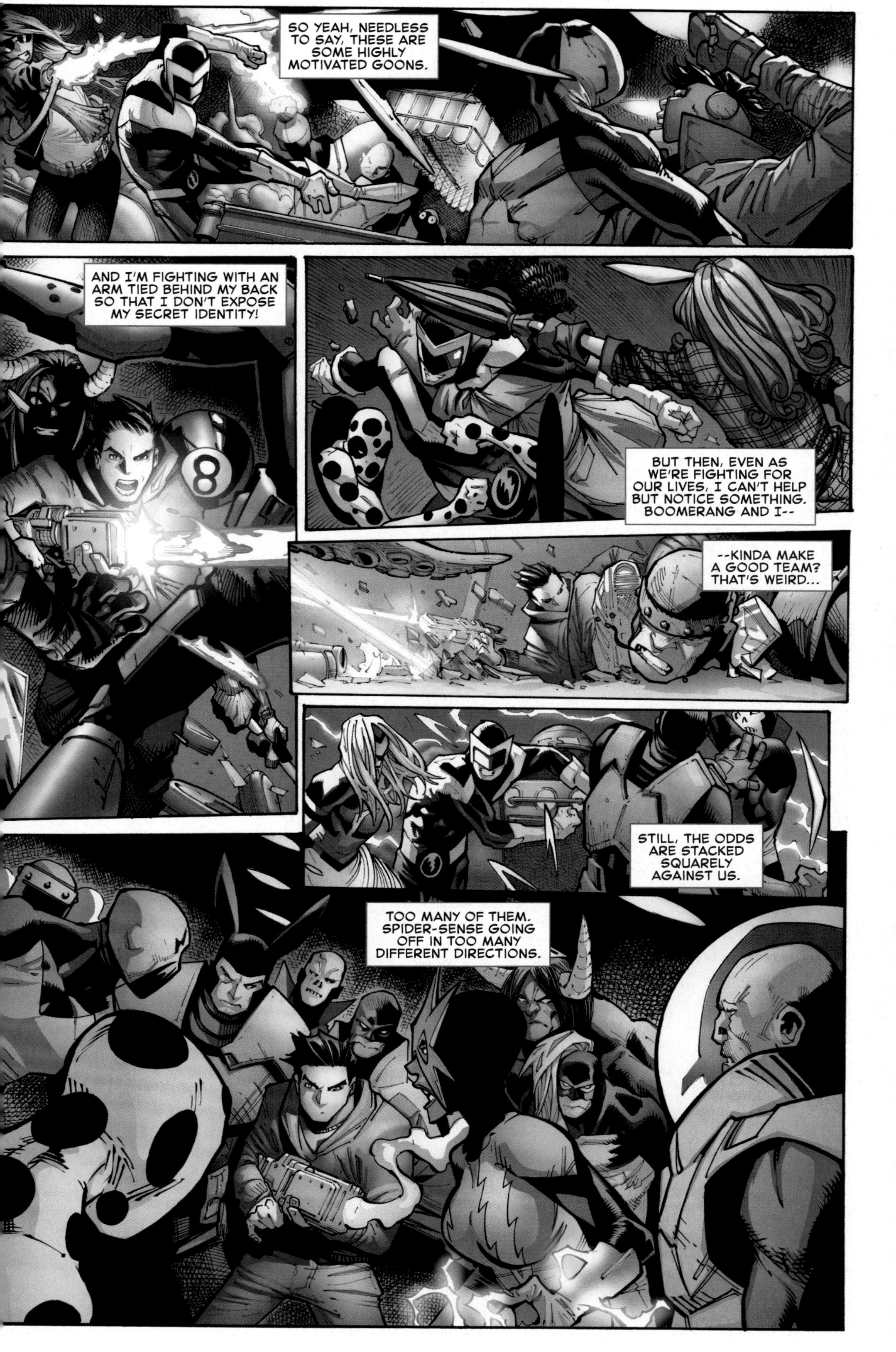
SO YEAH, NEEDLESS TO SAY, THESE ARE SOME HIGHLY MOTIVATED GOONS.
AND I'M FIGHTING WITH AN ARM TIED BEHIND MY BACK SO THAT I DON'T EXPOSE MY SECRET IDENTITY!
BUT THEN, EVEN AS WE'RE FIGHTING FOR OUR LIVES, I CAN'T HELP BUT NOTICE SOMETHING. BOOMERANG AND I--
--KINDA MAKE A GOOD TEAM? THAT'S WEIRD...
STILL, THE ODDS ARE STACKED SQUARELY AGAINST US.
TOO MANY OF THEM. SPIDER-SENSE GOING OFF IN TOO MANY DIFFERENT DIRECTIONS.

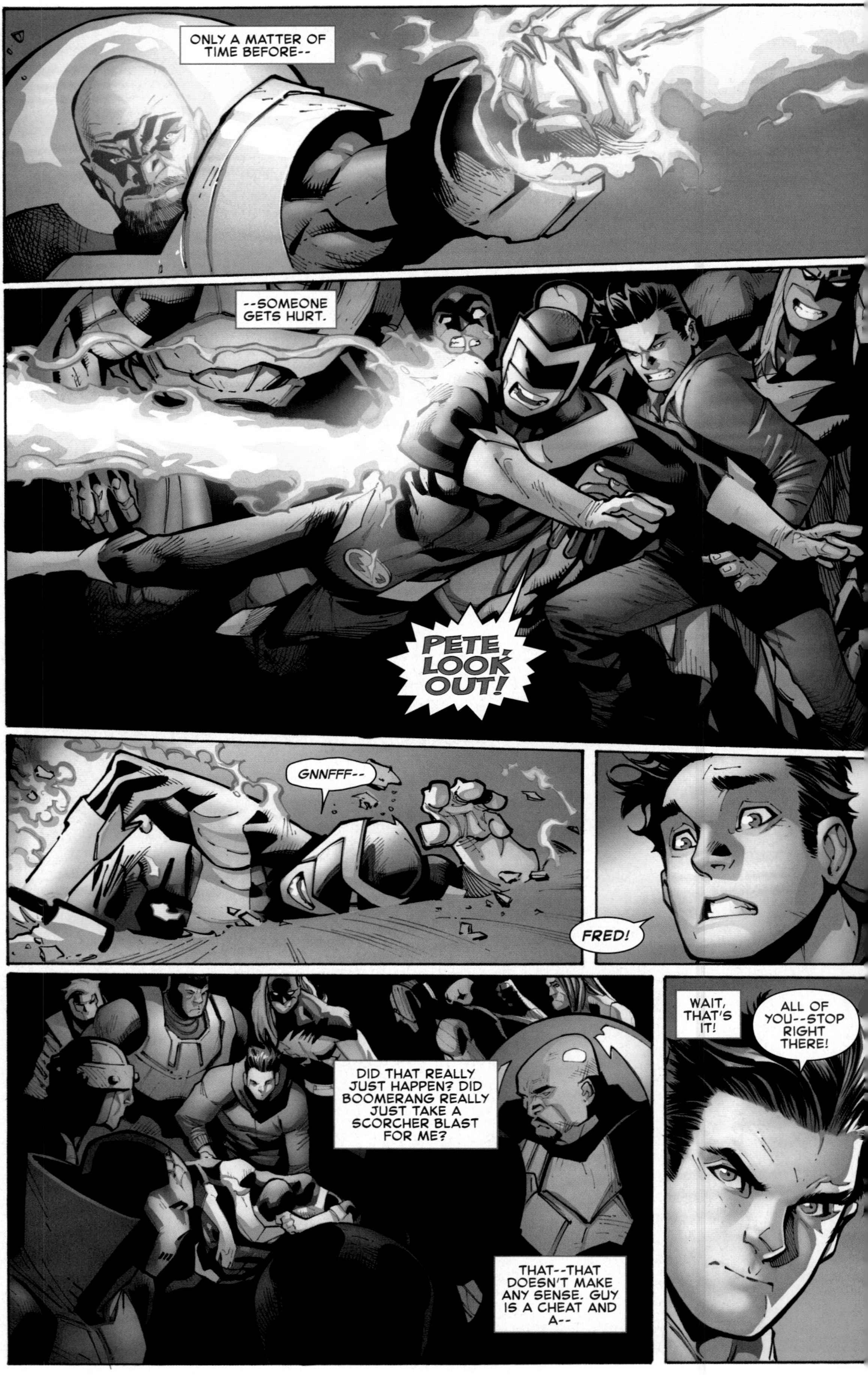
ONLY A MATTER OF TIME BEFORE--
--SOMEONE GETS HURT.
PETE, LOOK OUT!
GNNFFF--
FRED!
DID THAT REALLY JUST HAPPEN? DID BOOMERANG REALLY JUST TAKE A SCORCHER BLAST FOR ME?
THAT--THAT DOESN'T MAKE ANY SENSE. GUY IS A CHEAT AND A--
WAIT, THAT'S IT!
ALL OF YOU--STOP RIGHT THERE!

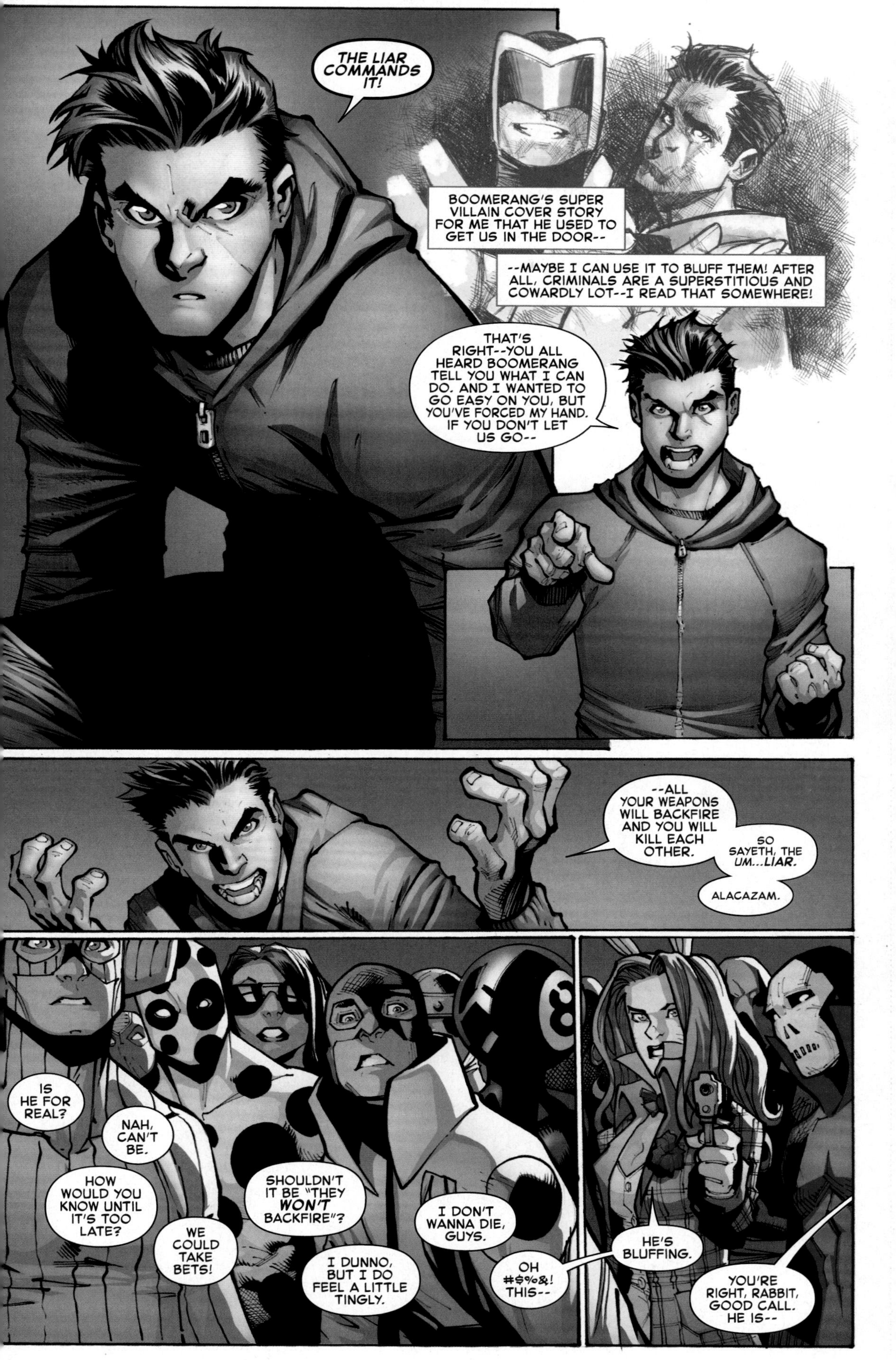
THE LIAR COMMANDS IT!
BOOMERANG'S SUPER VILLAIN COVER STORY FOR ME THAT HE USED TO GET US IN THE DOOR--
--MAYBE I CAN USE IT TO BLUFF THEM! AFTER ALL, CRIMINALS ARE A SUPERSTITIOUS AND COWARDLY LOT--I READ THAT SOMEWHERE!
THAT'S RIGHT--YOU ALL HEARD BOOMERANG TELL YOU WHAT I CAN DO. AND I WANTED TO GO EASY ON YOU, BUT YOU'VE FORCED MY HAND. IF YOU DON'T LET US GO--
--ALL YOUR WEAPONS WILL BACKFIRE AND YOU WILL KILL EACH OTHER.
SO SAYETH, THE *UM...LIAR.*
ALACAZAM.
IS HE FOR REAL?
NAH, CAN'T BE.
HOW WOULD YOU KNOW UNTIL IT'S TOO LATE?
WE COULD TAKE BETS!
SHOULDN'T IT BE "THEY *WON'T* BACKFIRE"?
I DUNNO, BUT I DO FEEL A LITTLE TINGLY.
I DON'T WANNA DIE, GUYS.
OH #$%&! THIS--
HE'S BLUFFING.
YOU'RE RIGHT, RABBIT, GOOD CALL. HE IS--

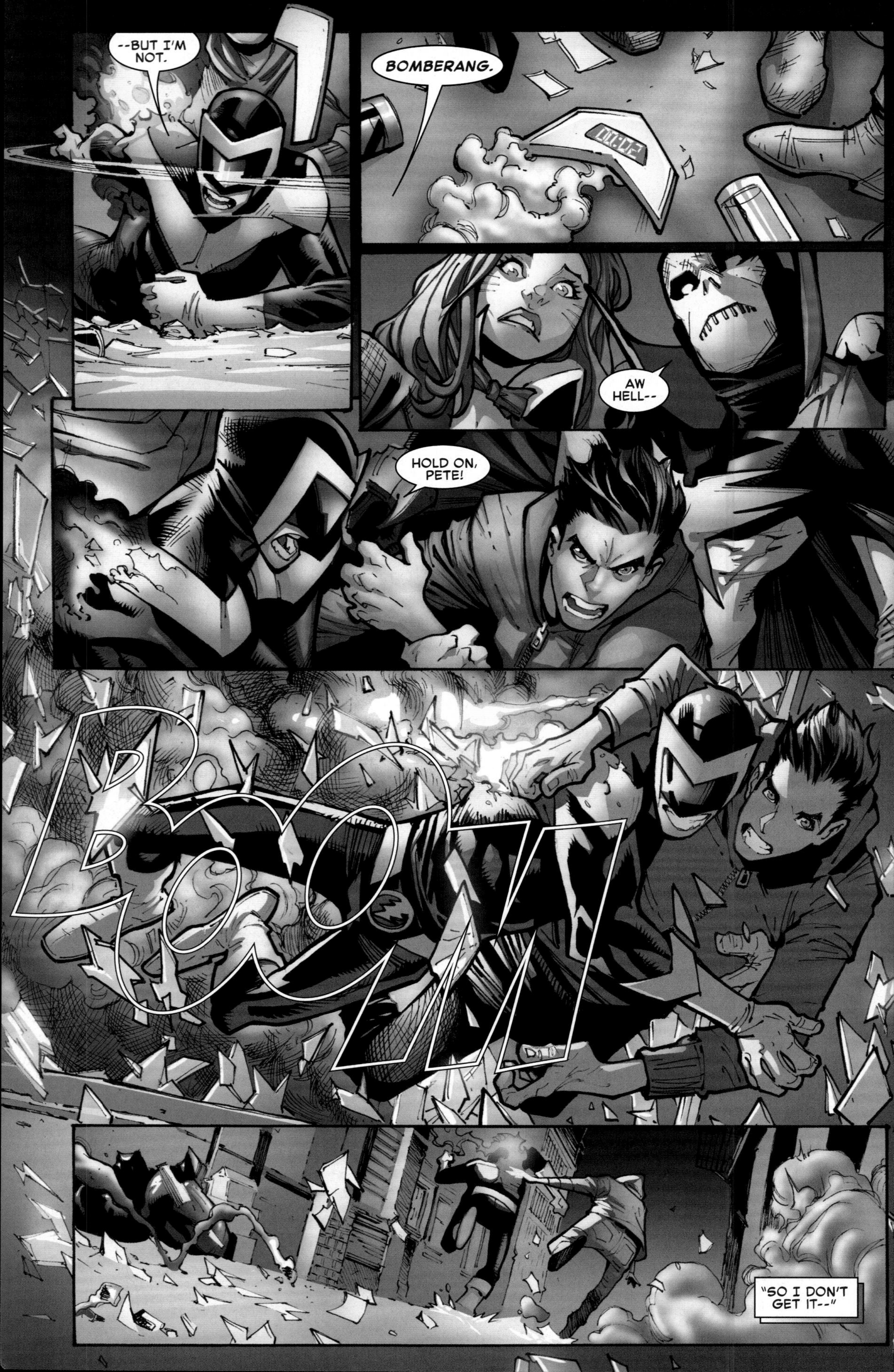
--BUT I'M NOT.
BOMBERANG.
AW HELL--
HOLD ON, PETE!
BOOM
"SO I DON'T GET IT--"

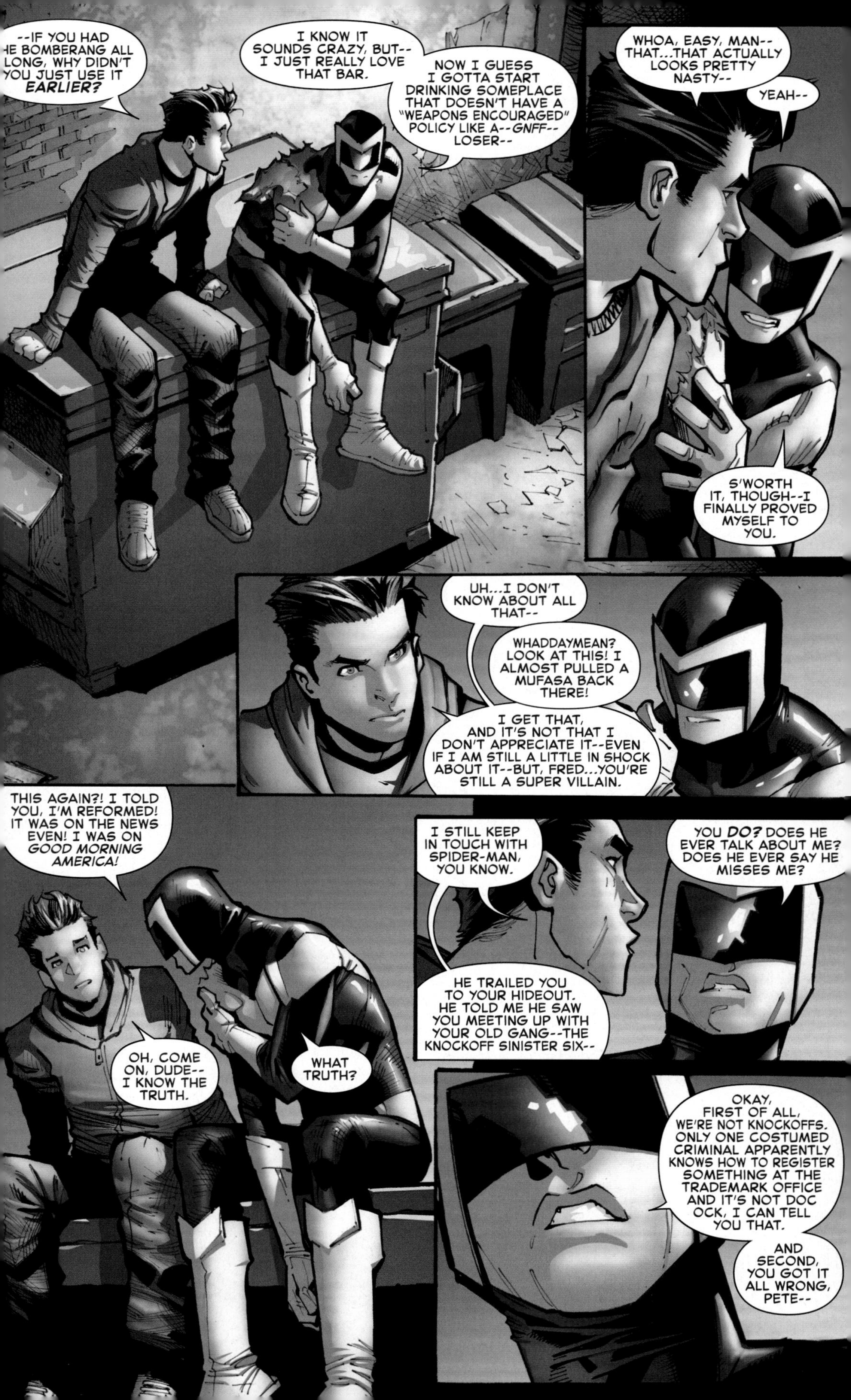
--IF YOU HAD THE BOMBERANG ALL ALONG, WHY DIDN'T YOU JUST USE IT *EARLIER?*
I KNOW IT SOUNDS CRAZY, BUT-- I JUST REALLY LOVE THAT BAR.
NOW I GUESS I GOTTA START DRINKING SOMEPLACE THAT DOESN'T HAVE A "WEAPONS ENCOURAGED" POLICY LIKE A--*GNFF*-- LOSER--
WHOA, EASY, MAN-- THAT...THAT ACTUALLY LOOKS PRETTY NASTY--
YEAH--
S'WORTH IT, THOUGH--I FINALLY PROVED MYSELF TO YOU.
UH...I DON'T KNOW ABOUT ALL THAT--
WHADDAYMEAN? LOOK AT THIS! I ALMOST PULLED A MUFASA BACK THERE!
I GET THAT, AND IT'S NOT THAT I DON'T APPRECIATE IT--EVEN IF I AM STILL A LITTLE IN SHOCK ABOUT IT--BUT, FRED...YOU'RE STILL A SUPER VILLAIN.
THIS AGAIN?! I TOLD YOU, I'M REFORMED! IT WAS ON THE NEWS EVEN! I WAS ON *GOOD MORNING AMERICA!*
OH, COME ON, DUDE-- I KNOW THE TRUTH.
WHAT TRUTH?
I STILL KEEP IN TOUCH WITH SPIDER-MAN, YOU KNOW.
YOU *DO?* DOES HE EVER TALK ABOUT ME? DOES HE EVER SAY HE MISSES ME?
HE TRAILED YOU TO YOUR HIDEOUT. HE TOLD ME HE SAW YOU MEETING UP WITH YOUR OLD GANG--THE KNOCKOFF SINISTER SIX--
OKAY, FIRST OF ALL, WE'RE NOT KNOCKOFFS. ONLY ONE COSTUMED CRIMINAL APPARENTLY KNOWS HOW TO REGISTER SOMETHING AT THE TRADEMARK OFFICE AND IT'S NOT DOC OCK, I CAN TELL YOU THAT.
AND SECOND, YOU GOT IT ALL WRONG, PETE--

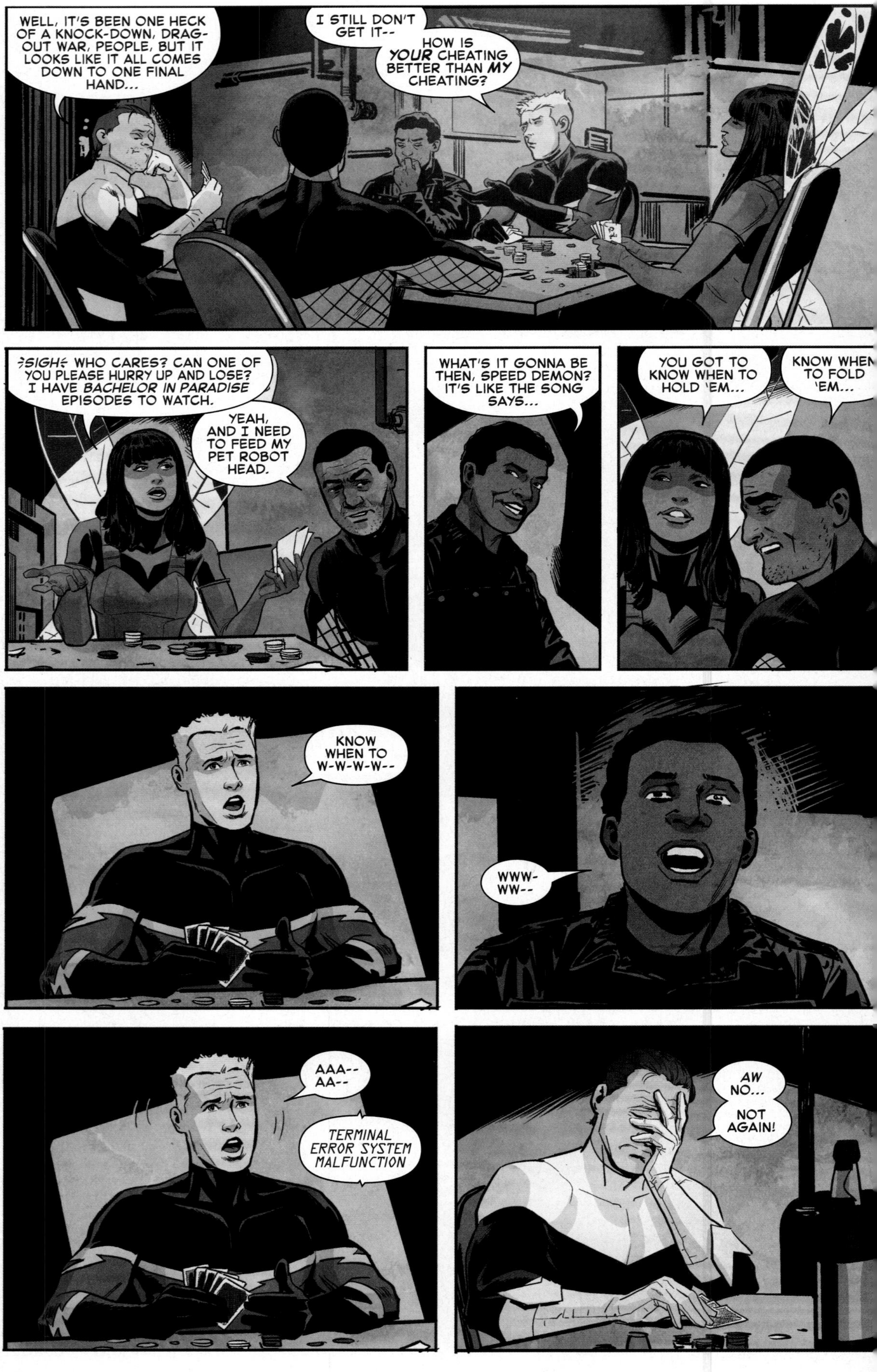
WELL, IT'S BEEN ONE HECK OF A KNOCK-DOWN, DRAG-OUT WAR, PEOPLE, BUT IT LOOKS LIKE IT ALL COMES DOWN TO ONE FINAL HAND...
I STILL DON'T GET IT--
HOW IS *YOUR* CHEATING BETTER THAN *MY* CHEATING?
SIGH WHO CARES? CAN ONE OF YOU PLEASE HURRY UP AND LOSE? I HAVE *BACHELOR IN PARADISE* EPISODES TO WATCH.
YEAH, AND I NEED TO FEED MY PET ROBOT HEAD.
WHAT'S IT GONNA BE THEN, SPEED DEMON? IT'S LIKE THE SONG SAYS...
YOU GOT TO KNOW WHEN TO HOLD 'EM...
KNOW WHEN TO FOLD 'EM...
KNOW WHEN TO W-W-W-W--
WWW-WW--
AAA--AA--
TERMINAL ERROR SYSTEM MALFUNCTION
AW NO...
NOT AGAIN!

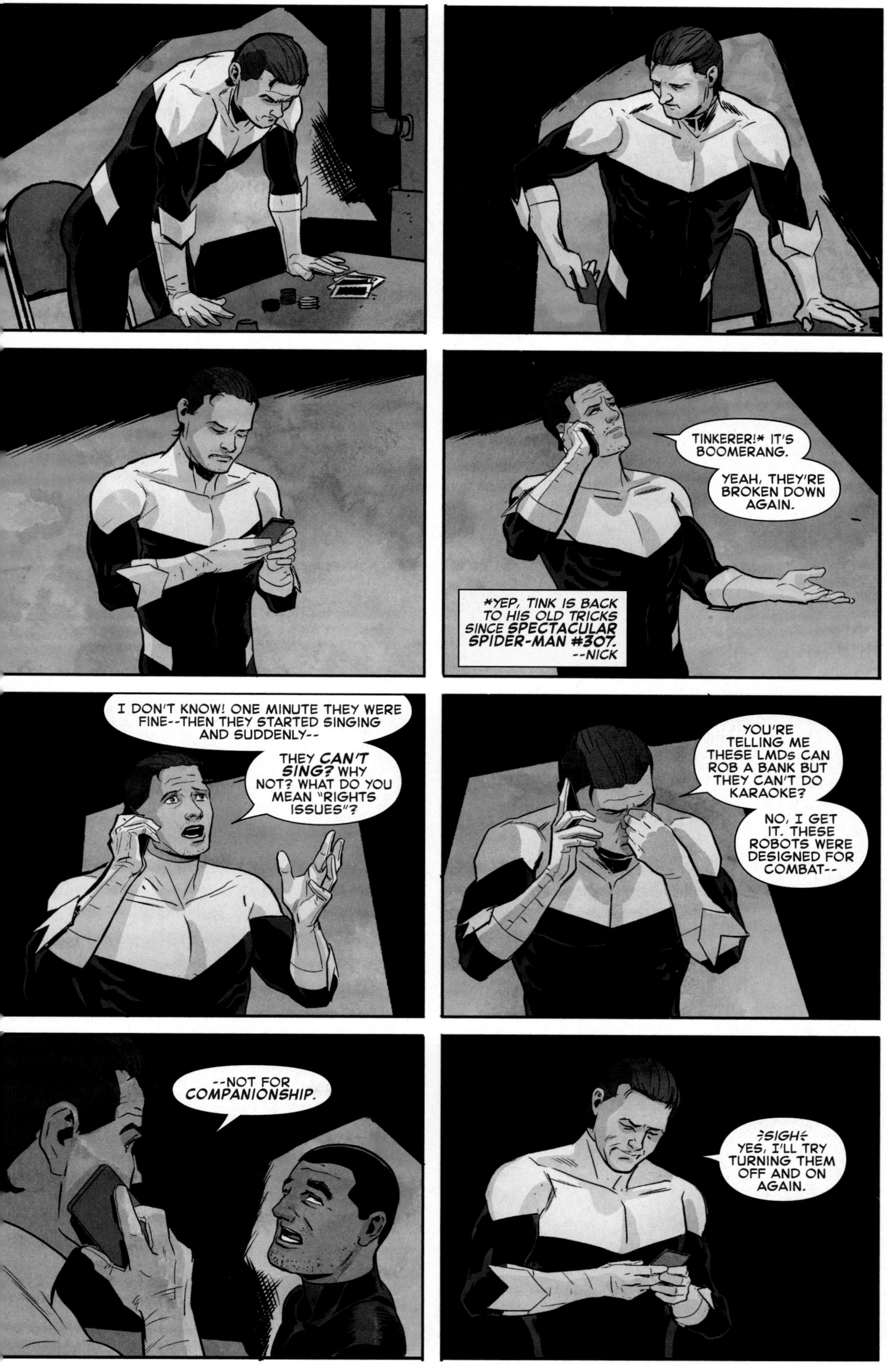
TINKERER!* IT'S BOOMERANG.
YEAH, THEY'RE BROKEN DOWN AGAIN.
*YEP, TINK IS BACK TO HIS OLD TRICKS SINCE SPECTACULAR SPIDER-MAN #307. --NICK
I DON'T KNOW! ONE MINUTE THEY WERE FINE--THEN THEY STARTED SINGING AND SUDDENLY--
THEY CAN'T SING? WHY NOT? WHAT DO YOU MEAN "RIGHTS ISSUES"?
YOU'RE TELLING ME THESE LMDs CAN ROB A BANK BUT THEY CAN'T DO KARAOKE?
NO, I GET IT. THESE ROBOTS WERE DESIGNED FOR COMBAT--
--NOT FOR COMPANIONSHIP.
SIGH YES, I'LL TRY TURNING THEM OFF AND ON AGAIN.

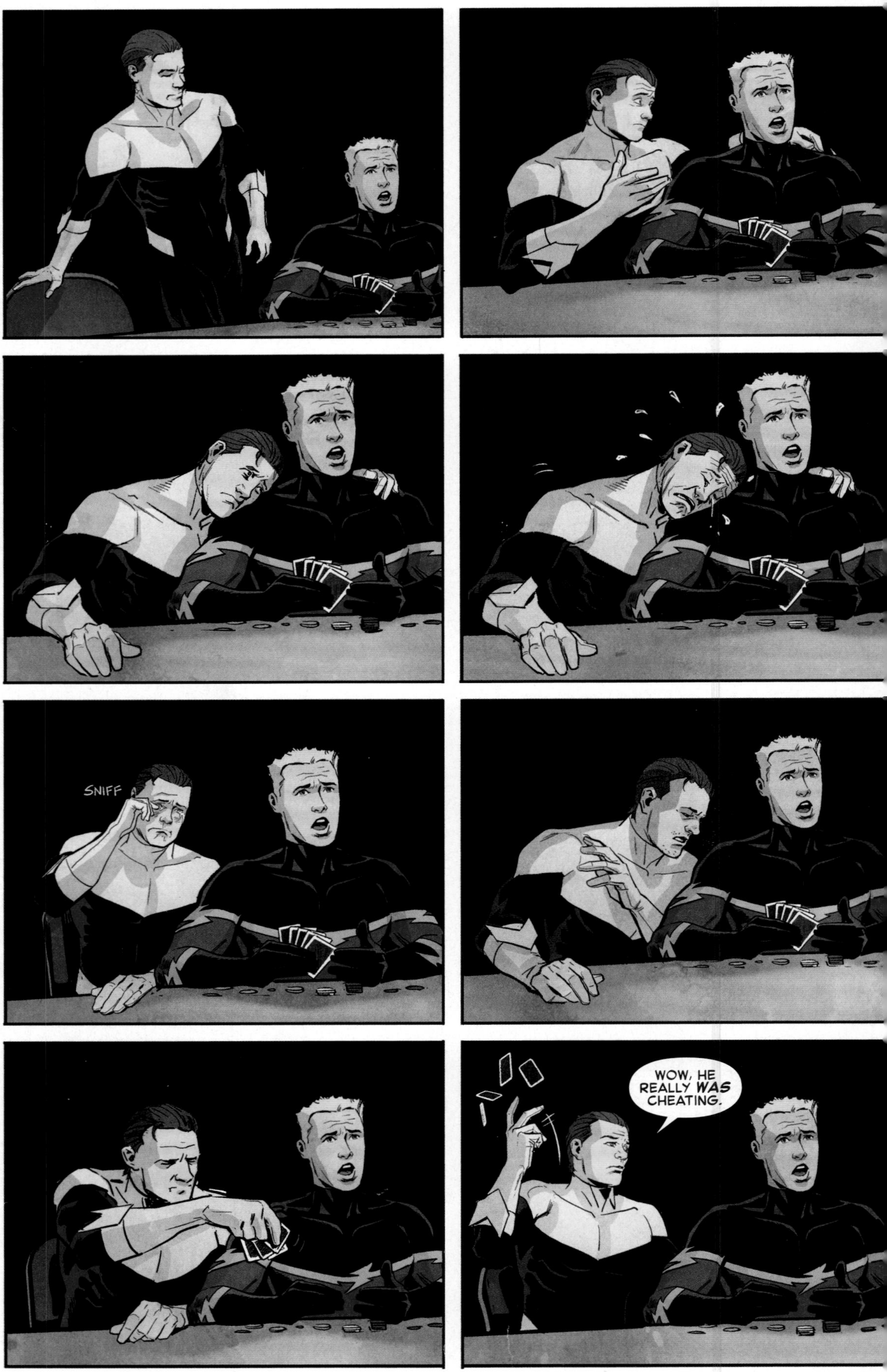
SNIFF
WOW, HE REALLY WAS CHEATING.

GEEZ, FRED... I--I DIDN'T KNOW, MAN. I'M SORRY.

EH, NO REASON TO APOLOGIZE. TRUTH IS, I *DESERVE* IT--

--THEY WERE MY GANG. I WAS THEIR LEADER. I WAS SUPPOSED TO LOOK OUT FOR THEM. BUT ALL I EVER DID WAS STAB THEM IN THE BACK, USE THEM AS PAWNS IN MY DUMB LITTLE ATTEMPT TO... HECK, I DON'T KNOW WHAT I WAS ATTEMPTING AT THIS POINT.

BY THE TIME IT WAS ALL OVER, I DIDN'T HAVE A SINGLE FRIEND LEFT. WHO COULD BLAME THEM?

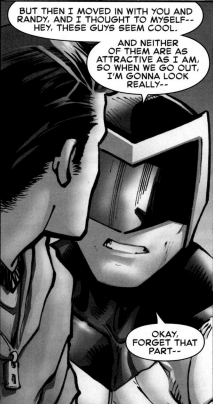

BUT THEN I MOVED IN WITH YOU AND RANDY, AND I THOUGHT TO MYSELF-- HEY, THESE GUYS SEEM COOL.

AND NEITHER OF THEM ARE AS ATTRACTIVE AS I AM, SO WHEN WE GO OUT, I'M GONNA LOOK REALLY--

OKAY, FORGET THAT PART--

MY POINT IS, I THOUGHT MAYBE I COULD GET IT RIGHT THIS TIME. BUT YOU'RE RIGHT, WHY WOULD ANYBODY TRUST ME AFTER EVERYTHING I'VE DONE?

IT'S TOO LATE...

≥SIGH≤ SUNDAYS.

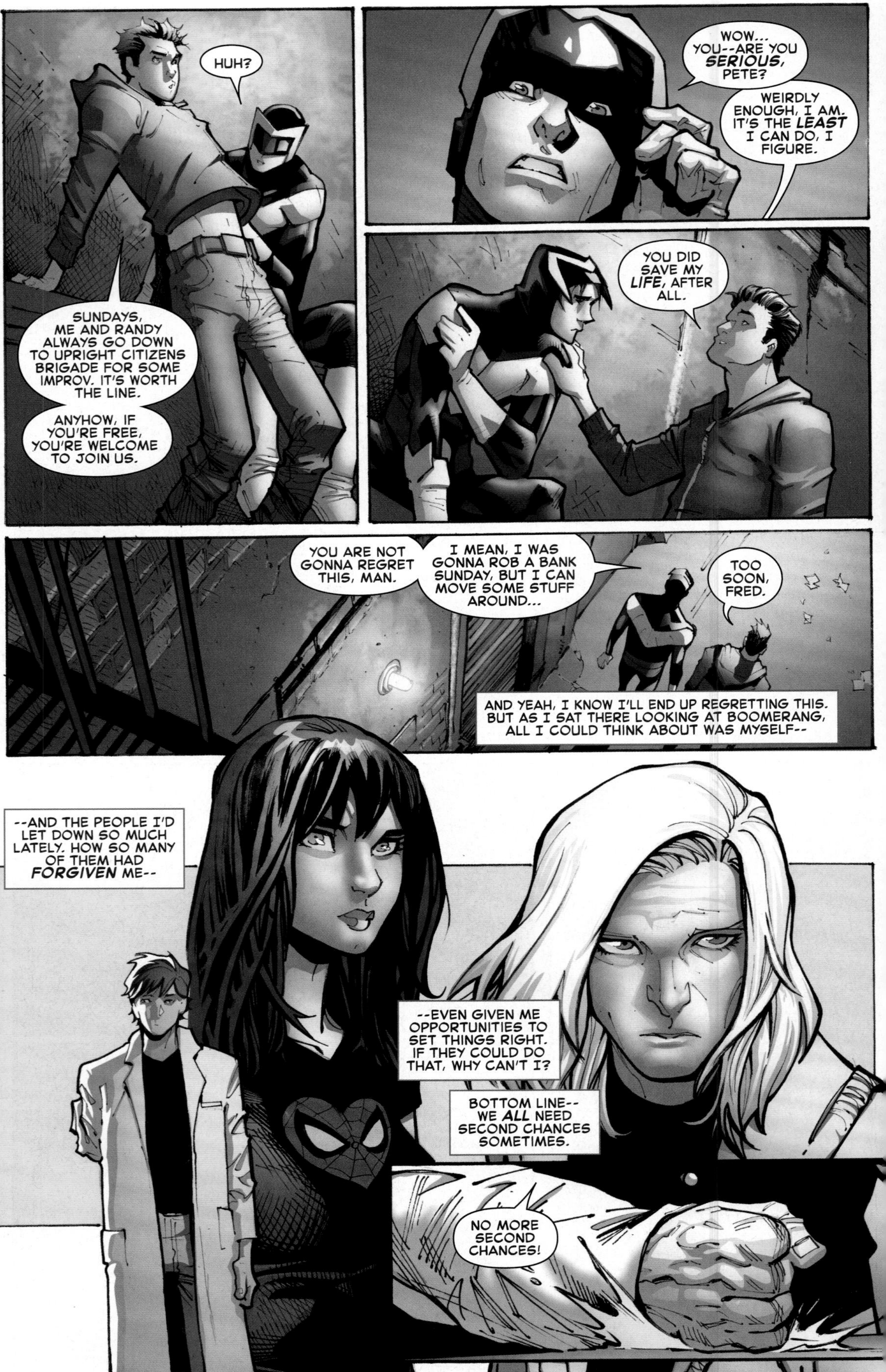
HUH?
SUNDAYS, ME AND RANDY ALWAYS GO DOWN TO UPRIGHT CITIZENS BRIGADE FOR SOME IMPROV. IT'S WORTH THE LINE.
ANYHOW, IF YOU'RE FREE, YOU'RE WELCOME TO JOIN US.
WOW... YOU--ARE YOU SERIOUS, PETE?
WEIRDLY ENOUGH, I AM. IT'S THE LEAST I CAN DO, I FIGURE.
YOU DID SAVE MY LIFE, AFTER ALL.
YOU ARE NOT GONNA REGRET THIS, MAN.
I MEAN, I WAS GONNA ROB A BANK SUNDAY, BUT I CAN MOVE SOME STUFF AROUND...
TOO SOON, FRED.
AND YEAH, I KNOW I'LL END UP REGRETTING THIS. BUT AS I SAT THERE LOOKING AT BOOMERANG, ALL I COULD THINK ABOUT WAS MYSELF--
--AND THE PEOPLE I'D LET DOWN SO MUCH LATELY. HOW SO MANY OF THEM HAD FORGIVEN ME--
--EVEN GIVEN ME OPPORTUNITIES TO SET THINGS RIGHT. IF THEY COULD DO THAT, WHY CAN'T I?
BOTTOM LINE-- WE ALL NEED SECOND CHANCES SOMETIMES.
NO MORE SECOND CHANCES!

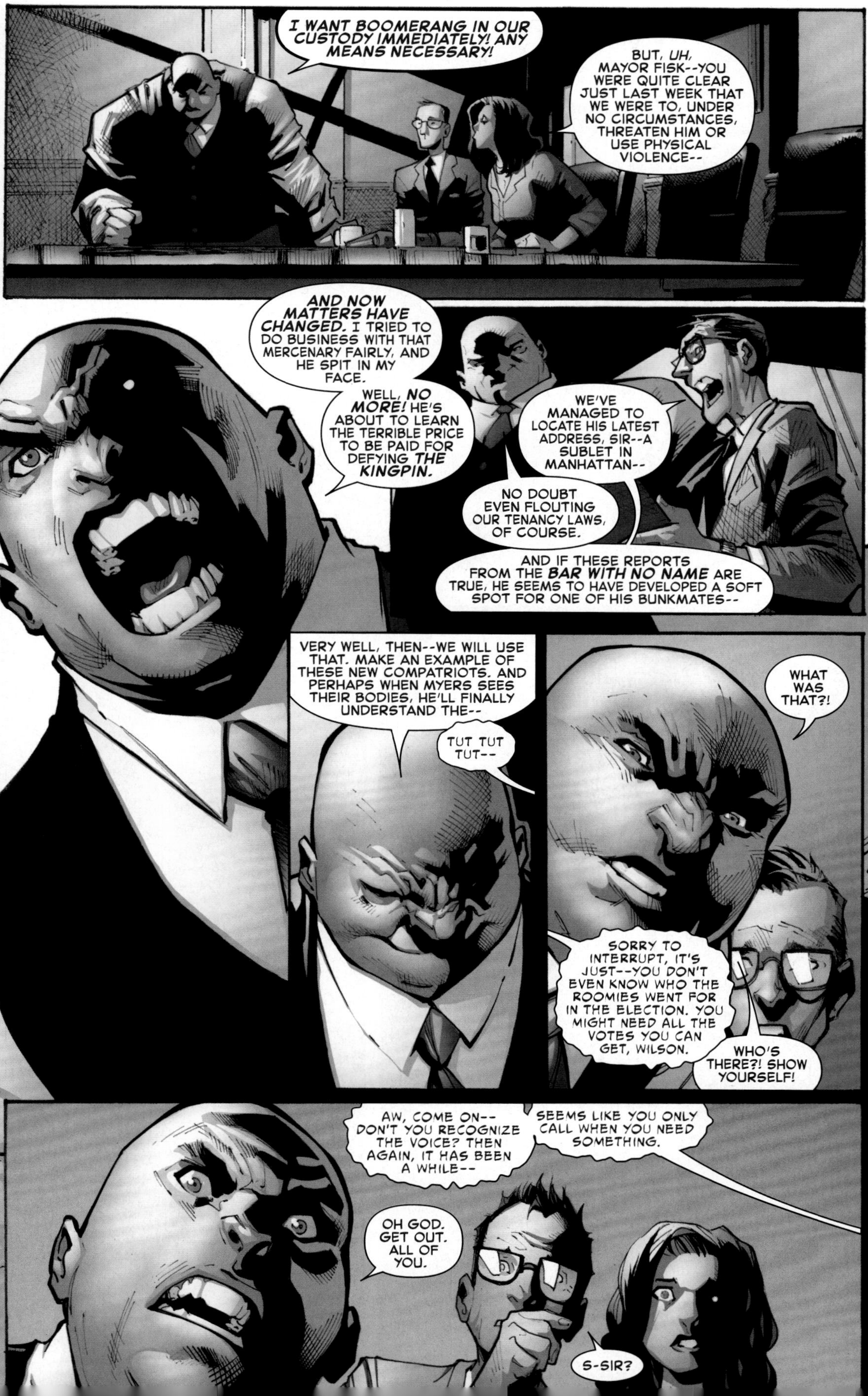

I WANT BOOMERANG IN OUR CUSTODY IMMEDIATELY! ANY MEANS NECESSARY!
BUT, UH, MAYOR FISK--YOU WERE QUITE CLEAR JUST LAST WEEK THAT WE WERE TO, UNDER NO CIRCUMSTANCES, THREATEN HIM OR USE PHYSICAL VIOLENCE--
AND NOW MATTERS HAVE CHANGED. I TRIED TO DO BUSINESS WITH THAT MERCENARY FAIRLY, AND HE SPIT IN MY FACE.
WELL, NO MORE! HE'S ABOUT TO LEARN THE TERRIBLE PRICE TO BE PAID FOR DEFYING THE KINGPIN.
WE'VE MANAGED TO LOCATE HIS LATEST ADDRESS, SIR--A SUBLET IN MANHATTAN--
NO DOUBT EVEN FLOUTING OUR TENANCY LAWS, OF COURSE.
AND IF THESE REPORTS FROM THE BAR WITH NO NAME ARE TRUE, HE SEEMS TO HAVE DEVELOPED A SOFT SPOT FOR ONE OF HIS BUNKMATES--
VERY WELL, THEN--WE WILL USE THAT. MAKE AN EXAMPLE OF THESE NEW COMPATRIOTS. AND PERHAPS WHEN MYERS SEES THEIR BODIES, HE'LL FINALLY UNDERSTAND THE--
TUT TUT TUT--
WHAT WAS THAT?!
SORRY TO INTERRUPT, IT'S JUST--YOU DON'T EVEN KNOW WHO THE ROOMIES WENT FOR IN THE ELECTION. YOU MIGHT NEED ALL THE VOTES YOU CAN GET, WILSON.
WHO'S THERE?! SHOW YOURSELF!
AW, COME ON--DON'T YOU RECOGNIZE THE VOICE? THEN AGAIN, IT HAS BEEN A WHILE--
SEEMS LIKE YOU ONLY CALL WHEN YOU NEED SOMETHING.
OH GOD. GET OUT. ALL OF YOU.
S-SIR?

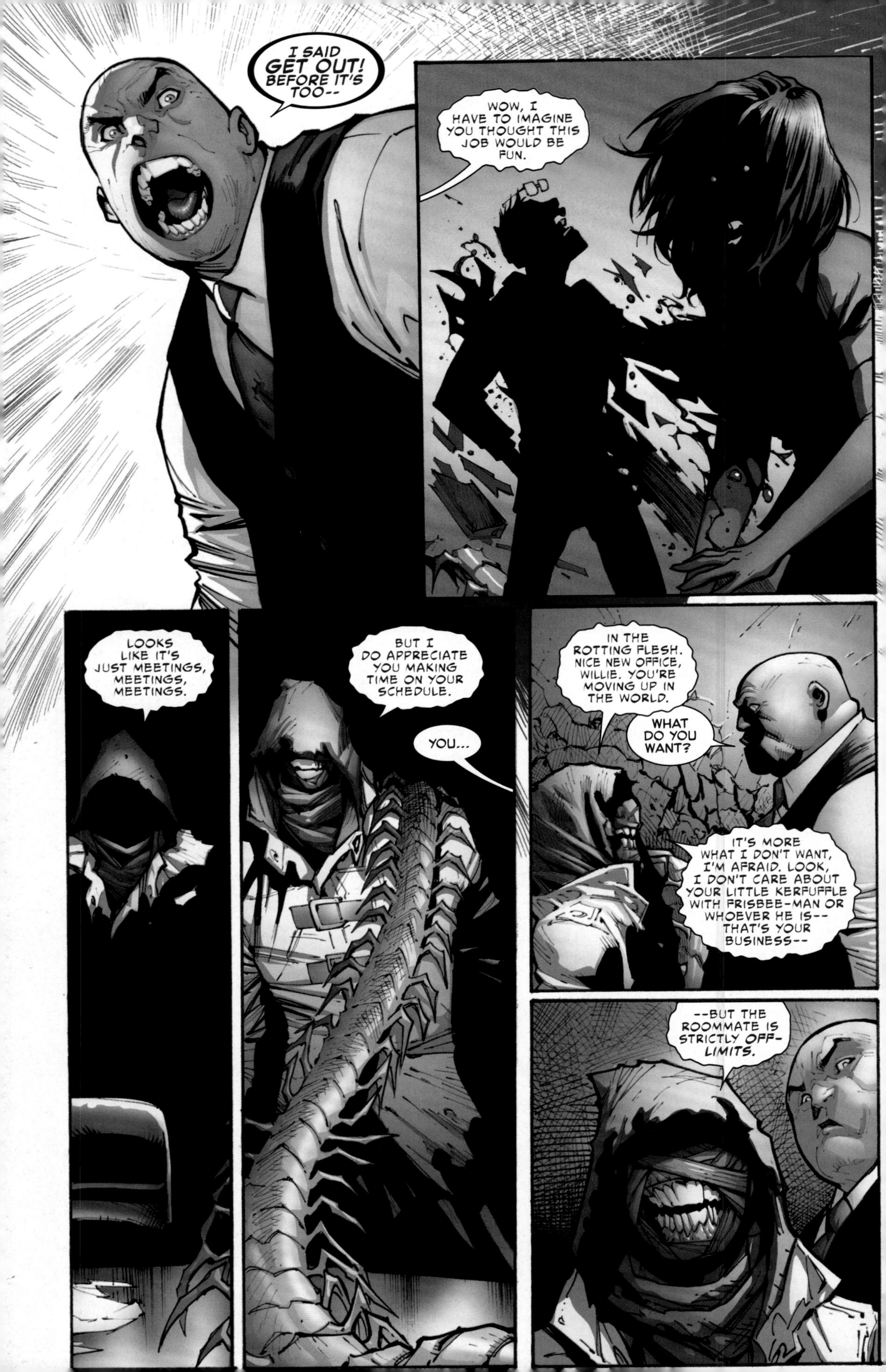
I SAID GET OUT! BEFORE IT'S TOO--
WOW, I HAVE TO IMAGINE YOU THOUGHT THIS JOB WOULD BE FUN.
LOOKS LIKE IT'S JUST MEETINGS, MEETINGS, MEETINGS.
BUT I DO APPRECIATE YOU MAKING TIME ON YOUR SCHEDULE.
YOU...
IN THE ROTTING FLESH. NICE NEW OFFICE, WILLIE. YOU'RE MOVING UP IN THE WORLD.
WHAT DO YOU WANT?
IT'S MORE WHAT I DON'T WANT, I'M AFRAID. LOOK, I DON'T CARE ABOUT YOUR LITTLE KERFUFFLE WITH FRISBEE-MAN OR WHOEVER HE IS-- THAT'S YOUR BUSINESS--
--BUT THE ROOMMATE IS STRICTLY OFF-LIMITS.

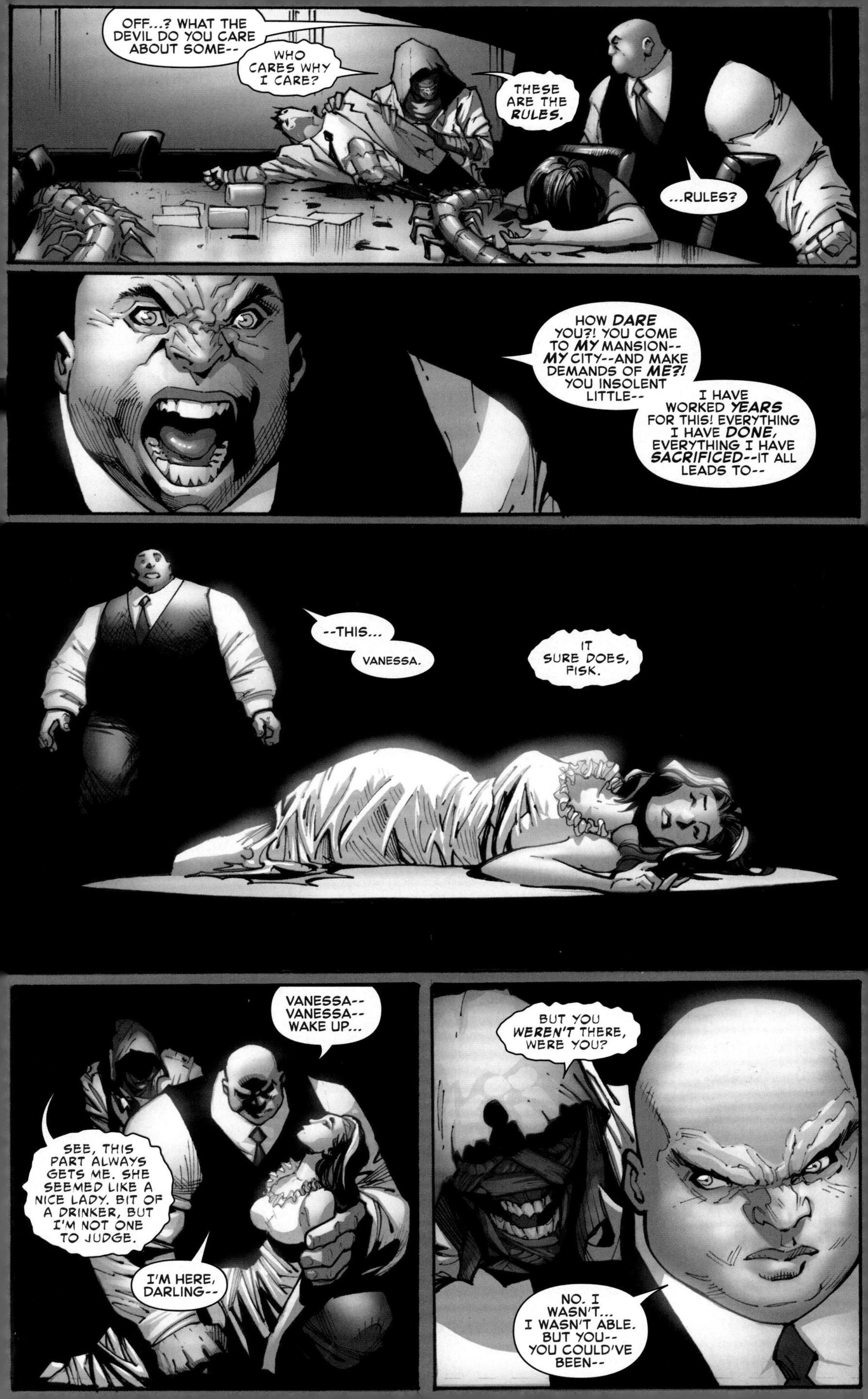

OFF...? WHAT THE DEVIL DO YOU CARE ABOUT SOME--
WHO CARES WHY I CARE?
THESE ARE THE **RULES**.
...RULES?
HOW **DARE** YOU?! YOU COME TO **MY** MANSION-- **MY** CITY--AND MAKE DEMANDS OF **ME?!** YOU INSOLENT LITTLE--
I HAVE WORKED **YEARS** FOR THIS! EVERYTHING I HAVE **DONE**, EVERYTHING I HAVE **SACRIFICED**--IT ALL LEADS TO--
--THIS...
VANESSA.
IT SURE DOES, FISK.
VANESSA-- VANESSA-- WAKE UP...
SEE, THIS PART ALWAYS GETS ME. SHE SEEMED LIKE A NICE LADY. BIT OF A DRINKER, BUT I'M NOT ONE TO JUDGE.
I'M HERE, DARLING--
BUT YOU **WEREN'T** THERE, WERE YOU?
NO. I WASN'T... I WASN'T ABLE. BUT YOU-- YOU COULD'VE BEEN--

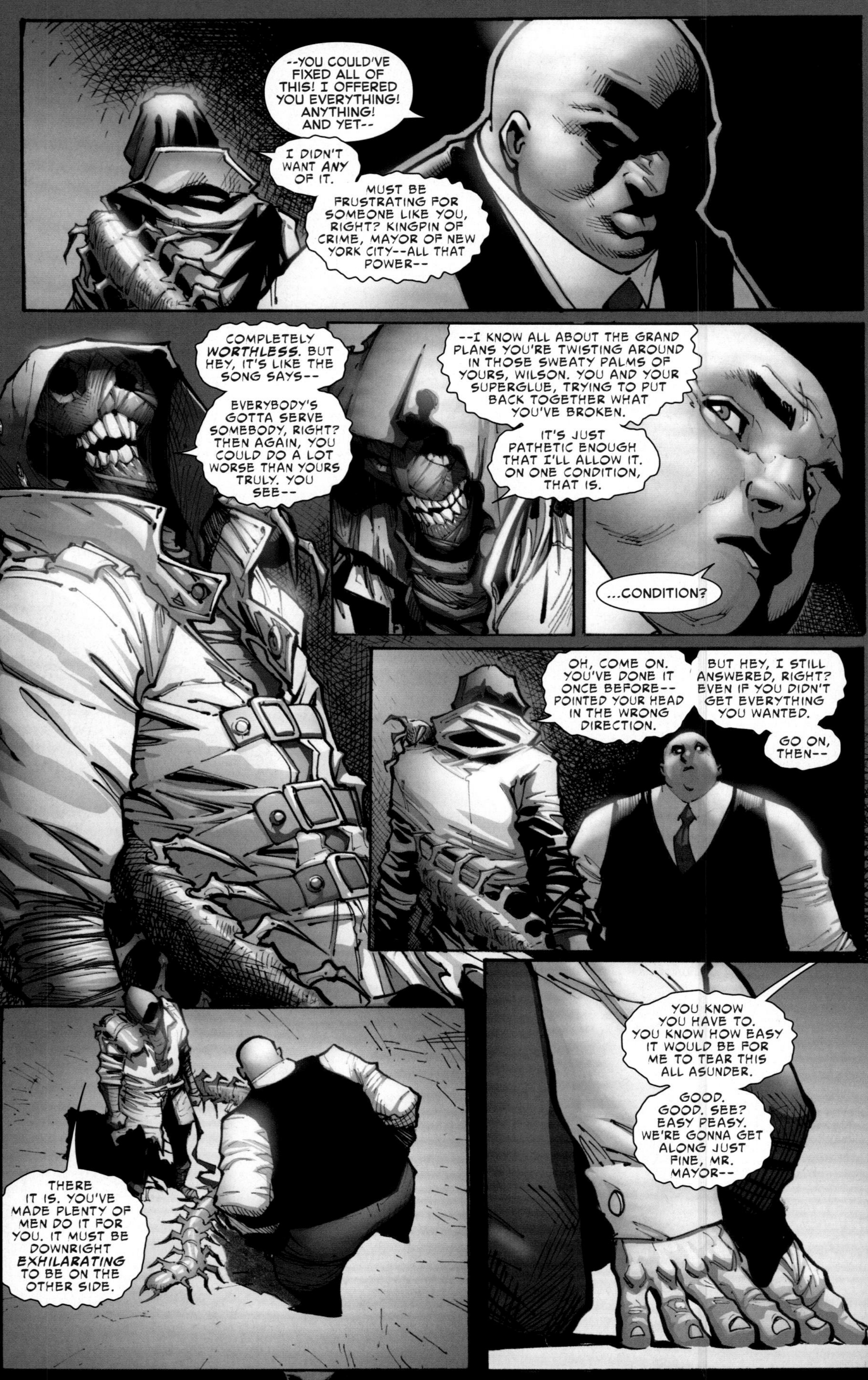

--YOU COULD'VE FIXED ALL OF THIS! I OFFERED YOU EVERYTHING! ANYTHING! AND YET--
I DIDN'T WANT ANY OF IT.
MUST BE FRUSTRATING FOR SOMEONE LIKE YOU, RIGHT? KINGPIN OF CRIME, MAYOR OF NEW YORK CITY--ALL THAT POWER--
COMPLETELY WORTHLESS. BUT HEY, IT'S LIKE THE SONG SAYS--
EVERYBODY'S GOTTA SERVE SOMEBODY, RIGHT? THEN AGAIN, YOU COULD DO A LOT WORSE THAN YOURS TRULY. YOU SEE--
--I KNOW ALL ABOUT THE GRAND PLANS YOU'RE TWISTING AROUND IN THOSE SWEATY PALMS OF YOURS, WILSON. YOU AND YOUR SUPERGLUE, TRYING TO PUT BACK TOGETHER WHAT YOU'VE BROKEN.
IT'S JUST PATHETIC ENOUGH THAT I'LL ALLOW IT. ON ONE CONDITION, THAT IS.
...CONDITION?
OH, COME ON. YOU'VE DONE IT ONCE BEFORE-- POINTED YOUR HEAD IN THE WRONG DIRECTION.
BUT HEY, I STILL ANSWERED, RIGHT? EVEN IF YOU DIDN'T GET EVERYTHING YOU WANTED.
GO ON, THEN--
YOU KNOW YOU HAVE TO. YOU KNOW HOW EASY IT WOULD BE FOR ME TO TEAR THIS ALL ASUNDER.
GOOD. GOOD. SEE? EASY PEASY. WE'RE GONNA GET ALONG JUST FINE, MR. MAYOR--
THERE IT IS. YOU'VE MADE PLENTY OF MEN DO IT FOR YOU. IT MUST BE DOWNRIGHT EXHILARATING TO BE ON THE OTHER SIDE.

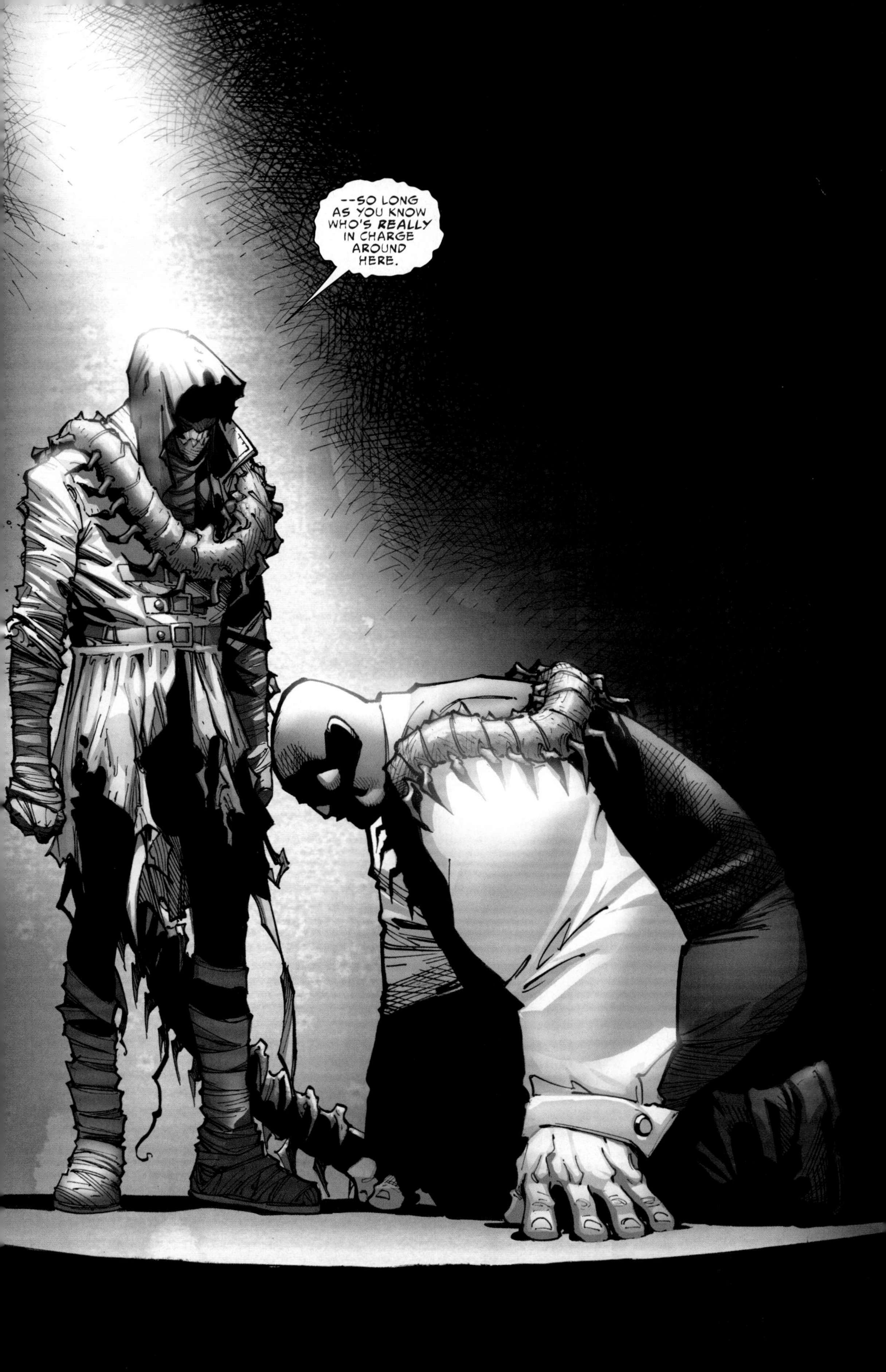
--SO LONG AS YOU KNOW WHO'S REALLY IN CHARGE AROUND HERE.

8

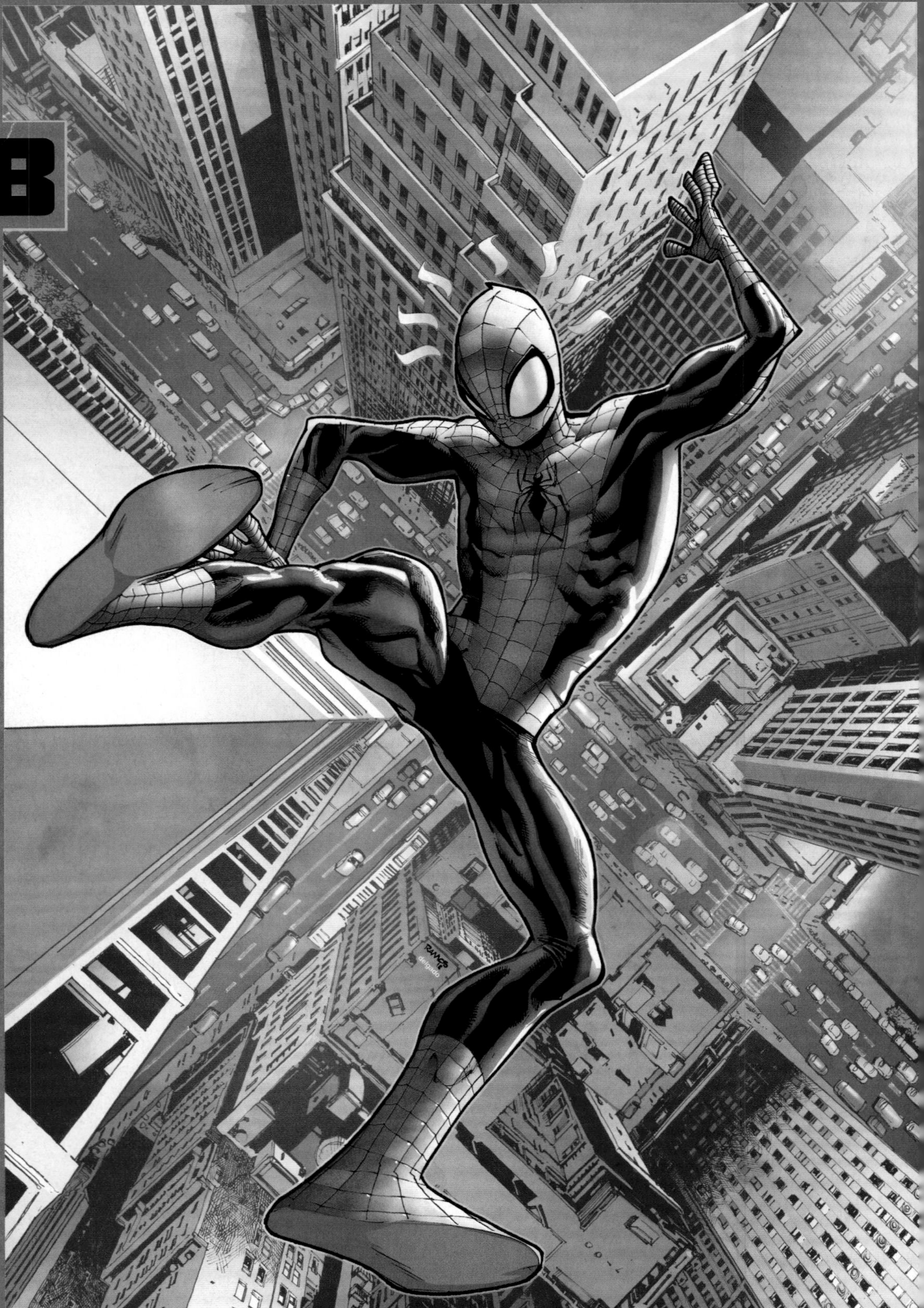

HEIST PART 1

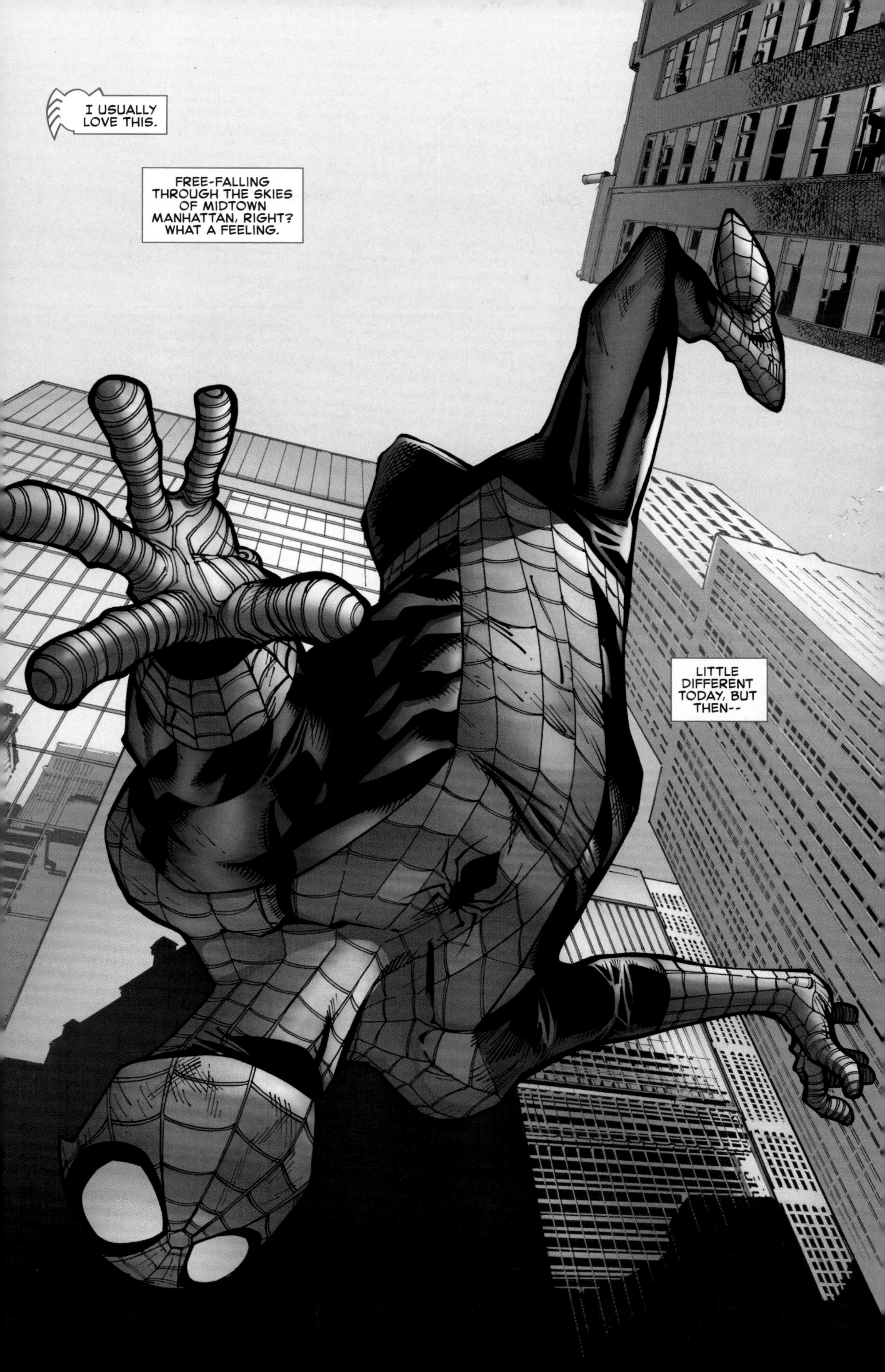
I USUALLY LOVE THIS.
FREE-FALLING THROUGH THE SKIES OF MIDTOWN MANHATTAN, RIGHT? WHAT A FEELING.
LITTLE DIFFERENT TODAY, BUT THEN--

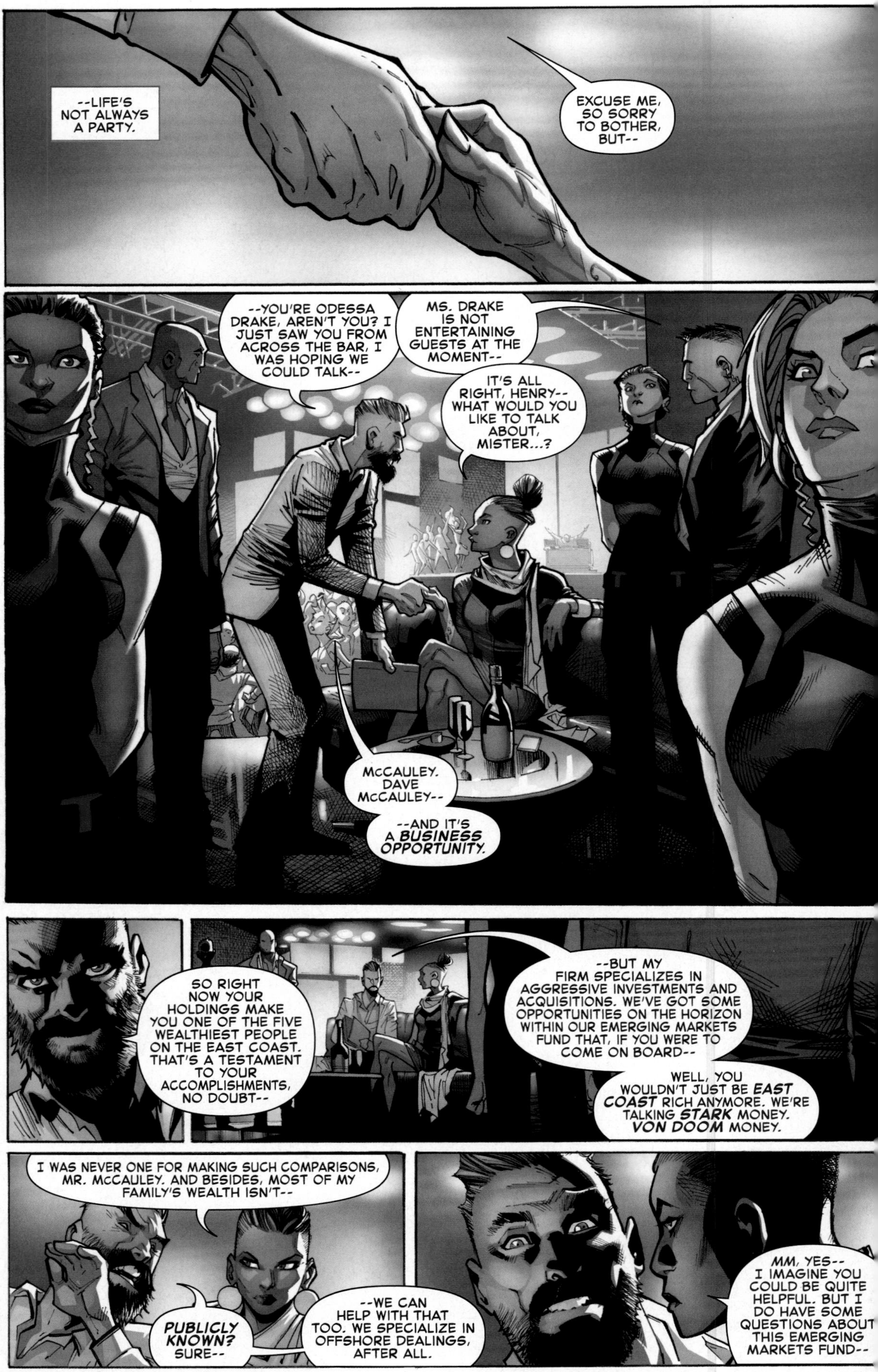
--LIFE'S NOT ALWAYS A PARTY.
EXCUSE ME, SO SORRY TO BOTHER, BUT--
--YOU'RE ODESSA DRAKE, AREN'T YOU? I JUST SAW YOU FROM ACROSS THE BAR, I WAS HOPING WE COULD TALK--
MS. DRAKE IS NOT ENTERTAINING GUESTS AT THE MOMENT--
IT'S ALL RIGHT, HENRY-- WHAT WOULD YOU LIKE TO TALK ABOUT, MISTER...?
McCAULEY. DAVE McCAULEY--
--AND IT'S A BUSINESS OPPORTUNITY.
SO RIGHT NOW YOUR HOLDINGS MAKE YOU ONE OF THE FIVE WEALTHIEST PEOPLE ON THE EAST COAST. THAT'S A TESTAMENT TO YOUR ACCOMPLISHMENTS, NO DOUBT--
--BUT MY FIRM SPECIALIZES IN AGGRESSIVE INVESTMENTS AND ACQUISITIONS. WE'VE GOT SOME OPPORTUNITIES ON THE HORIZON WITHIN OUR EMERGING MARKETS FUND THAT, IF YOU WERE TO COME ON BOARD--
WELL, YOU WOULDN'T JUST BE EAST COAST RICH ANYMORE. WE'RE TALKING STARK MONEY. VON DOOM MONEY.
I WAS NEVER ONE FOR MAKING SUCH COMPARISONS, MR. McCAULEY. AND BESIDES, MOST OF MY FAMILY'S WEALTH ISN'T--
PUBLICLY KNOWN? SURE--
--WE CAN HELP WITH THAT TOO. WE SPECIALIZE IN OFFSHORE DEALINGS, AFTER ALL.
MM, YES-- I IMAGINE YOU COULD BE QUITE HELPFUL. BUT I DO HAVE SOME QUESTIONS ABOUT THIS EMERGING MARKETS FUND--

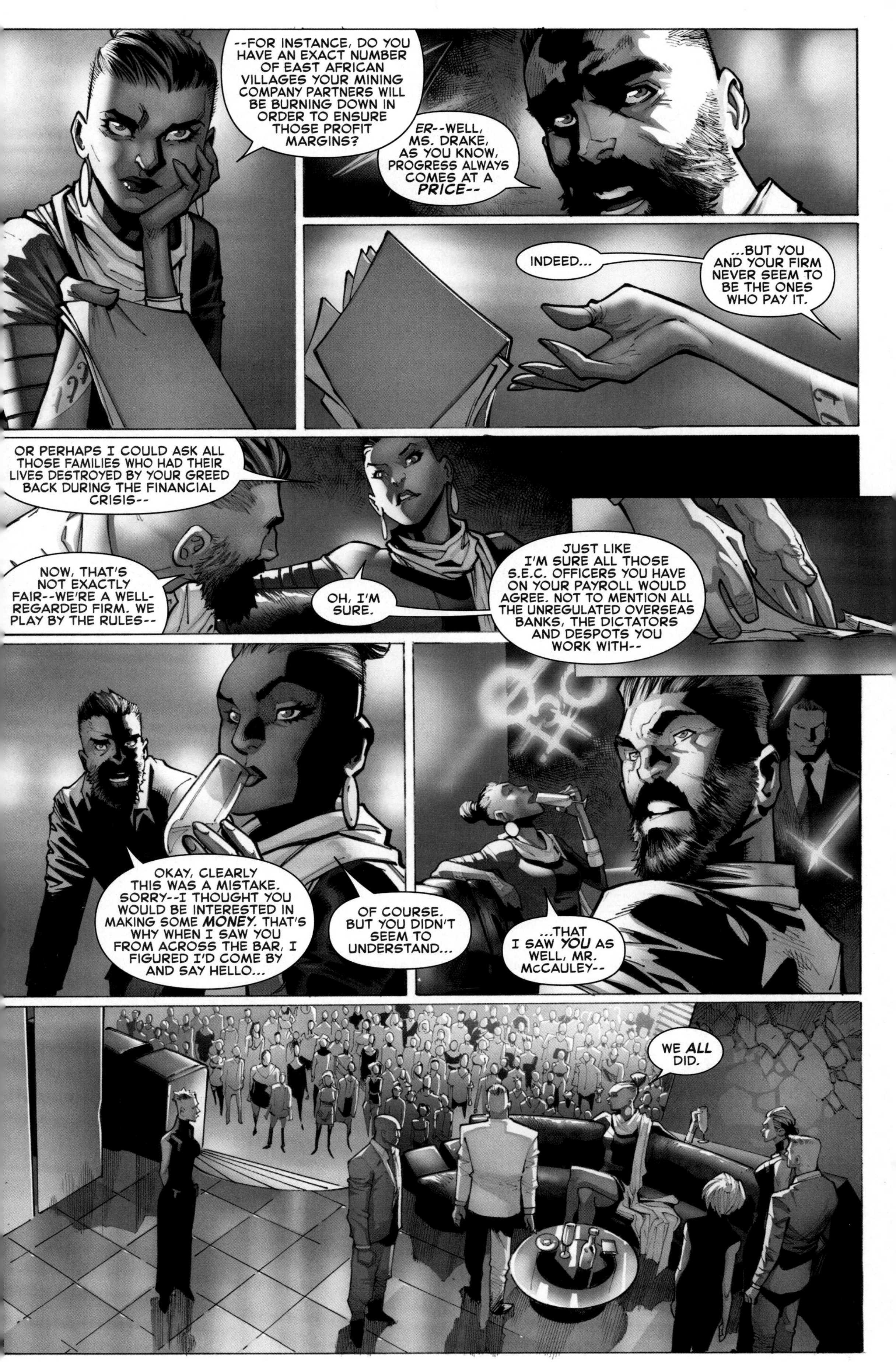

--FOR INSTANCE, DO YOU HAVE AN EXACT NUMBER OF EAST AFRICAN VILLAGES YOUR MINING COMPANY PARTNERS WILL BE BURNING DOWN IN ORDER TO ENSURE THOSE PROFIT MARGINS?
ER--WELL, MS. DRAKE, AS YOU KNOW, PROGRESS ALWAYS COMES AT A PRICE--
INDEED...
...BUT YOU AND YOUR FIRM NEVER SEEM TO BE THE ONES WHO PAY IT.
OR PERHAPS I COULD ASK ALL THOSE FAMILIES WHO HAD THEIR LIVES DESTROYED BY YOUR GREED BACK DURING THE FINANCIAL CRISIS--
NOW, THAT'S NOT EXACTLY FAIR--WE'RE A WELL-REGARDED FIRM. WE PLAY BY THE RULES--
OH, I'M SURE.
JUST LIKE I'M SURE ALL THOSE S.E.C. OFFICERS YOU HAVE ON YOUR PAYROLL WOULD AGREE. NOT TO MENTION ALL THE UNREGULATED OVERSEAS BANKS, THE DICTATORS AND DESPOTS YOU WORK WITH--
OKAY, CLEARLY THIS WAS A MISTAKE. SORRY--I THOUGHT YOU WOULD BE INTERESTED IN MAKING SOME MONEY. THAT'S WHY WHEN I SAW YOU FROM ACROSS THE BAR, I FIGURED I'D COME BY AND SAY HELLO...
OF COURSE. BUT YOU DIDN'T SEEM TO UNDERSTAND...
...THAT I SAW YOU AS WELL, MR. McCAULEY--
WE ALL DID.

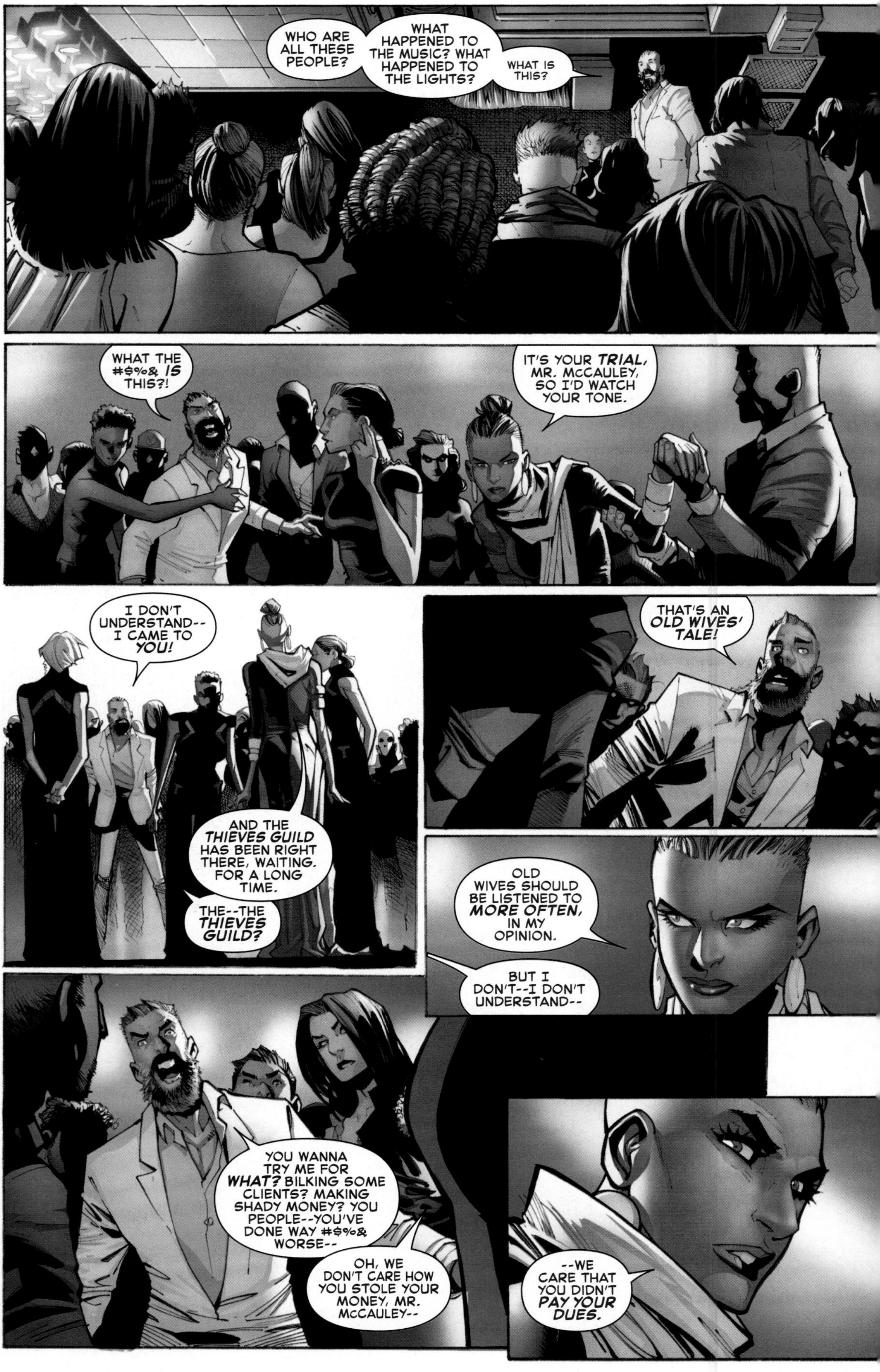
WHO ARE ALL THESE PEOPLE?
WHAT HAPPENED TO THE MUSIC? WHAT HAPPENED TO THE LIGHTS?
WHAT IS THIS?
WHAT THE #$%& *IS* THIS?!
IT'S YOUR *TRIAL,* MR. McCAULEY, SO I'D WATCH YOUR TONE.
I DON'T UNDERSTAND-- I CAME TO *YOU!*
AND THE *THIEVES GUILD* HAS BEEN RIGHT THERE, WAITING. FOR A LONG TIME.
THE--THE *THIEVES GUILD?*
THAT'S AN *OLD WIVES' TALE!*
OLD WIVES SHOULD BE LISTENED TO *MORE OFTEN,* IN MY OPINION.
BUT I DON'T--I DON'T UNDERSTAND--
YOU WANNA TRY ME FOR *WHAT?* BILKING SOME CLIENTS? MAKING SHADY MONEY? YOU PEOPLE--YOU'VE DONE WAY #$%& WORSE--
OH, WE DON'T CARE HOW YOU STOLE YOUR MONEY, MR. McCAULEY--
--WE CARE THAT YOU DIDN'T *PAY YOUR DUES.*

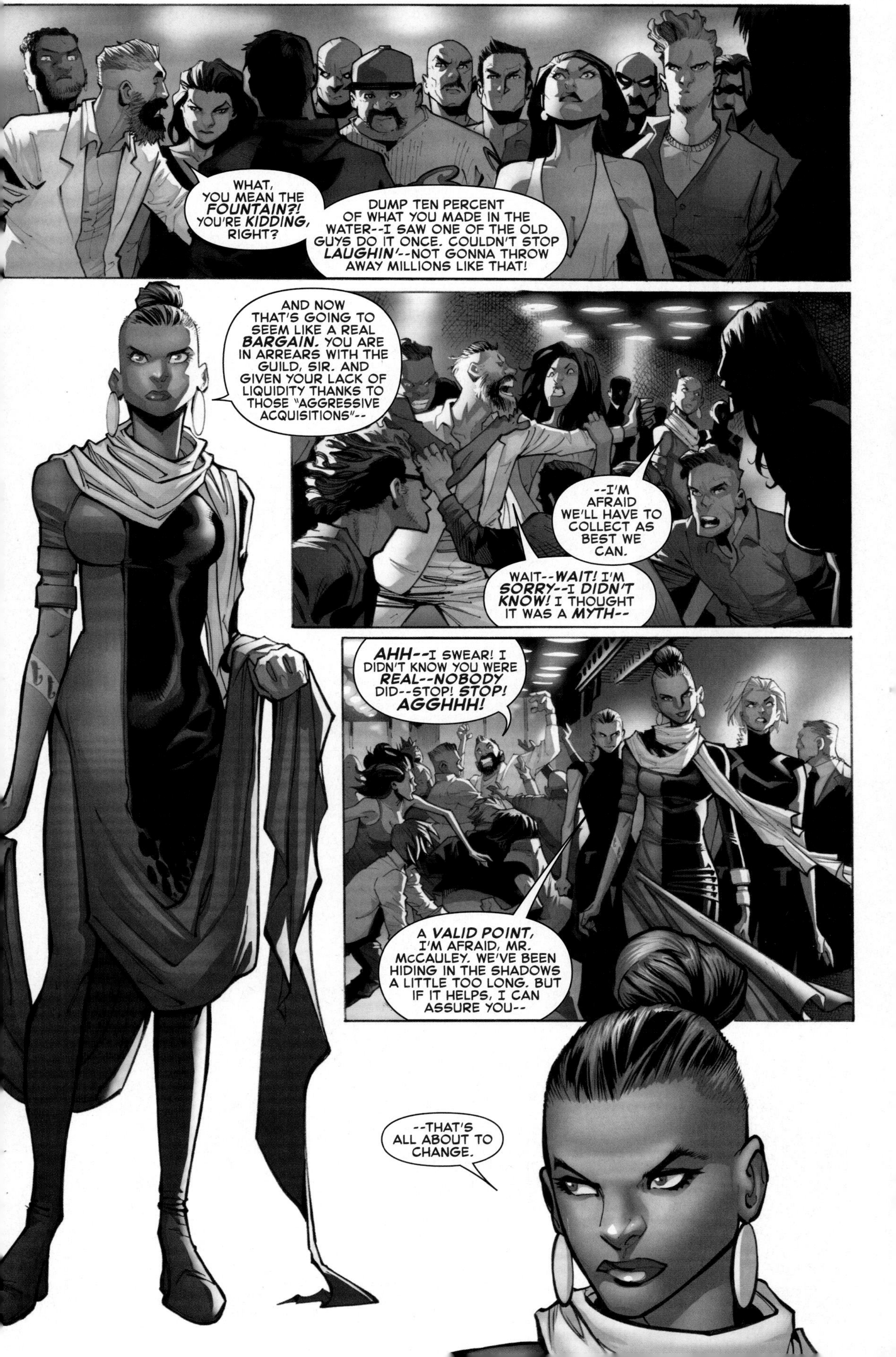
WHAT, YOU MEAN THE FOUNTAIN?! YOU'RE KIDDING, RIGHT?
DUMP TEN PERCENT OF WHAT YOU MADE IN THE WATER--I SAW ONE OF THE OLD GUYS DO IT ONCE. COULDN'T STOP LAUGHIN'--NOT GONNA THROW AWAY MILLIONS LIKE THAT!
AND NOW THAT'S GOING TO SEEM LIKE A REAL BARGAIN. YOU ARE IN ARREARS WITH THE GUILD, SIR. AND GIVEN YOUR LACK OF LIQUIDITY THANKS TO THOSE "AGGRESSIVE ACQUISITIONS"--
--I'M AFRAID WE'LL HAVE TO COLLECT AS BEST WE CAN.
WAIT--WAIT! I'M SORRY--I DIDN'T KNOW! I THOUGHT IT WAS A MYTH--
AHH--I SWEAR! I DIDN'T KNOW YOU WERE REAL--NOBODY DID--STOP! STOP! AGGHHH!
A VALID POINT, I'M AFRAID, MR. McCAULEY. WE'VE BEEN HIDING IN THE SHADOWS A LITTLE TOO LONG. BUT IF IT HELPS, I CAN ASSURE YOU--
--THAT'S ALL ABOUT TO CHANGE.

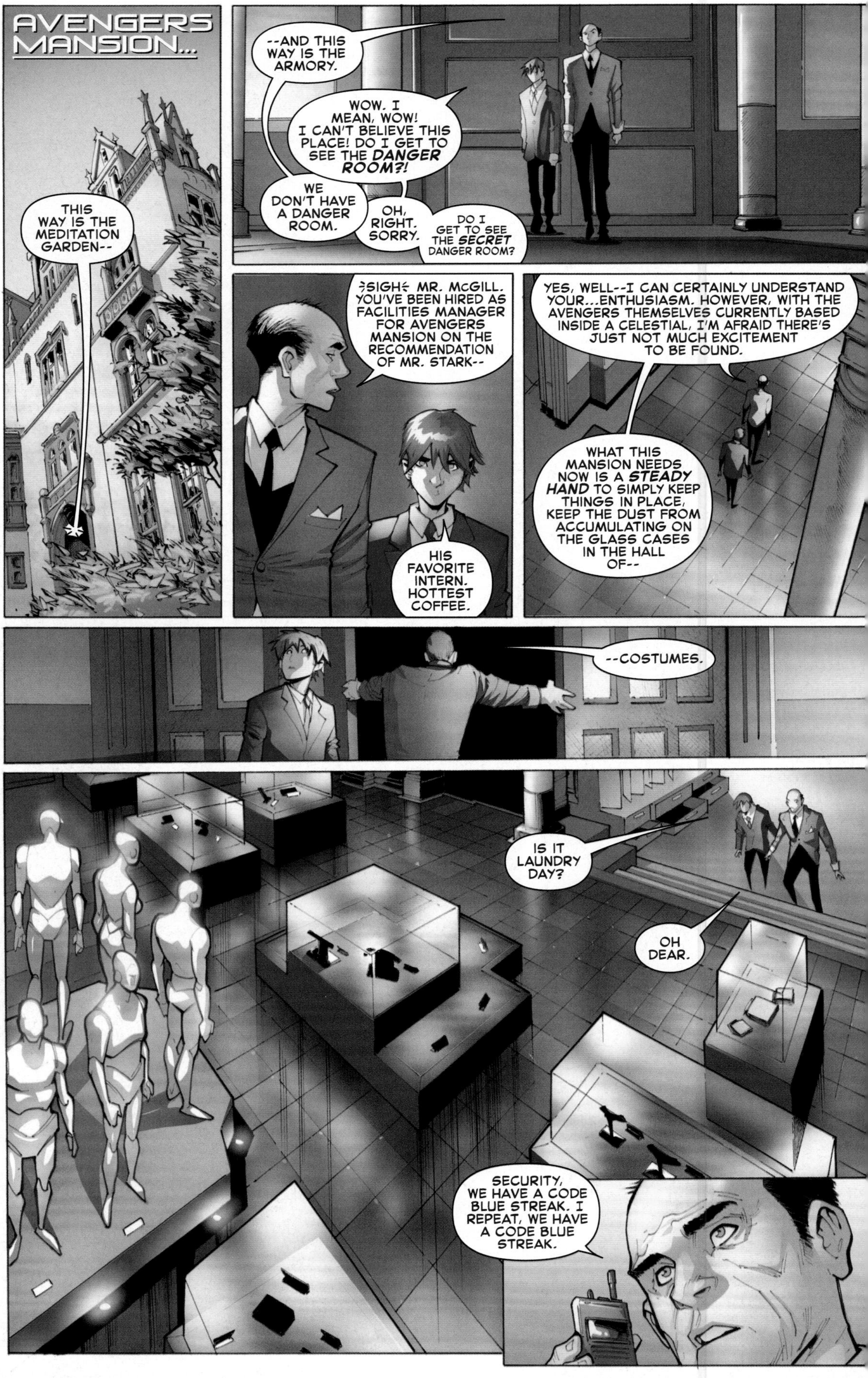
AVENGERS MANSION...
THIS WAY IS THE MEDITATION GARDEN--
--AND THIS WAY IS THE ARMORY.
WOW. I MEAN, WOW! I CAN'T BELIEVE THIS PLACE! DO I GET TO SEE THE DANGER ROOM?!
WE DON'T HAVE A DANGER ROOM.
OH, RIGHT. SORRY.
DO I GET TO SEE THE SECRET DANGER ROOM?
≯SIGH≮ MR. McGILL. YOU'VE BEEN HIRED AS FACILITIES MANAGER FOR AVENGERS MANSION ON THE RECOMMENDATION OF MR. STARK--
HIS FAVORITE INTERN. HOTTEST COFFEE.
YES, WELL--I CAN CERTAINLY UNDERSTAND YOUR...ENTHUSIASM. HOWEVER, WITH THE AVENGERS THEMSELVES CURRENTLY BASED INSIDE A CELESTIAL, I'M AFRAID THERE'S JUST NOT MUCH EXCITEMENT TO BE FOUND.
WHAT THIS MANSION NEEDS NOW IS A STEADY HAND TO SIMPLY KEEP THINGS IN PLACE, KEEP THE DUST FROM ACCUMULATING ON THE GLASS CASES IN THE HALL OF--
--COSTUMES.
IS IT LAUNDRY DAY?
OH DEAR.
SECURITY, WE HAVE A CODE BLUE STREAK. I REPEAT, WE HAVE A CODE BLUE STREAK.

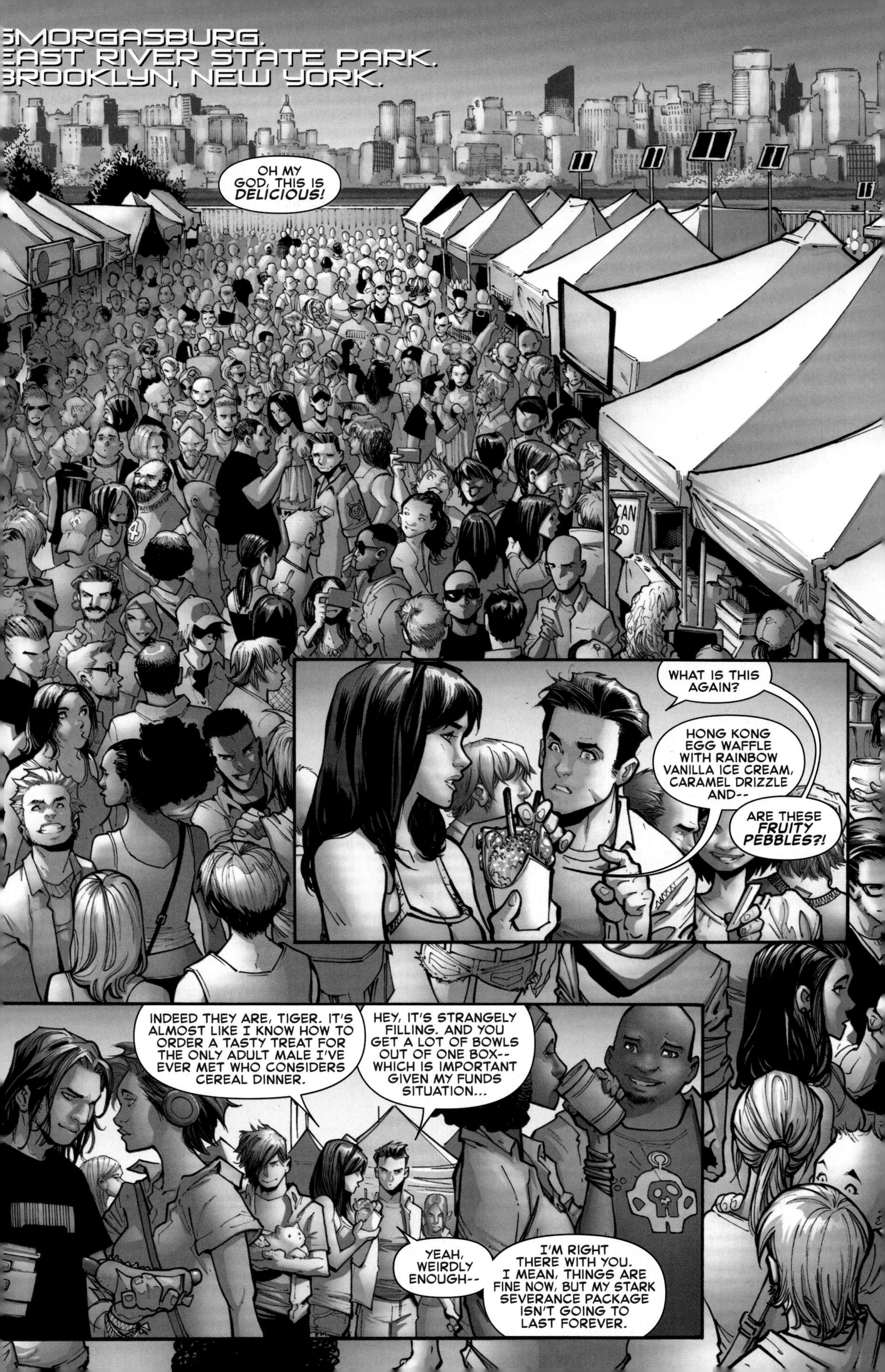
SMORGASBURG.
EAST RIVER STATE PARK.
BROOKLYN, NEW YORK.
OH MY GOD, THIS IS DELICIOUS!
WHAT IS THIS AGAIN?
HONG KONG EGG WAFFLE WITH RAINBOW VANILLA ICE CREAM, CARAMEL DRIZZLE AND--
ARE THESE FRUITY PEBBLES?!
INDEED THEY ARE, TIGER. IT'S ALMOST LIKE I KNOW HOW TO ORDER A TASTY TREAT FOR THE ONLY ADULT MALE I'VE EVER MET WHO CONSIDERS CEREAL DINNER.
HEY, IT'S STRANGELY FILLING. AND YOU GET A LOT OF BOWLS OUT OF ONE BOX-- WHICH IS IMPORTANT GIVEN MY FUNDS SITUATION...
YEAH, WEIRDLY ENOUGH--
I'M RIGHT THERE WITH YOU. I MEAN, THINGS ARE FINE NOW, BUT MY STARK SEVERANCE PACKAGE ISN'T GOING TO LAST FOREVER.

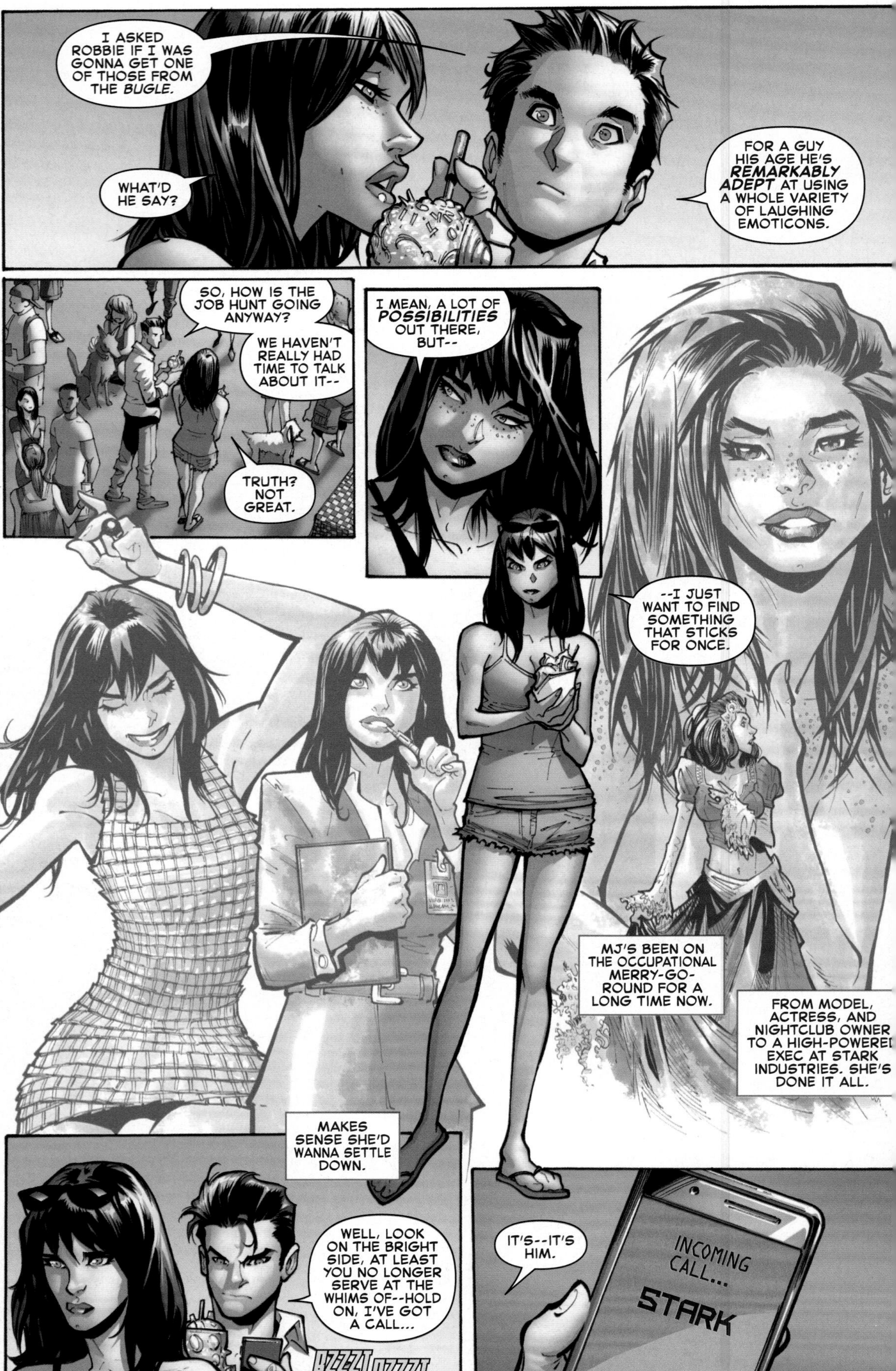

I ASKED ROBBIE IF I WAS GONNA GET ONE OF THOSE FROM THE *BUGLE*.
WHAT'D HE SAY?
FOR A GUY HIS AGE HE'S ***REMARKABLY ADEPT*** AT USING A WHOLE VARIETY OF LAUGHING EMOTICONS.
SO, HOW IS THE JOB HUNT GOING ANYWAY?
WE HAVEN'T REALLY HAD TIME TO TALK ABOUT IT--
TRUTH? NOT GREAT.
I MEAN, A LOT OF ***POSSIBILITIES*** OUT THERE, BUT--
--I JUST WANT TO FIND SOMETHING THAT STICKS FOR ONCE.
MJ'S BEEN ON THE OCCUPATIONAL MERRY-GO-ROUND FOR A LONG TIME NOW.
FROM MODEL, ACTRESS, AND NIGHTCLUB OWNER TO A HIGH-POWERED EXEC AT STARK INDUSTRIES. SHE'S DONE IT ALL.
MAKES SENSE SHE'D WANNA SETTLE DOWN.
WELL, LOOK ON THE BRIGHT SIDE, AT LEAST YOU NO LONGER SERVE AT THE WHIMS OF--HOLD ON, I'VE GOT A CALL...
BZZZZT BZZZZT
IT'S--IT'S HIM.
INCOMING CALL...
STARK

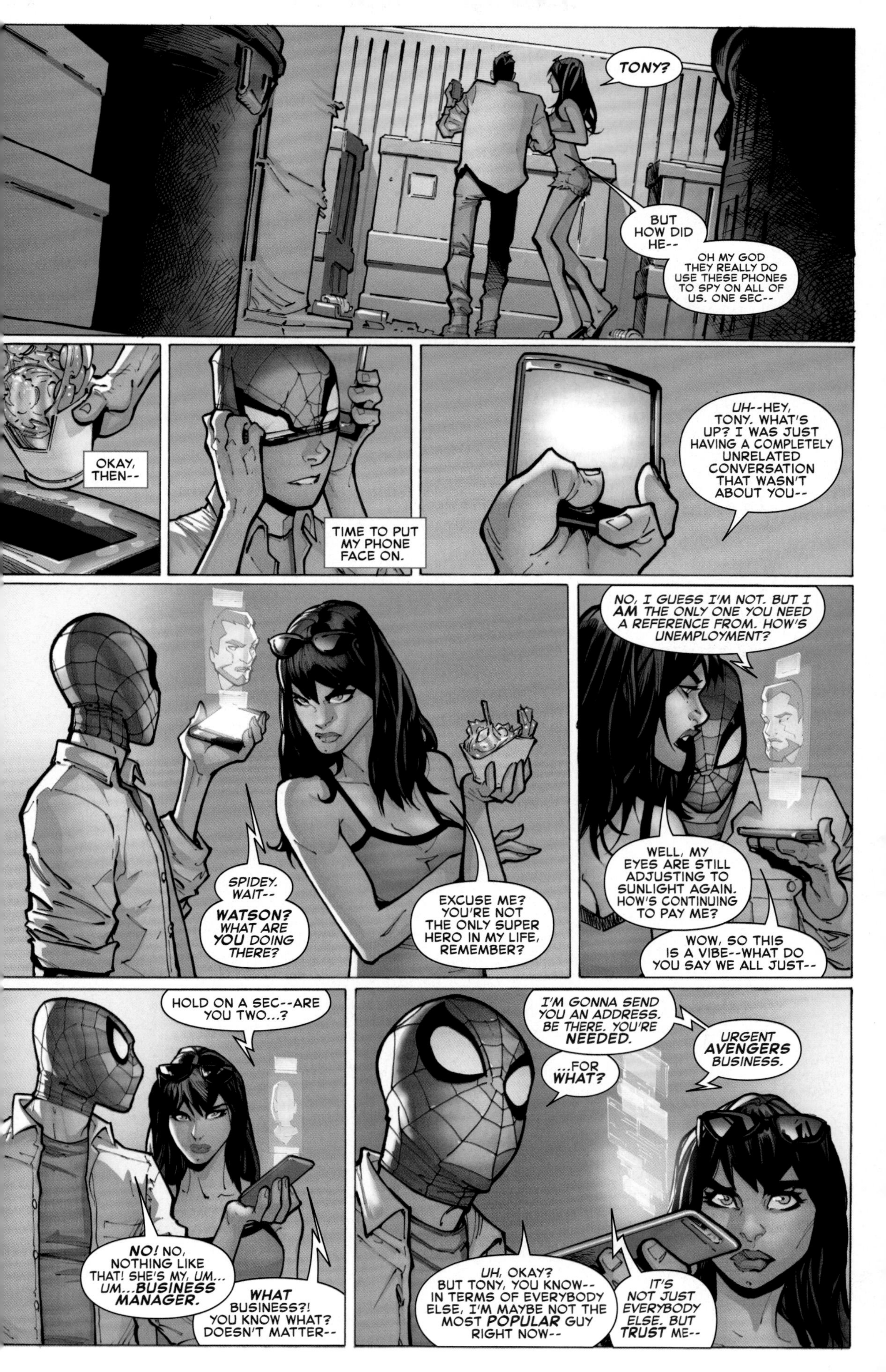
TONY?
BUT HOW DID HE--
OH MY GOD THEY REALLY DO USE THESE PHONES TO SPY ON ALL OF US. ONE SEC--
OKAY, THEN--
TIME TO PUT MY PHONE FACE ON.
UH--HEY, TONY. WHAT'S UP? I WAS JUST HAVING A COMPLETELY UNRELATED CONVERSATION THAT WASN'T ABOUT YOU--
SPIDEY. WAIT--
WATSON? WHAT ARE YOU DOING THERE?
EXCUSE ME? YOU'RE NOT THE ONLY SUPER HERO IN MY LIFE, REMEMBER?
NO, I GUESS I'M NOT. BUT I AM THE ONLY ONE YOU NEED A REFERENCE FROM. HOW'S UNEMPLOYMENT?
WELL, MY EYES ARE STILL ADJUSTING TO SUNLIGHT AGAIN. HOW'S CONTINUING TO PAY ME?
WOW, SO THIS IS A VIBE--WHAT DO YOU SAY WE ALL JUST--
HOLD ON A SEC--ARE YOU TWO...?
NO! NO, NOTHING LIKE THAT! SHE'S MY, UM... UM...BUSINESS MANAGER.
WHAT BUSINESS?! YOU KNOW WHAT? DOESN'T MATTER--
I'M GONNA SEND YOU AN ADDRESS. BE THERE. YOU'RE NEEDED.
URGENT AVENGERS BUSINESS.
...FOR WHAT?
UH, OKAY? BUT TONY, YOU KNOW-- IN TERMS OF EVERYBODY ELSE, I'M MAYBE NOT THE MOST POPULAR GUY RIGHT NOW--
IT'S NOT JUST EVERYBODY ELSE. BUT TRUST ME--

"--THIS AFFECTS *ALL OF US.*"

STARK TOWER. EARLIER THAT MORNING.

LET'S GO OVER THE CALENDAR FOR TODAY.

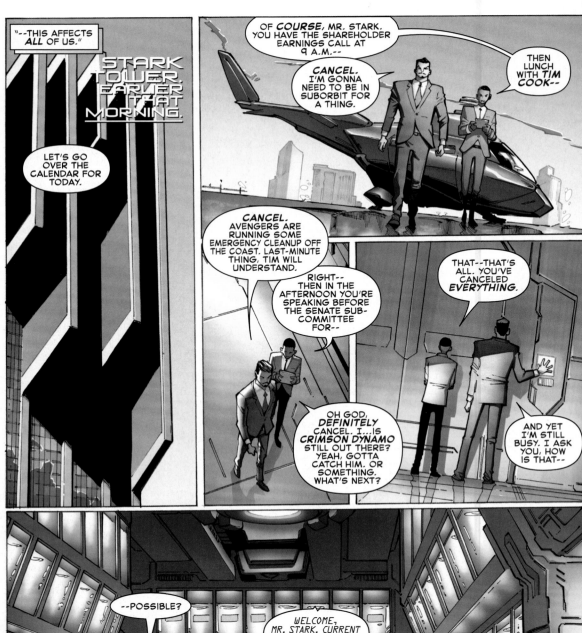

OF *COURSE,* MR. STARK. YOU HAVE THE SHAREHOLDER EARNINGS CALL AT 9 A.M.--

CANCEL. I'M GONNA NEED TO BE IN SUBORBIT FOR A THING.

THEN LUNCH WITH *TIM COOK--*

CANCEL. AVENGERS ARE RUNNING SOME EMERGENCY CLEANUP OFF THE COAST. LAST-MINUTE THING, TIM WILL UNDERSTAND.

RIGHT-- THEN IN THE AFTERNOON YOU'RE SPEAKING BEFORE THE SENATE SUB-COMMITTEE FOR--

THAT--THAT'S ALL. YOU'VE CANCELED *EVERYTHING.*

OH GOD, *DEFINITELY* CANCEL. I...IS *CRIMSON DYNAMO* STILL OUT THERE? YEAH, GOTTA CATCH HIM. OR SOMETHING. WHAT'S NEXT?

AND YET I'M STILL BUSY. I ASK YOU, HOW IS THAT--

--POSSIBLE?

WELCOME, MR. STARK. CURRENT ARMOR INVENTORY IS: 0.

SCRATCH THAT. I MIGHT HAVE MORE TIME THAN I THOUGHT.

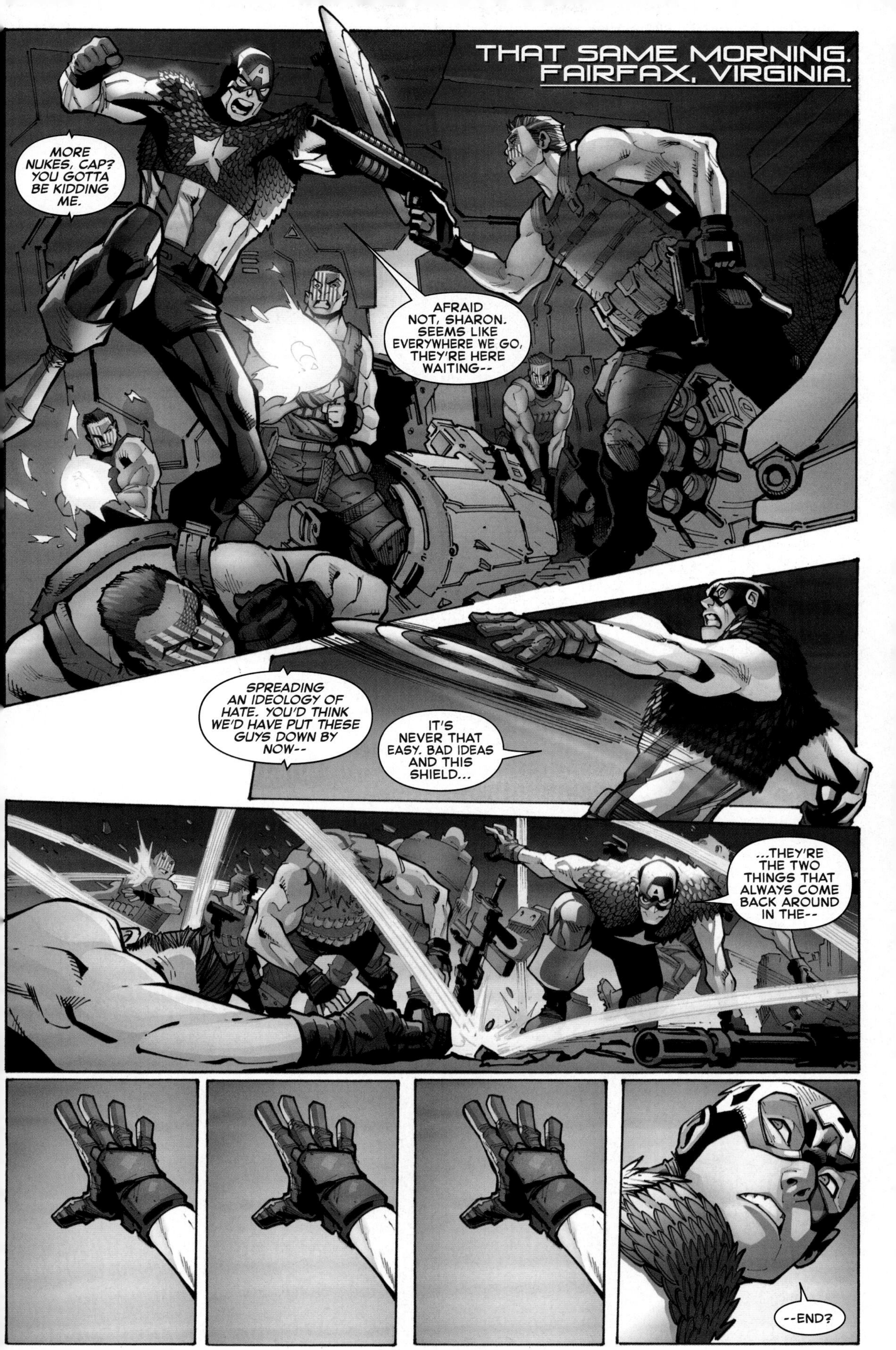
THAT SAME MORNING. FAIRFAX, VIRGINIA.
MORE NUKES, CAP? YOU GOTTA BE KIDDING ME.
AFRAID NOT, SHARON. SEEMS LIKE EVERYWHERE WE GO, THEY'RE HERE WAITING--
SPREADING AN IDEOLOGY OF HATE. YOU'D THINK WE'D HAVE PUT THESE GUYS DOWN BY NOW--
IT'S NEVER THAT EASY. BAD IDEAS AND THIS SHIELD...
...THEY'RE THE TWO THINGS THAT ALWAYS COME BACK AROUND IN THE--
--END?

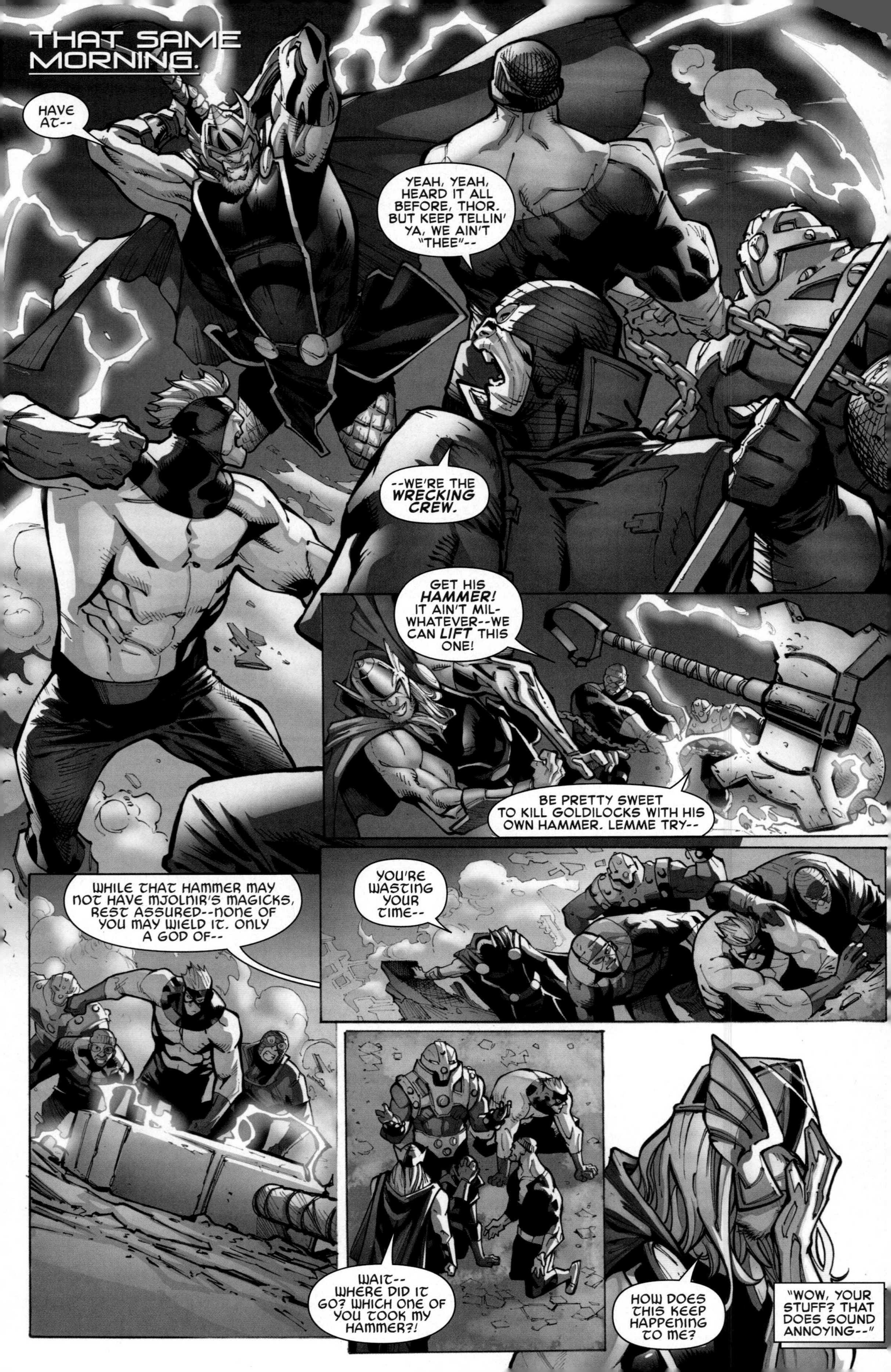
THAT SAME MORNING.
HAVE AT--
YEAH, YEAH, HEARD IT ALL BEFORE, THOR. BUT KEEP TELLIN' YA, WE AIN'T "THEE"--
--WE'RE THE WRECKING CREW.
GET HIS HAMMER! IT AIN'T MIL-WHATEVER--WE CAN LIFT THIS ONE!
BE PRETTY SWEET TO KILL GOLDILOCKS WITH HIS OWN HAMMER. LEMME TRY--
WHILE THAT HAMMER MAY NOT HAVE MJOLNIR'S MAGICKS, REST ASSURED--NONE OF YOU MAY WIELD IT. ONLY A GOD OF--
YOU'RE WASTING YOUR TIME--
WAIT-- WHERE DID IT GO? WHICH ONE OF YOU TOOK MY HAMMER?!
HOW DOES THIS KEEP HAPPENING TO ME?
"WOW, YOUR STUFF? THAT DOES SOUND ANNOYING--"

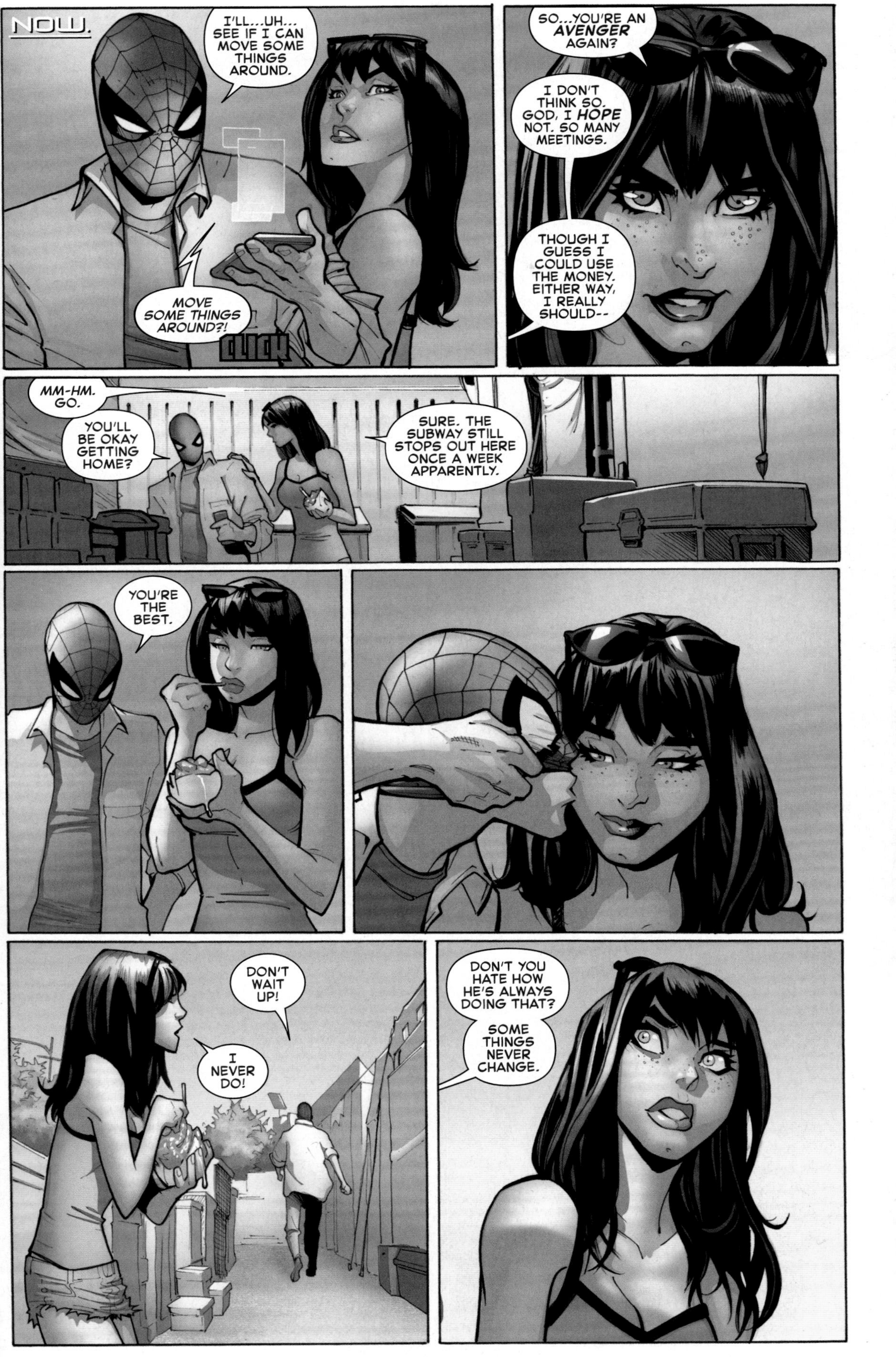
NOW.
I'LL...UH... SEE IF I CAN MOVE SOME THINGS AROUND.
MOVE SOME THINGS AROUND?!
CLICK
SO...YOU'RE AN AVENGER AGAIN?
I DON'T THINK SO. GOD, I HOPE NOT. SO MANY MEETINGS.
THOUGH I GUESS I COULD USE THE MONEY. EITHER WAY, I REALLY SHOULD--
MM-HM. GO.
YOU'LL BE OKAY GETTING HOME?
SURE. THE SUBWAY STILL STOPS OUT HERE ONCE A WEEK APPARENTLY.
YOU'RE THE BEST.
DON'T WAIT UP!
I NEVER DO!
DON'T YOU HATE HOW HE'S ALWAYS DOING THAT?
SOME THINGS NEVER CHANGE.

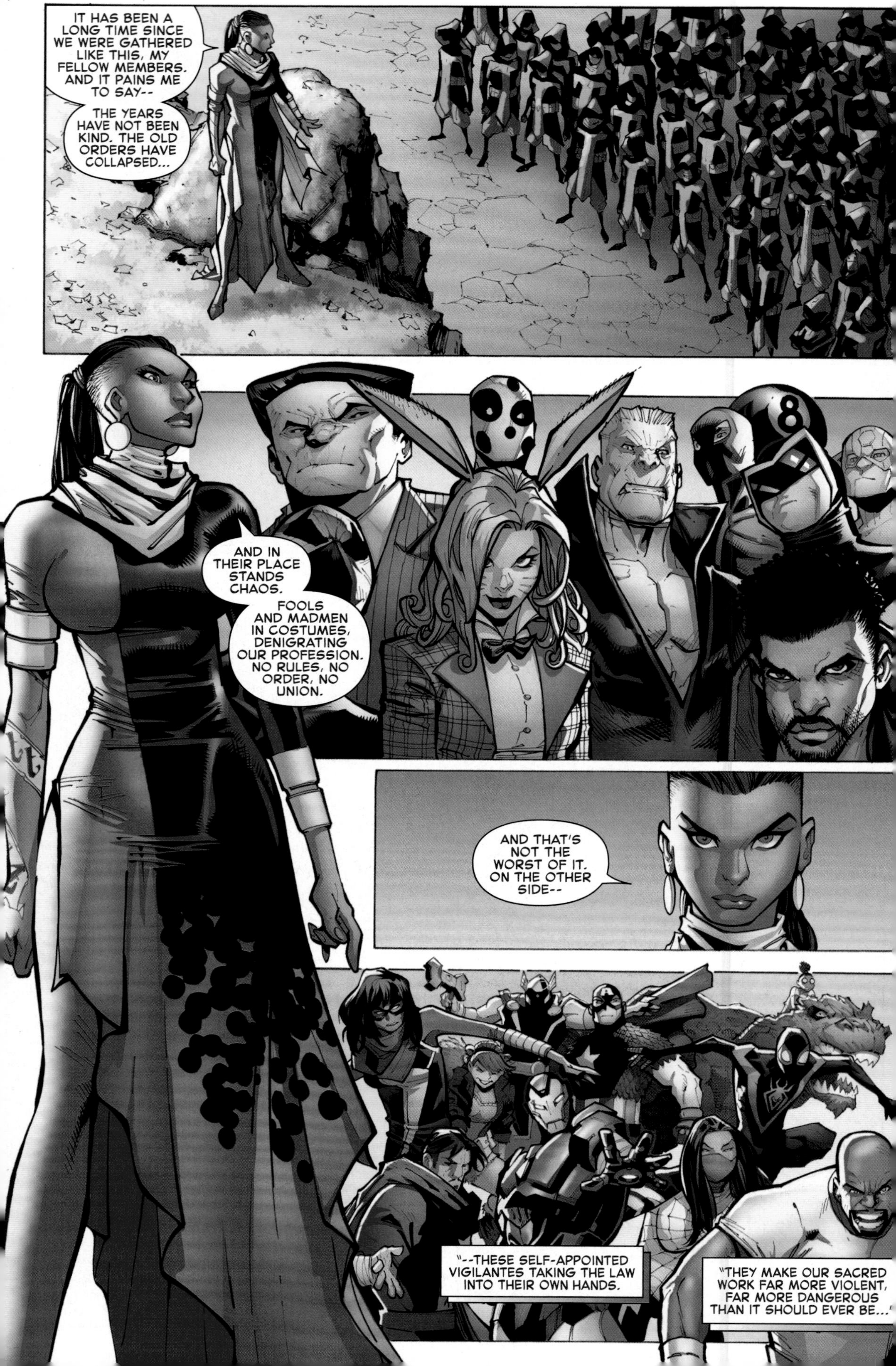
IT HAS BEEN A LONG TIME SINCE WE WERE GATHERED LIKE THIS, MY FELLOW MEMBERS. AND IT PAINS ME TO SAY--
THE YEARS HAVE NOT BEEN KIND. THE OLD ORDERS HAVE COLLAPSED...
AND IN THEIR PLACE STANDS CHAOS.
FOOLS AND MADMEN IN COSTUMES, DENIGRATING OUR PROFESSION. NO RULES, NO ORDER, NO UNION.
8
AND THAT'S NOT THE WORST OF IT. ON THE OTHER SIDE--
"--THESE SELF-APPOINTED VIGILANTES TAKING THE LAW INTO THEIR OWN HANDS.
"THEY MAKE OUR SACRED WORK FAR MORE VIOLENT, FAR MORE DANGEROUS THAN IT SHOULD EVER BE..."

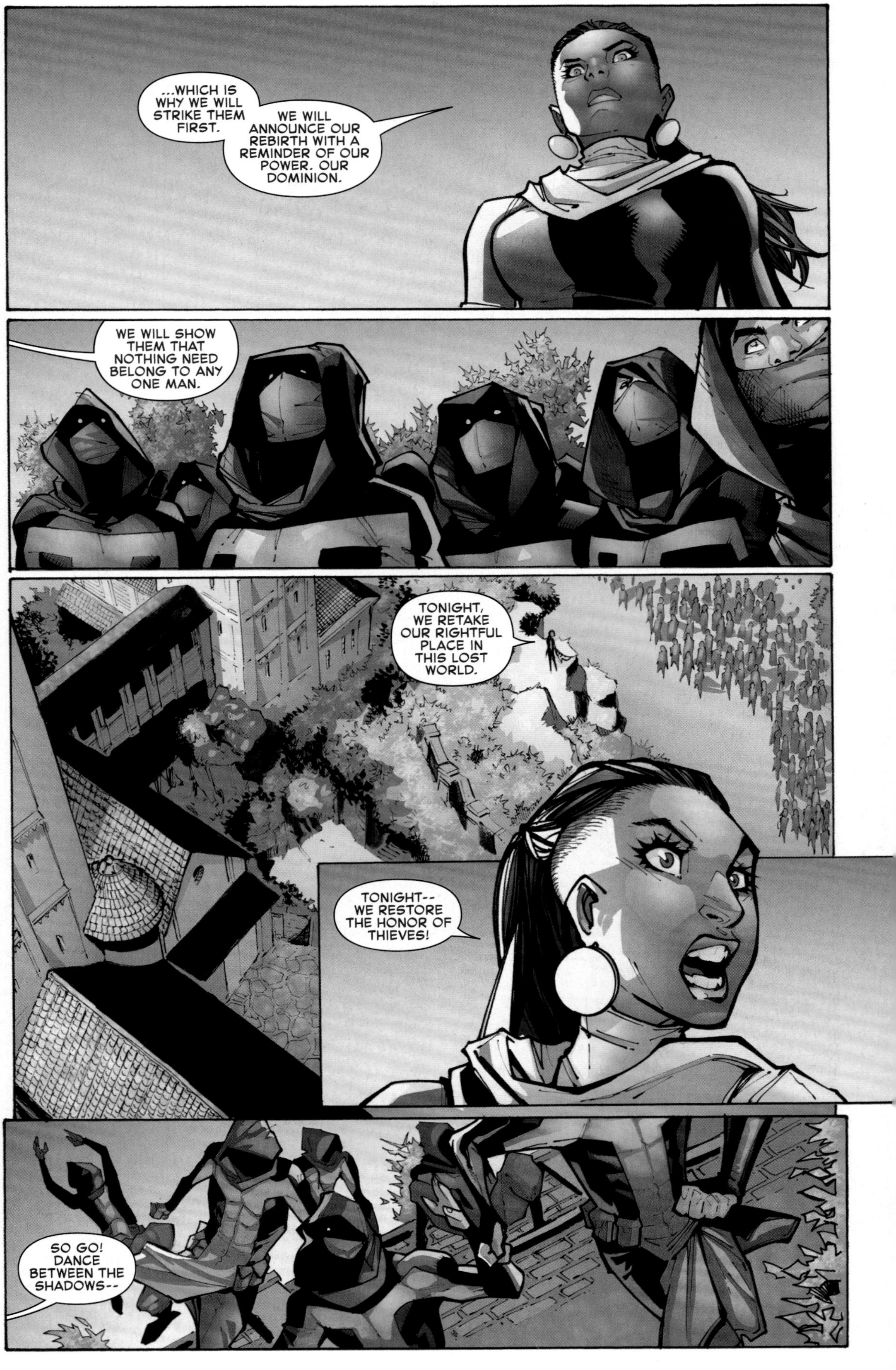
...WHICH IS WHY WE WILL STRIKE THEM FIRST.
WE WILL ANNOUNCE OUR REBIRTH WITH A REMINDER OF OUR POWER. OUR DOMINION.
WE WILL SHOW THEM THAT NOTHING NEED BELONG TO ANY ONE MAN.
TONIGHT, WE RETAKE OUR RIGHTFUL PLACE IN THIS LOST WORLD.
TONIGHT-- WE RESTORE THE HONOR OF THIEVES!
SO GO! DANCE BETWEEN THE SHADOWS--

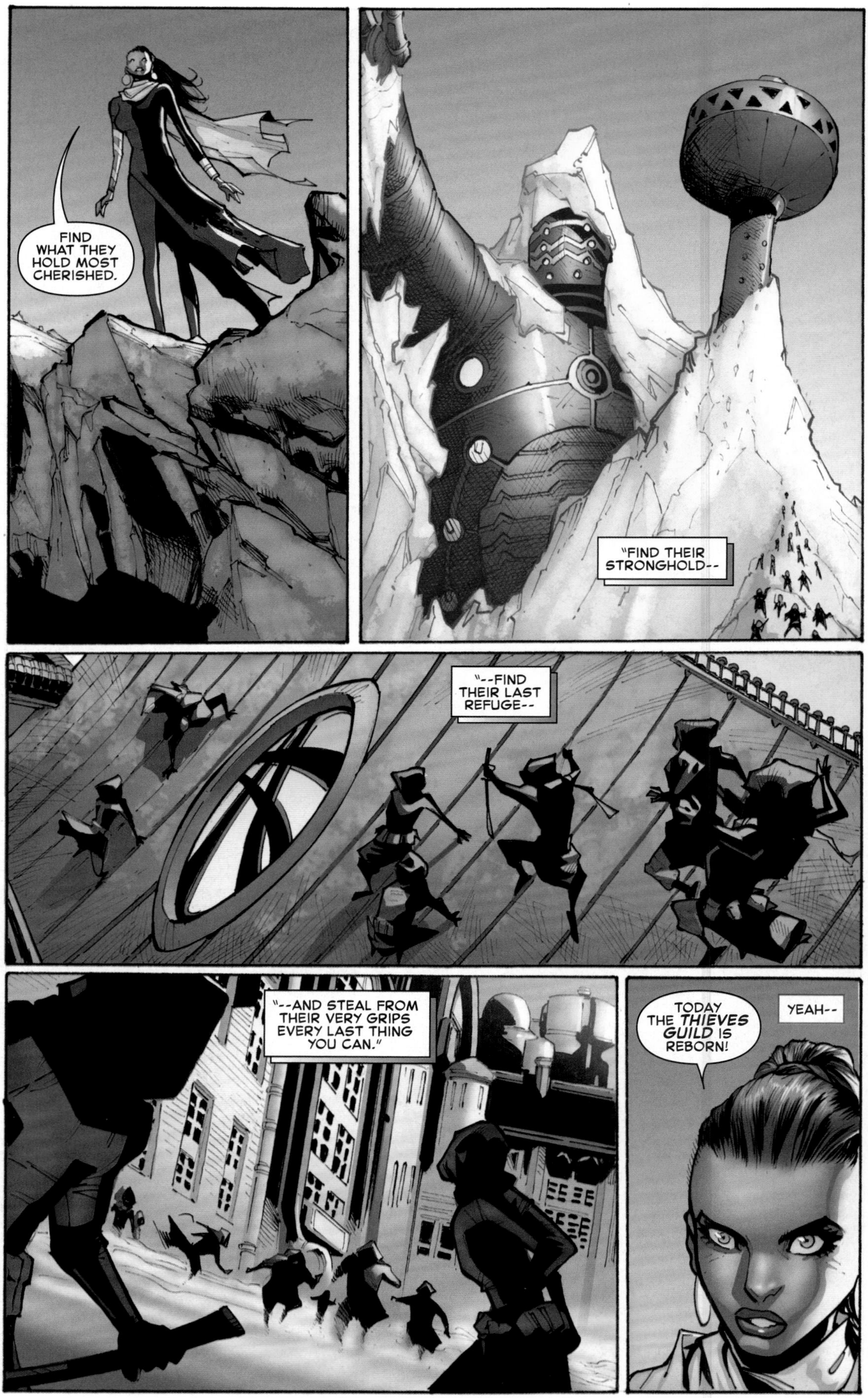
FIND WHAT THEY HOLD MOST CHERISHED.
"FIND THEIR STRONGHOLD--
"--FIND THEIR LAST REFUGE--
"--AND STEAL FROM THEIR VERY GRIPS EVERY LAST THING YOU CAN."
YEAH--
TODAY THE *THIEVES GUILD* IS REBORN!

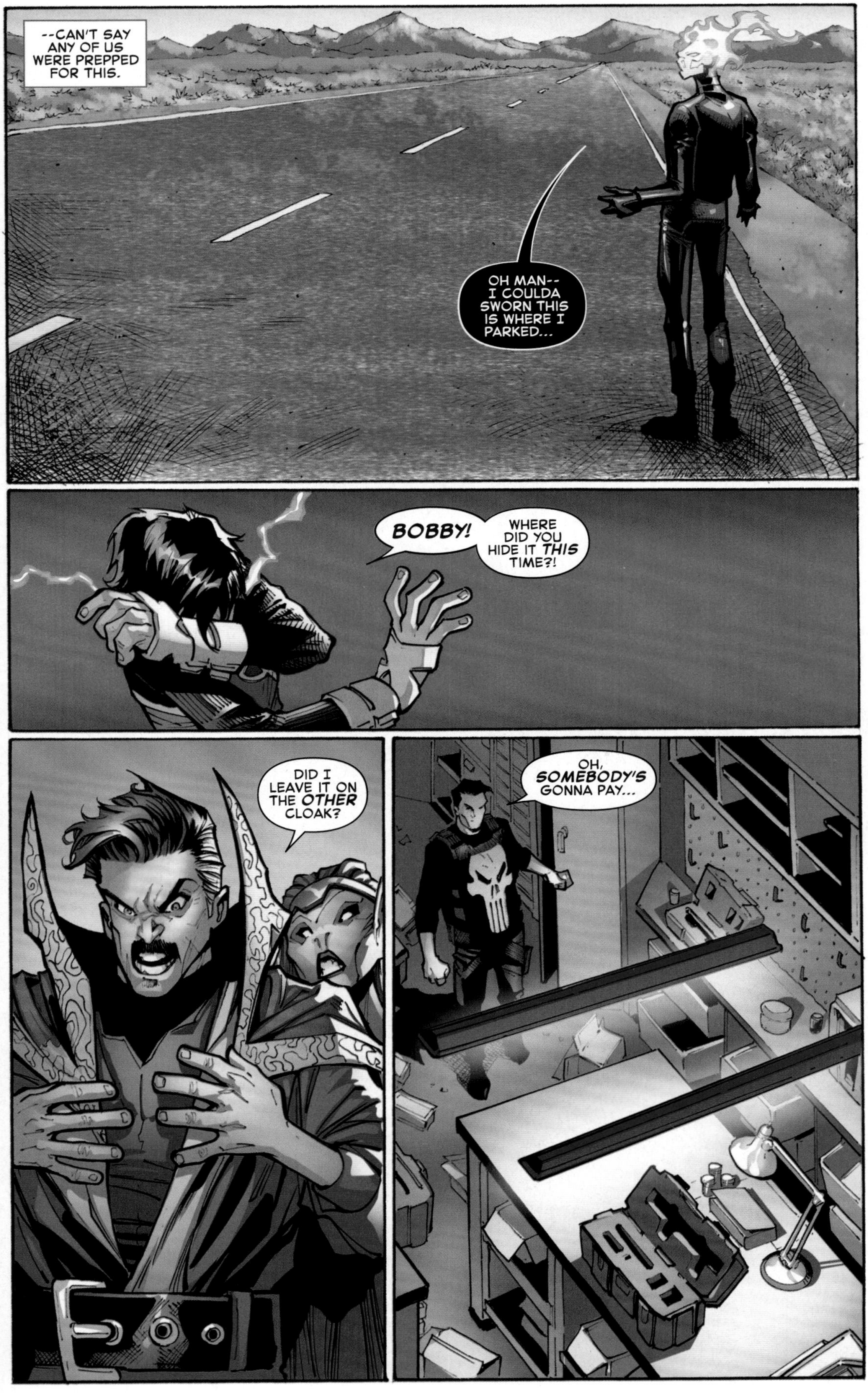
--CAN'T SAY ANY OF US WERE PREPPED FOR THIS.
OH MAN-- I COULDA SWORN THIS IS WHERE I PARKED...
BOBBY!
WHERE DID YOU HIDE IT THIS TIME?!
DID I LEAVE IT ON THE OTHER CLOAK?
OH, SOMEBODY'S GONNA PAY...

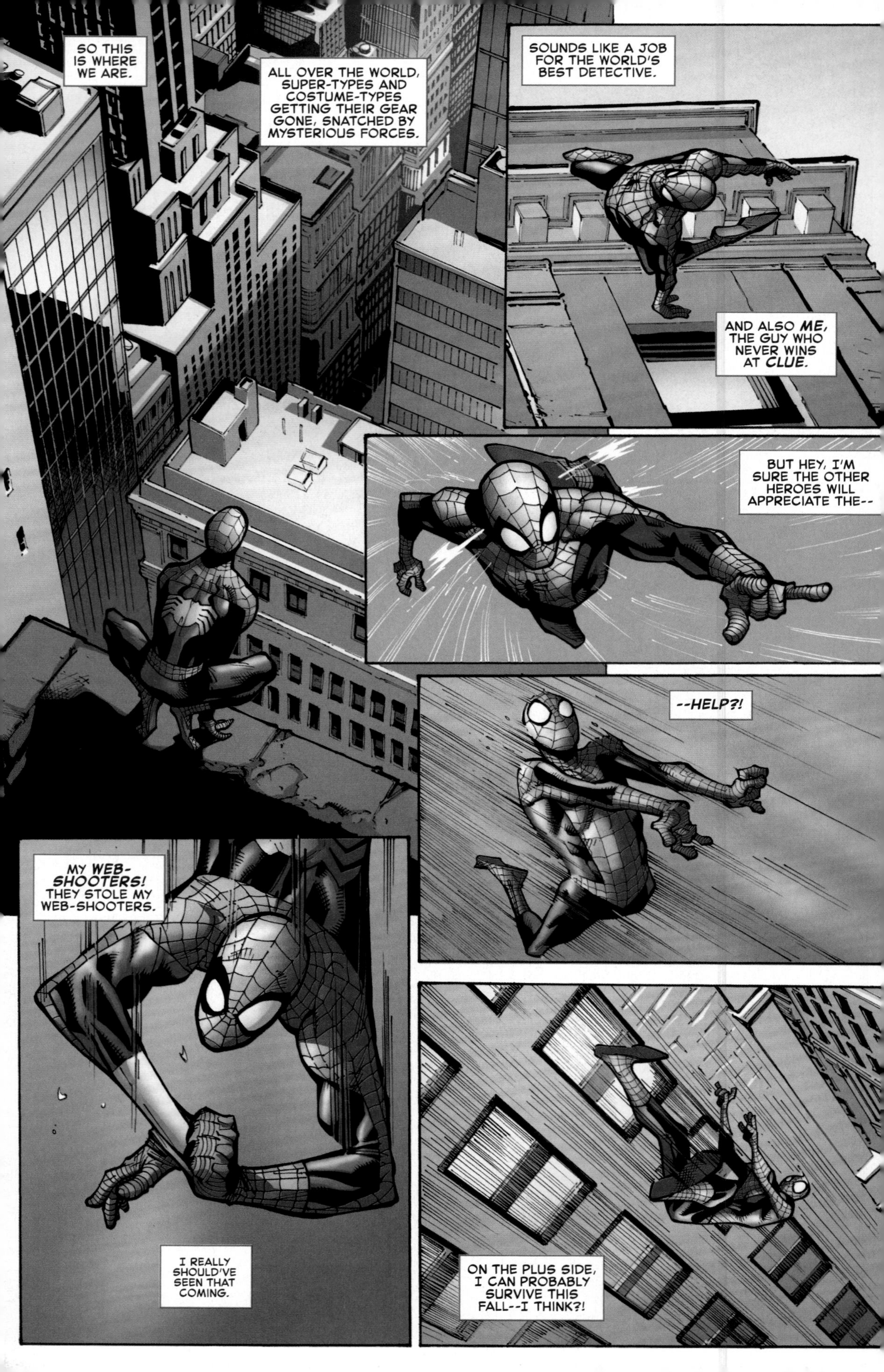
SO THIS IS WHERE WE ARE.
ALL OVER THE WORLD, SUPER-TYPES AND COSTUME-TYPES GETTING THEIR GEAR GONE, SNATCHED BY MYSTERIOUS FORCES.
SOUNDS LIKE A JOB FOR THE WORLD'S BEST DETECTIVE.
AND ALSO ME, THE GUY WHO NEVER WINS AT CLUE.
BUT HEY, I'M SURE THE OTHER HEROES WILL APPRECIATE THE--
--HELP?!
MY WEB-SHOOTERS! THEY STOLE MY WEB-SHOOTERS.
I REALLY SHOULD'VE SEEN THAT COMING.
ON THE PLUS SIDE, I CAN PROBABLY SURVIVE THIS FALL--I THINK?!

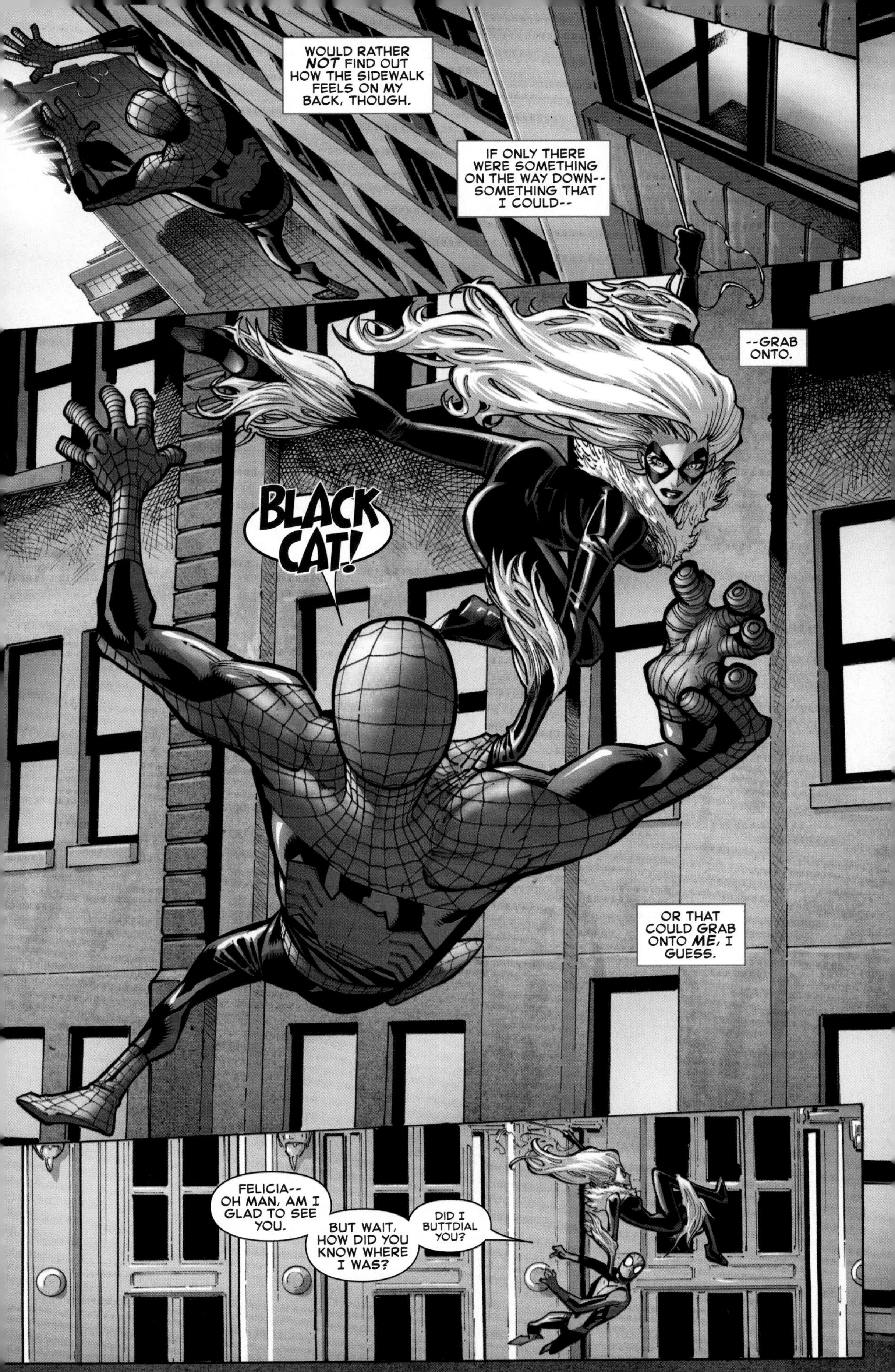

WOULD RATHER NOT FIND OUT HOW THE SIDEWALK FEELS ON MY BACK, THOUGH.
IF ONLY THERE WERE SOMETHING ON THE WAY DOWN-- SOMETHING THAT I COULD--
--GRAB ONTO.
BLACK CAT!
OR THAT COULD GRAB ONTO ME, I GUESS.
FELICIA-- OH MAN, AM I GLAD TO SEE YOU.
BUT WAIT, HOW DID YOU KNOW WHERE I WAS?
DID I BUTTDIAL YOU?

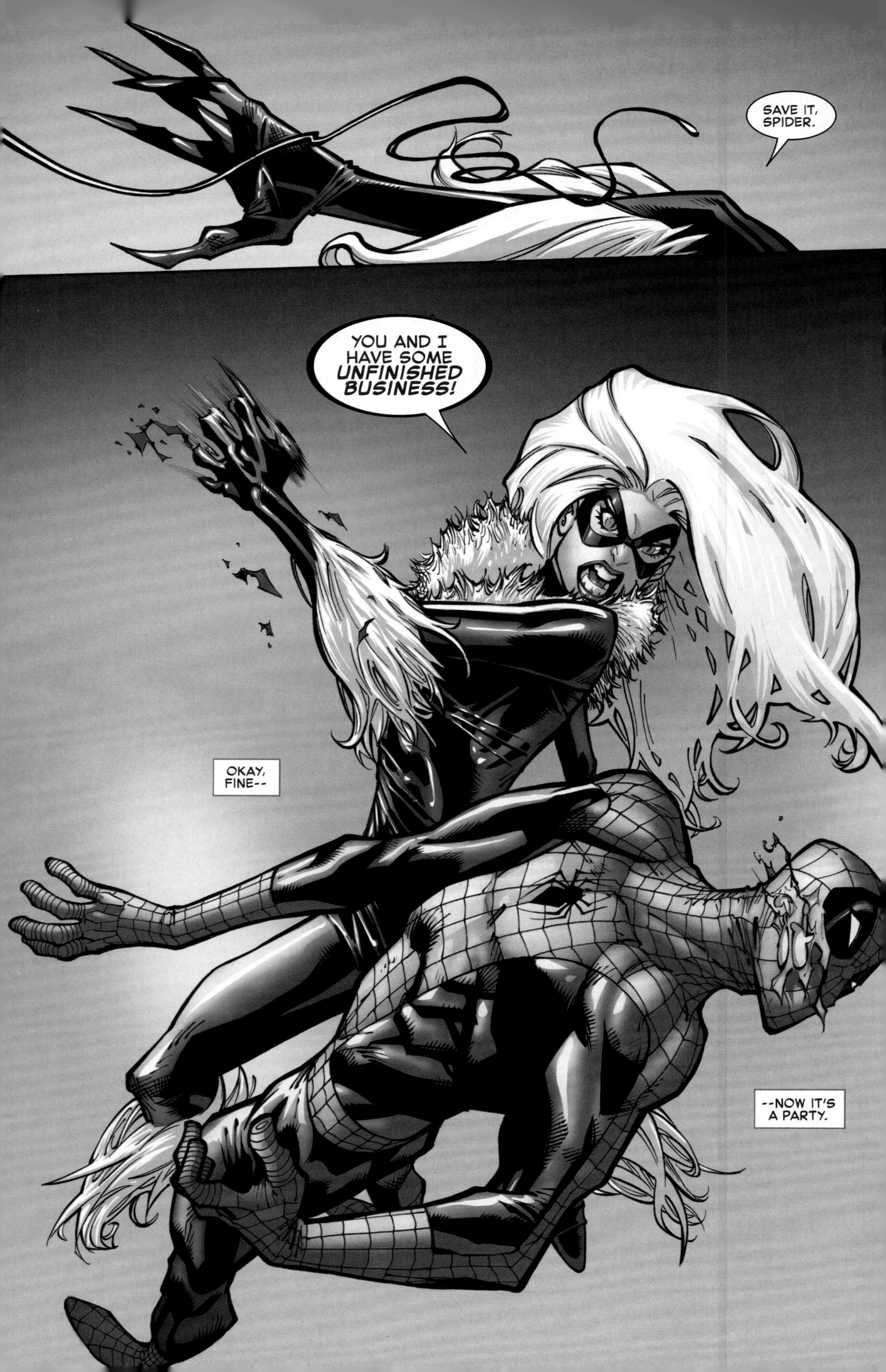
SAVE IT, SPIDER.
YOU AND I HAVE SOME UNFINISHED BUSINESS!
OKAY, FINE--
--NOW IT'S A PARTY.

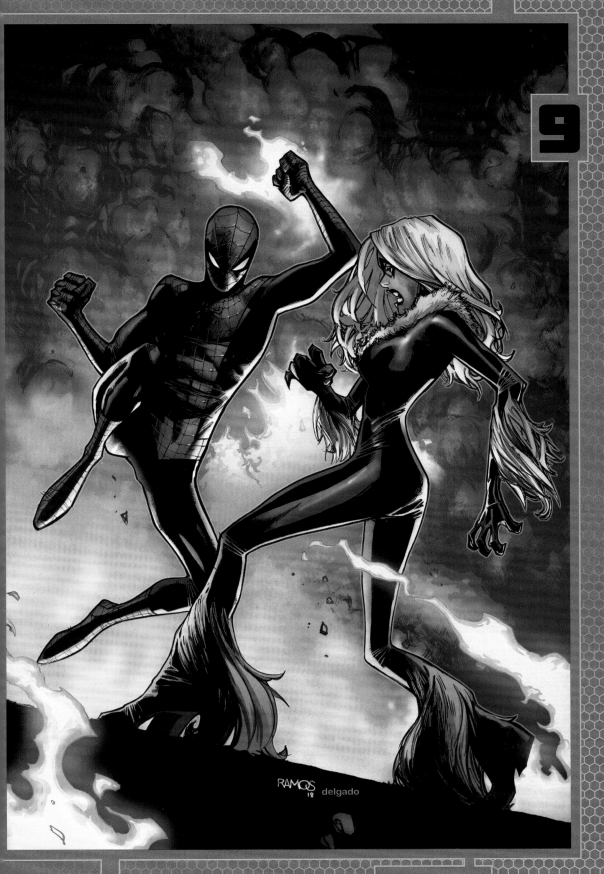

RAMOS 18 delgado

HEIST PART 2

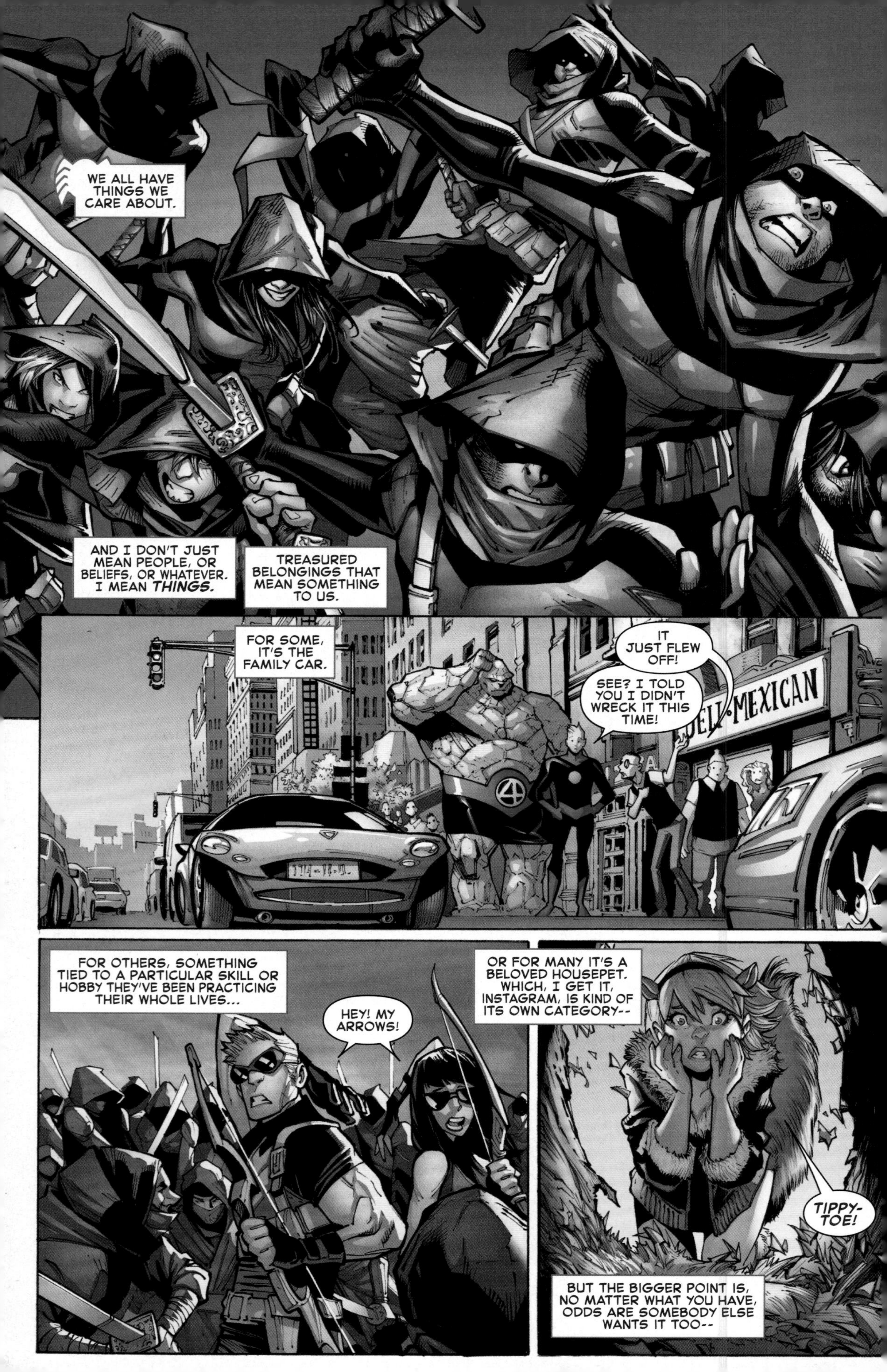

WE ALL HAVE THINGS WE CARE ABOUT.
AND I DON'T JUST MEAN PEOPLE, OR BELIEFS, OR WHATEVER. I MEAN *THINGS.*
TREASURED BELONGINGS THAT MEAN SOMETHING TO US.
FOR SOME, IT'S THE FAMILY CAR.
IT JUST FLEW OFF!
SEE? I TOLD YOU I DIDN'T WRECK IT THIS TIME!
DELI MEXICAN
FOR OTHERS, SOMETHING TIED TO A PARTICULAR SKILL OR HOBBY THEY'VE BEEN PRACTICING THEIR WHOLE LIVES...
HEY! MY ARROWS!
OR FOR MANY IT'S A BELOVED HOUSEPET. WHICH, I GET IT, INSTAGRAM, IS KIND OF ITS OWN CATEGORY--
TIPPY-TOE!
BUT THE BIGGER POINT IS, NO MATTER WHAT YOU HAVE, ODDS ARE SOMEBODY ELSE WANTS IT TOO--

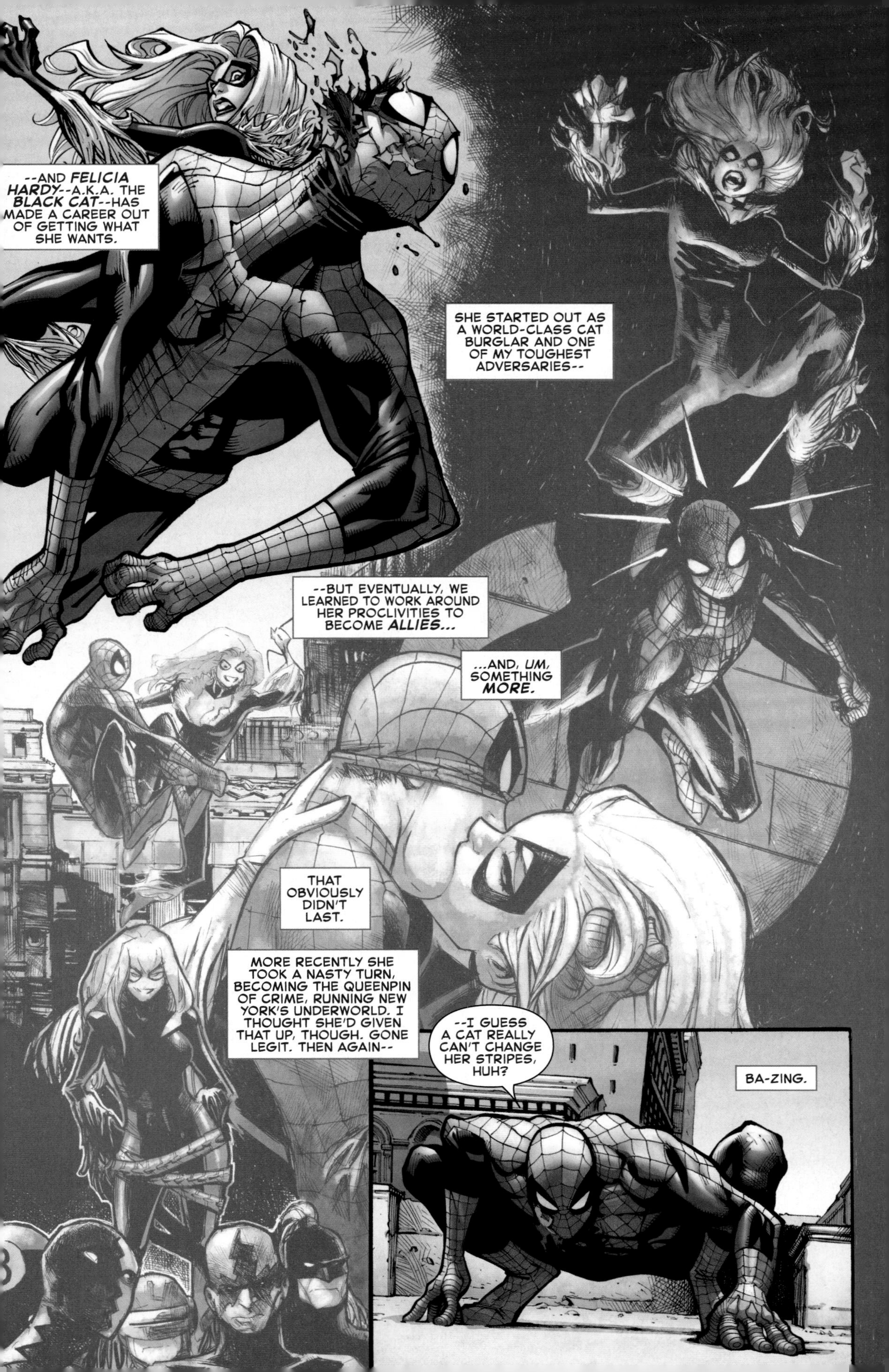
--AND FELICIA HARDY--A.K.A. THE BLACK CAT--HAS MADE A CAREER OUT OF GETTING WHAT SHE WANTS.
SHE STARTED OUT AS A WORLD-CLASS CAT BURGLAR AND ONE OF MY TOUGHEST ADVERSARIES--
--BUT EVENTUALLY, WE LEARNED TO WORK AROUND HER PROCLIVITIES TO BECOME ALLIES...
...AND, UM, SOMETHING MORE.
THAT OBVIOUSLY DIDN'T LAST.
MORE RECENTLY SHE TOOK A NASTY TURN, BECOMING THE QUEENPIN OF CRIME, RUNNING NEW YORK'S UNDERWORLD. I THOUGHT SHE'D GIVEN THAT UP, THOUGH. GONE LEGIT. THEN AGAIN--
--I GUESS A CAT REALLY CAN'T CHANGE HER STRIPES, HUH?
BA-ZING.

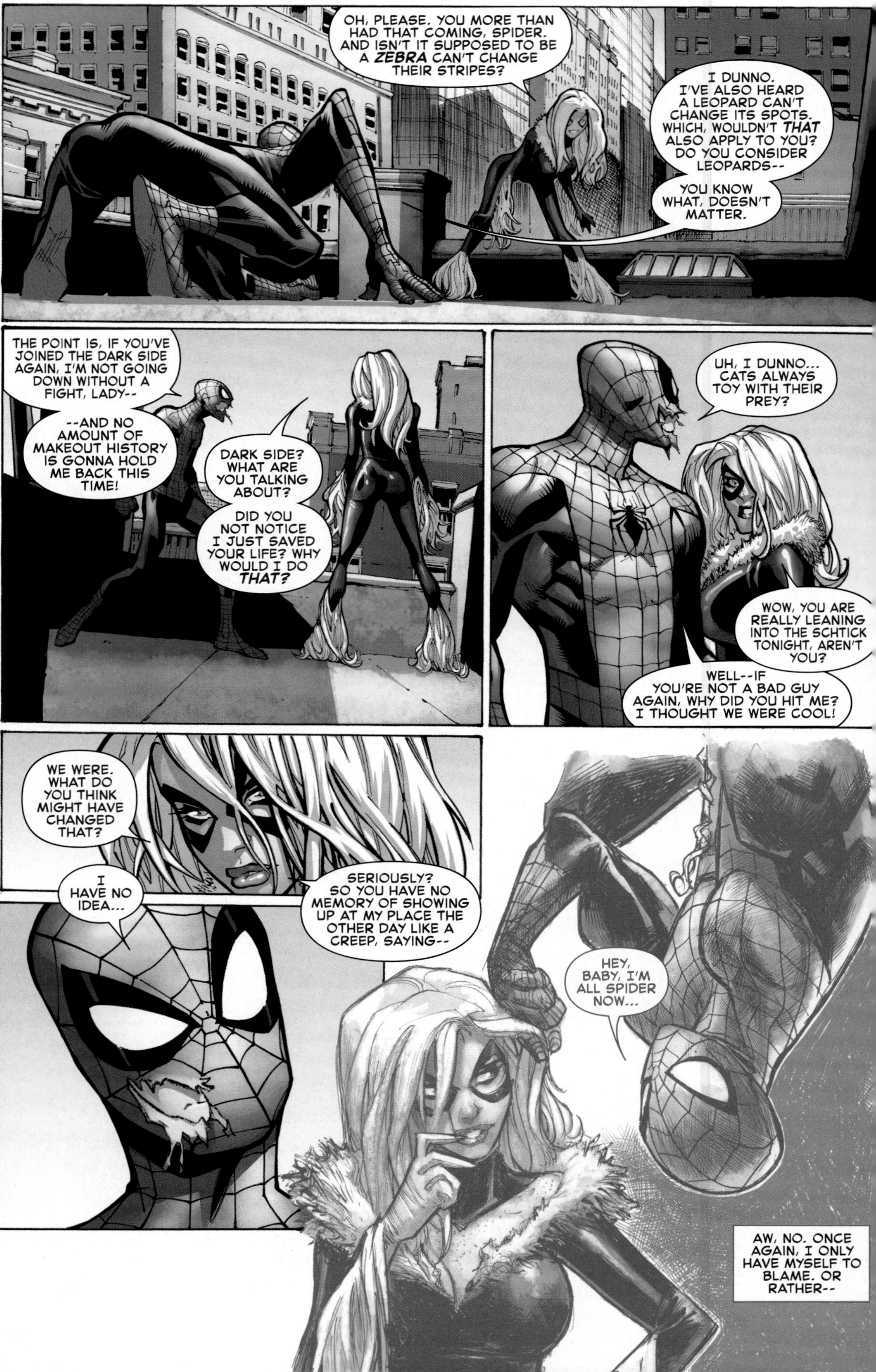
OH, PLEASE. YOU MORE THAN HAD THAT COMING, SPIDER. AND ISN'T IT SUPPOSED TO BE A ZEBRA CAN'T CHANGE THEIR STRIPES?
I DUNNO. I'VE ALSO HEARD A LEOPARD CAN'T CHANGE ITS SPOTS. WHICH, WOULDN'T THAT ALSO APPLY TO YOU? DO YOU CONSIDER LEOPARDS--
YOU KNOW WHAT, DOESN'T MATTER.
THE POINT IS, IF YOU'VE JOINED THE DARK SIDE AGAIN, I'M NOT GOING DOWN WITHOUT A FIGHT, LADY--
--AND NO AMOUNT OF MAKEOUT HISTORY IS GONNA HOLD ME BACK THIS TIME!
DARK SIDE? WHAT ARE YOU TALKING ABOUT?
DID YOU NOT NOTICE I JUST SAVED YOUR LIFE? WHY WOULD I DO THAT?
UH, I DUNNO... CATS ALWAYS TOY WITH THEIR PREY?
WOW, YOU ARE REALLY LEANING INTO THE SCHTICK TONIGHT, AREN'T YOU?
WELL--IF YOU'RE NOT A BAD GUY AGAIN, WHY DID YOU HIT ME? I THOUGHT WE WERE COOL!
WE WERE. WHAT DO YOU THINK MIGHT HAVE CHANGED THAT?
I HAVE NO IDEA...
SERIOUSLY? SO YOU HAVE NO MEMORY OF SHOWING UP AT MY PLACE THE OTHER DAY LIKE A CREEP, SAYING--
HEY, BABY, I'M ALL SPIDER NOW...
AW, NO. ONCE AGAIN, I ONLY HAVE MYSELF TO BLAME. OR RATHER--

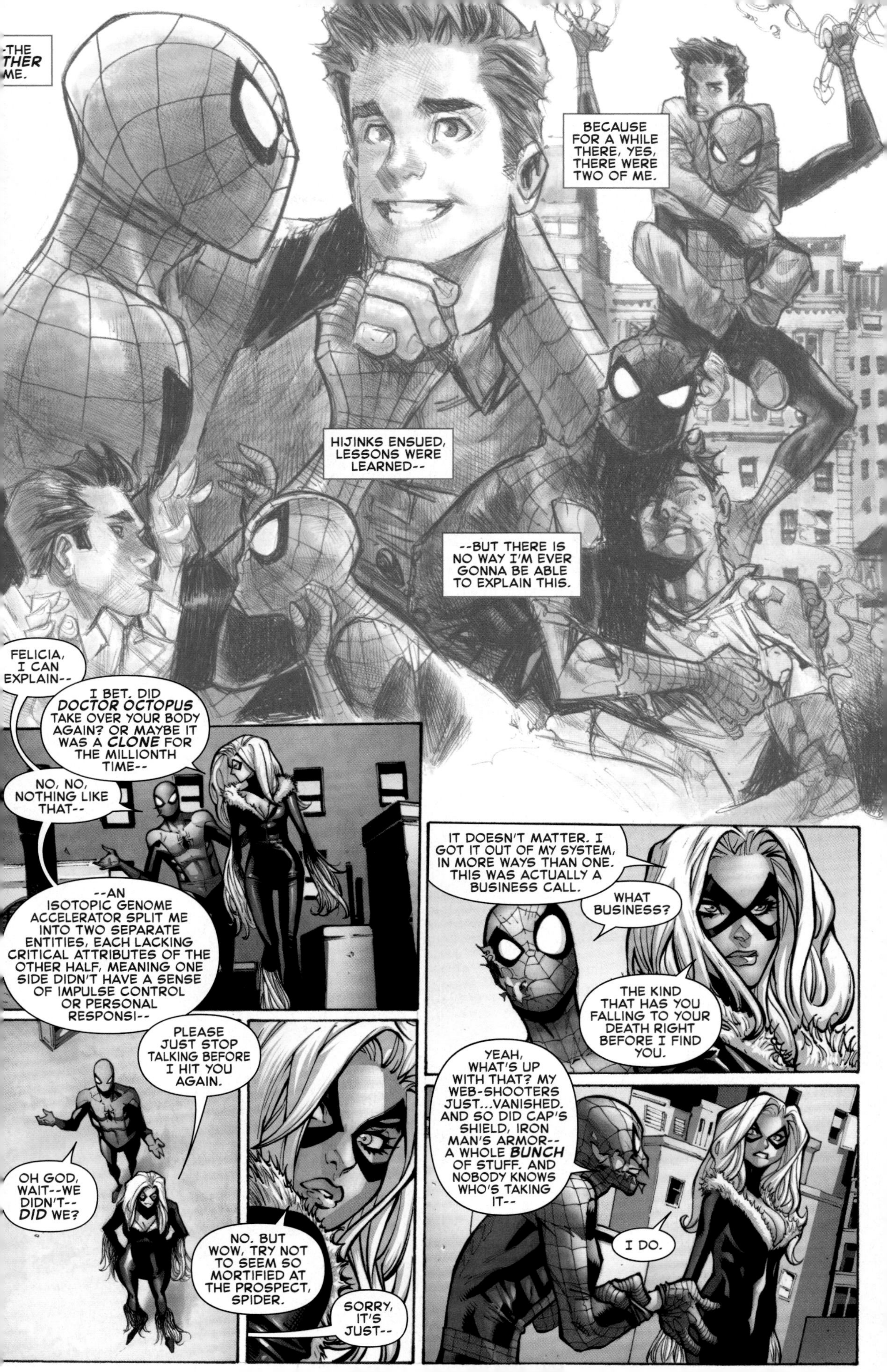

-THE
OTHER
ME.
BECAUSE FOR A WHILE THERE, YES, THERE WERE TWO OF ME.
HIJINKS ENSUED, LESSONS WERE LEARNED--
--BUT THERE IS NO WAY I'M EVER GONNA BE ABLE TO EXPLAIN THIS.
FELICIA, I CAN EXPLAIN--
I BET. DID DOCTOR OCTOPUS TAKE OVER YOUR BODY AGAIN? OR MAYBE IT WAS A CLONE FOR THE MILLIONTH TIME--
NO, NO, NOTHING LIKE THAT--
--AN ISOTOPIC GENOME ACCELERATOR SPLIT ME INTO TWO SEPARATE ENTITIES, EACH LACKING CRITICAL ATTRIBUTES OF THE OTHER HALF, MEANING ONE SIDE DIDN'T HAVE A SENSE OF IMPULSE CONTROL OR PERSONAL RESPONSI--
PLEASE JUST STOP TALKING BEFORE I HIT YOU AGAIN.
OH GOD, WAIT--WE DIDN'T--DID WE?
NO. BUT WOW, TRY NOT TO SEEM SO MORTIFIED AT THE PROSPECT, SPIDER.
SORRY, IT'S JUST--
IT DOESN'T MATTER. I GOT IT OUT OF MY SYSTEM, IN MORE WAYS THAN ONE. THIS WAS ACTUALLY A BUSINESS CALL.
WHAT BUSINESS?
THE KIND THAT HAS YOU FALLING TO YOUR DEATH RIGHT BEFORE I FIND YOU.
YEAH, WHAT'S UP WITH THAT? MY WEB-SHOOTERS JUST...VANISHED. AND SO DID CAP'S SHIELD, IRON MAN'S ARMOR--A WHOLE BUNCH OF STUFF. AND NOBODY KNOWS WHO'S TAKING IT--
I DO.

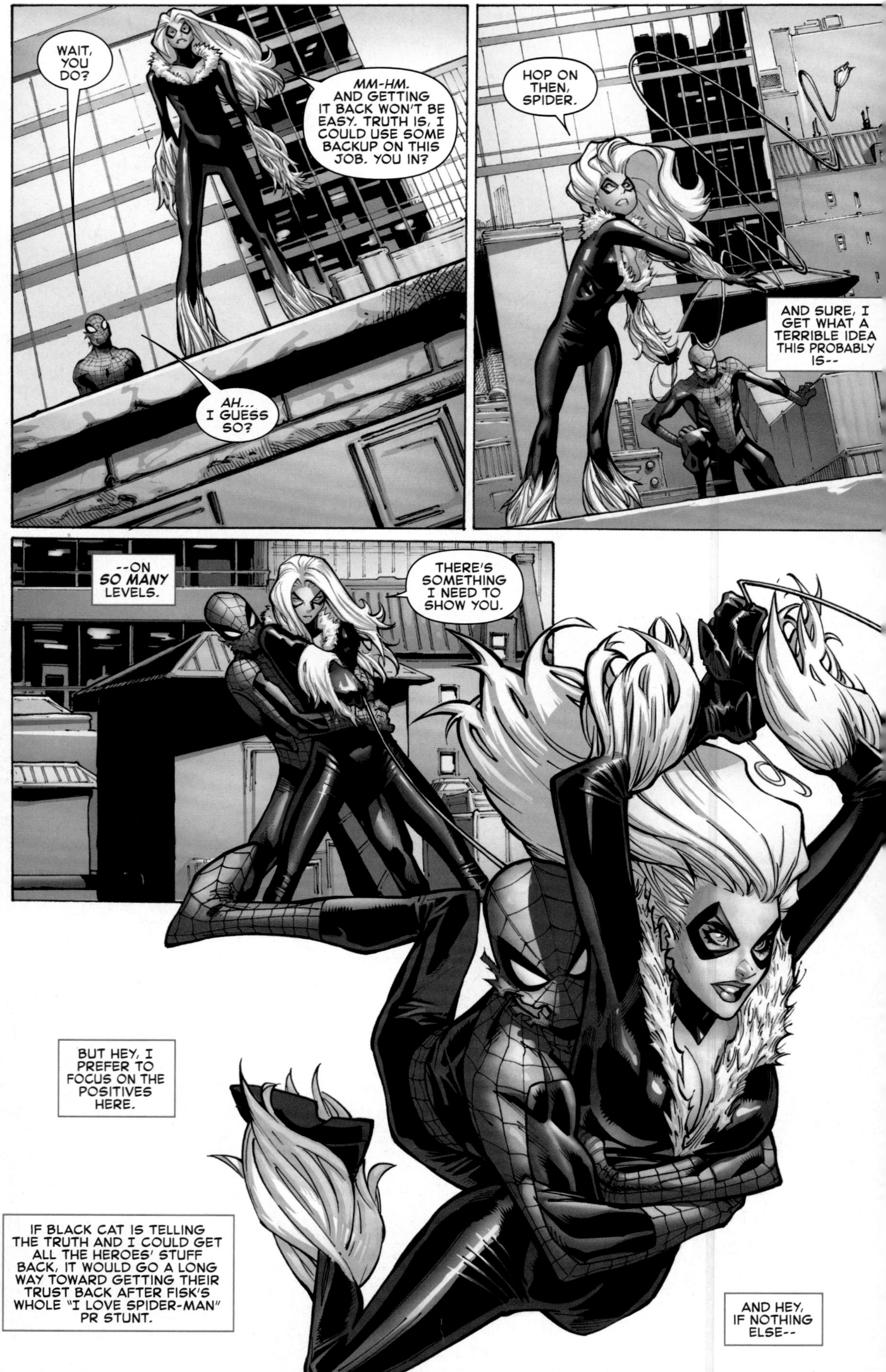
WAIT, YOU DO?
MM-HM. AND GETTING IT BACK WON'T BE EASY. TRUTH IS, I COULD USE SOME BACKUP ON THIS JOB. YOU IN?
AH... I GUESS SO?
HOP ON THEN, SPIDER.
AND SURE, I GET WHAT A TERRIBLE IDEA THIS PROBABLY IS--
--ON SO MANY LEVELS.
THERE'S SOMETHING I NEED TO SHOW YOU.
BUT HEY, I PREFER TO FOCUS ON THE POSITIVES HERE.
IF BLACK CAT IS TELLING THE TRUTH AND I COULD GET ALL THE HEROES' STUFF BACK, IT WOULD GO A LONG WAY TOWARD GETTING THEIR TRUST BACK AFTER FISK'S WHOLE "I LOVE SPIDER-MAN" PR STUNT.
AND HEY, IF NOTHING ELSE--

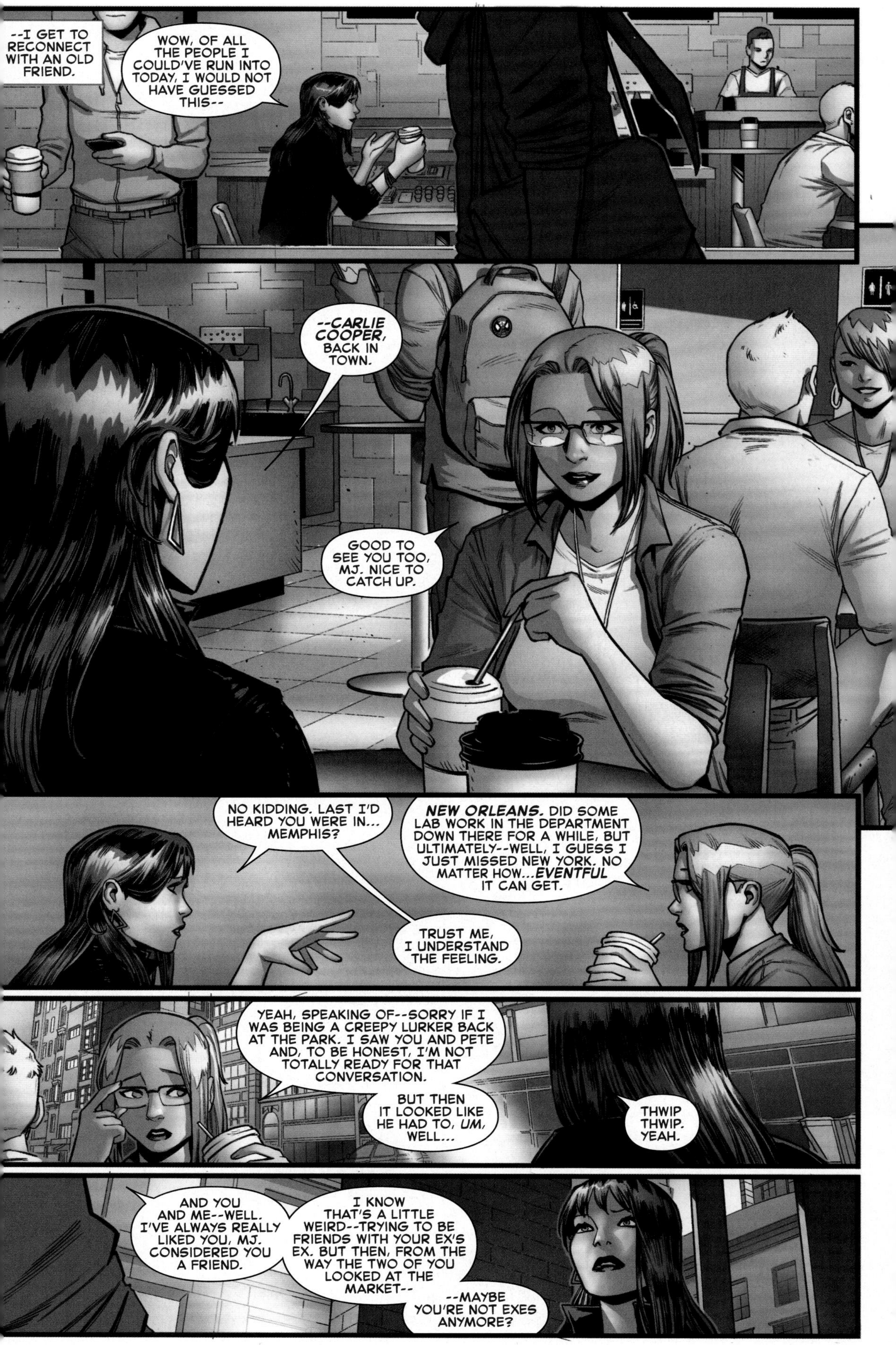
--I GET TO RECONNECT WITH AN OLD FRIEND.
WOW, OF ALL THE PEOPLE I COULD'VE RUN INTO TODAY, I WOULD NOT HAVE GUESSED THIS--
--CARLIE COOPER, BACK IN TOWN.
GOOD TO SEE YOU TOO, MJ. NICE TO CATCH UP.
NO KIDDING. LAST I'D HEARD YOU WERE IN... MEMPHIS?
NEW ORLEANS. DID SOME LAB WORK IN THE DEPARTMENT DOWN THERE FOR A WHILE, BUT ULTIMATELY--WELL, I GUESS I JUST MISSED NEW YORK. NO MATTER HOW...EVENTFUL IT CAN GET.
TRUST ME, I UNDERSTAND THE FEELING.
YEAH, SPEAKING OF--SORRY IF I WAS BEING A CREEPY LURKER BACK AT THE PARK. I SAW YOU AND PETE AND, TO BE HONEST, I'M NOT TOTALLY READY FOR THAT CONVERSATION.
BUT THEN IT LOOKED LIKE HE HAD TO, UM, WELL...
THWIP THWIP. YEAH.
AND YOU AND ME--WELL. I'VE ALWAYS REALLY LIKED YOU, MJ. CONSIDERED YOU A FRIEND.
I KNOW THAT'S A LITTLE WEIRD--TRYING TO BE FRIENDS WITH YOUR EX'S EX. BUT THEN, FROM THE WAY THE TWO OF YOU LOOKED AT THE MARKET--
--MAYBE YOU'RE NOT EXES ANYMORE?

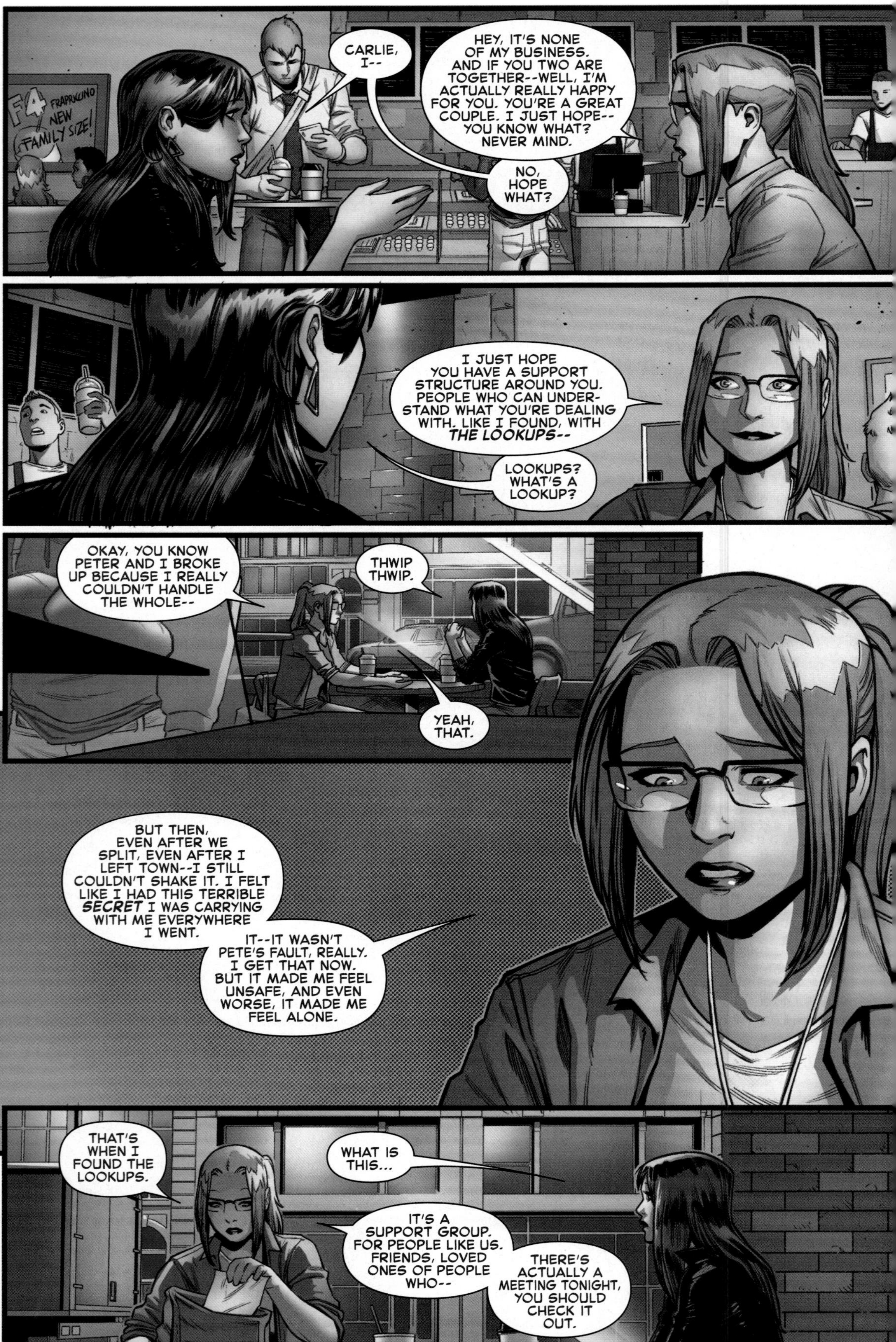
CARLIE, I--
HEY, IT'S NONE OF MY BUSINESS. AND IF YOU TWO ARE TOGETHER--WELL, I'M ACTUALLY REALLY HAPPY FOR YOU. YOU'RE A GREAT COUPLE. I JUST HOPE-- YOU KNOW WHAT? NEVER MIND.
NO, HOPE WHAT?
F4 FRAPPUCCINO NEW FAMILY SIZE!
I JUST HOPE YOU HAVE A SUPPORT STRUCTURE AROUND YOU. PEOPLE WHO CAN UNDERSTAND WHAT YOU'RE DEALING WITH. LIKE I FOUND, WITH *THE LOOKUPS--*
LOOKUPS? WHAT'S A LOOKUP?
OKAY, YOU KNOW PETER AND I BROKE UP BECAUSE I REALLY COULDN'T HANDLE THE WHOLE--
THWIP THWIP.
YEAH, THAT.
BUT THEN, EVEN AFTER WE SPLIT, EVEN AFTER I LEFT TOWN--I STILL COULDN'T SHAKE IT. I FELT LIKE I HAD THIS TERRIBLE *SECRET* I WAS CARRYING WITH ME EVERYWHERE I WENT.
IT--IT WASN'T PETE'S FAULT, REALLY. I GET THAT NOW. BUT IT MADE ME FEEL UNSAFE, AND EVEN WORSE, IT MADE ME FEEL ALONE.
THAT'S WHEN I FOUND THE LOOKUPS.
WHAT IS THIS...
IT'S A SUPPORT GROUP. FOR PEOPLE LIKE US. FRIENDS, LOVED ONES OF PEOPLE WHO--
THERE'S ACTUALLY A MEETING TONIGHT, YOU SHOULD CHECK IT OUT.

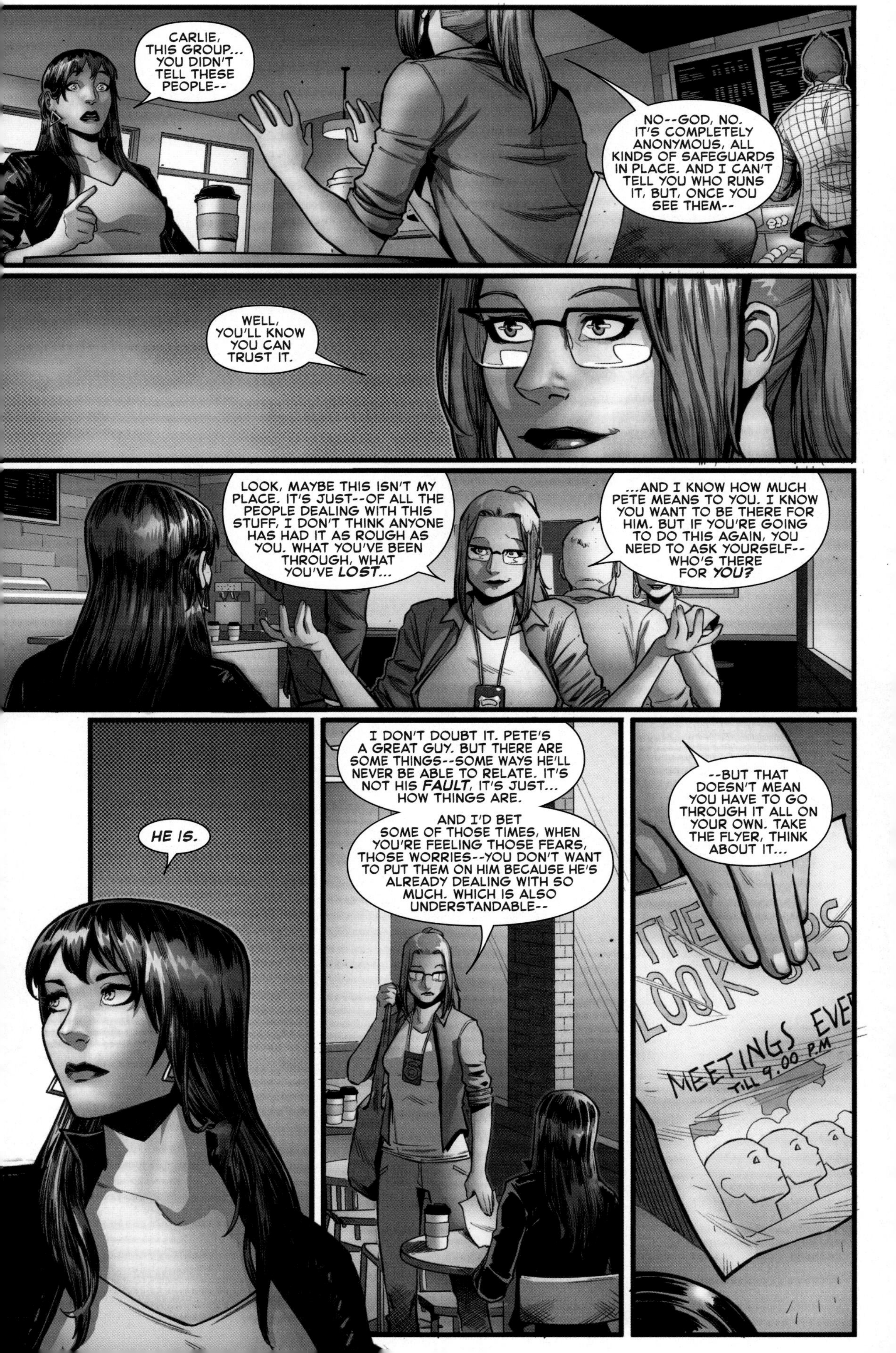
CARLIE, THIS GROUP... YOU DIDN'T TELL THESE PEOPLE--
NO--GOD, NO. IT'S COMPLETELY ANONYMOUS, ALL KINDS OF SAFEGUARDS IN PLACE. AND I CAN'T TELL YOU WHO RUNS IT, BUT, ONCE YOU SEE THEM--
WELL, YOU'LL KNOW YOU CAN TRUST IT.
LOOK, MAYBE THIS ISN'T MY PLACE. IT'S JUST--OF ALL THE PEOPLE DEALING WITH THIS STUFF, I DON'T THINK ANYONE HAS HAD IT AS ROUGH AS YOU. WHAT YOU'VE BEEN THROUGH, WHAT YOU'VE LOST...
...AND I KNOW HOW MUCH PETE MEANS TO YOU. I KNOW YOU WANT TO BE THERE FOR HIM. BUT IF YOU'RE GOING TO DO THIS AGAIN, YOU NEED TO ASK YOURSELF-- WHO'S THERE FOR YOU?
HE IS.
I DON'T DOUBT IT. PETE'S A GREAT GUY. BUT THERE ARE SOME THINGS--SOME WAYS HE'LL NEVER BE ABLE TO RELATE. IT'S NOT HIS FAULT, IT'S JUST... HOW THINGS ARE.
AND I'D BET SOME OF THOSE TIMES, WHEN YOU'RE FEELING THOSE FEARS, THOSE WORRIES--YOU DON'T WANT TO PUT THEM ON HIM BECAUSE HE'S ALREADY DEALING WITH SO MUCH. WHICH IS ALSO UNDERSTANDABLE--
--BUT THAT DOESN'T MEAN YOU HAVE TO GO THROUGH IT ALL ON YOUR OWN. TAKE THE FLYER, THINK ABOUT IT...
MEETINGS EVE
TILL 9.00 P.M

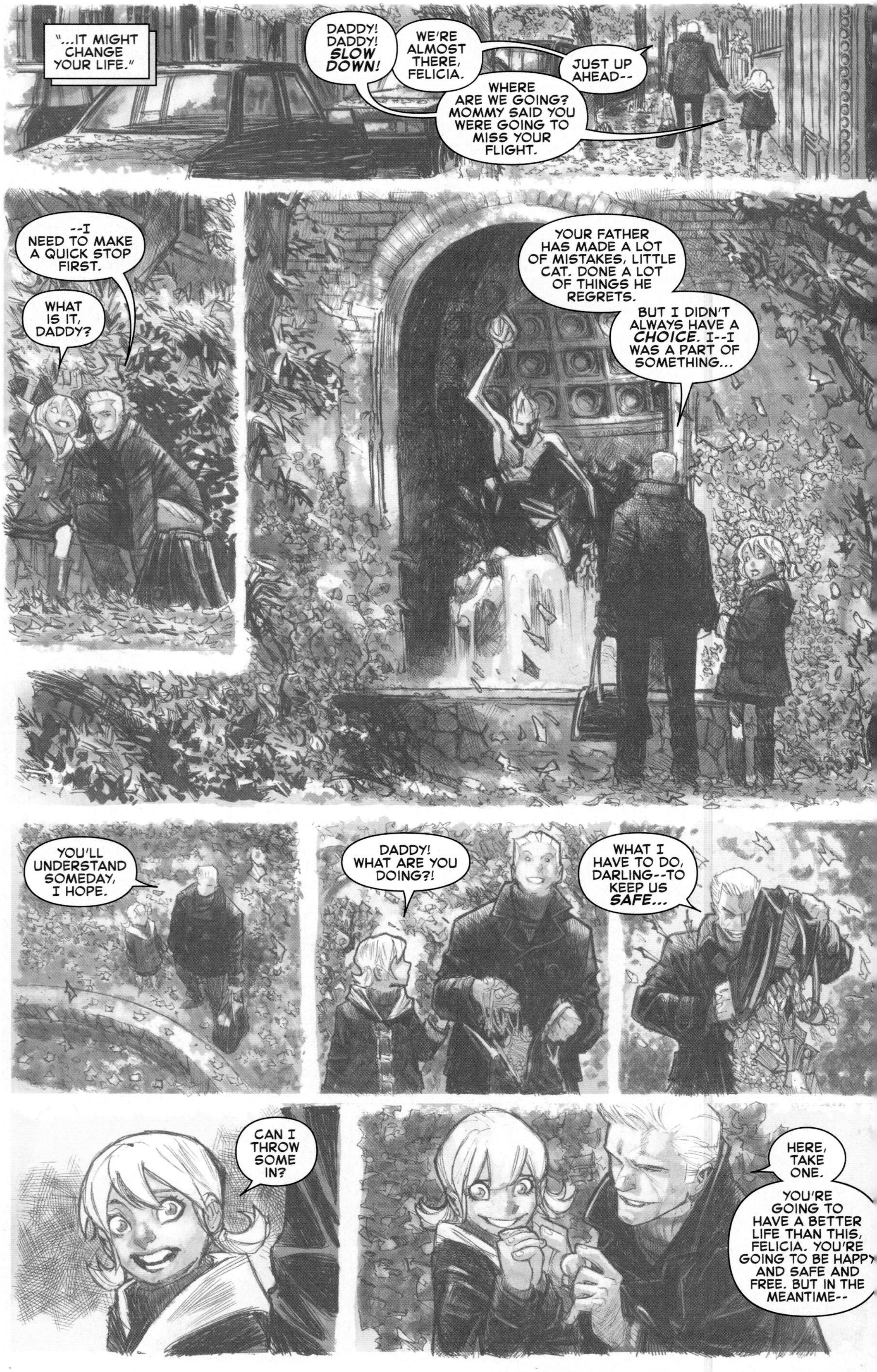
"...IT MIGHT CHANGE YOUR LIFE."
DADDY! DADDY! SLOW DOWN!
WE'RE ALMOST THERE, FELICIA.
JUST UP AHEAD--
WHERE ARE WE GOING? MOMMY SAID YOU WERE GOING TO MISS YOUR FLIGHT.
--I NEED TO MAKE A QUICK STOP FIRST.
WHAT IS IT, DADDY?
YOUR FATHER HAS MADE A LOT OF MISTAKES, LITTLE CAT. DONE A LOT OF THINGS HE REGRETS.
BUT I DIDN'T ALWAYS HAVE A CHOICE. I--I WAS A PART OF SOMETHING...
YOU'LL UNDERSTAND SOMEDAY, I HOPE.
DADDY! WHAT ARE YOU DOING?!
WHAT I HAVE TO DO, DARLING--TO KEEP US SAFE...
CAN I THROW SOME IN?
HERE, TAKE ONE.
YOU'RE GOING TO HAVE A BETTER LIFE THAN THIS, FELICIA. YOU'RE GOING TO BE HAPPY AND SAFE AND FREE. BUT IN THE MEANTIME--

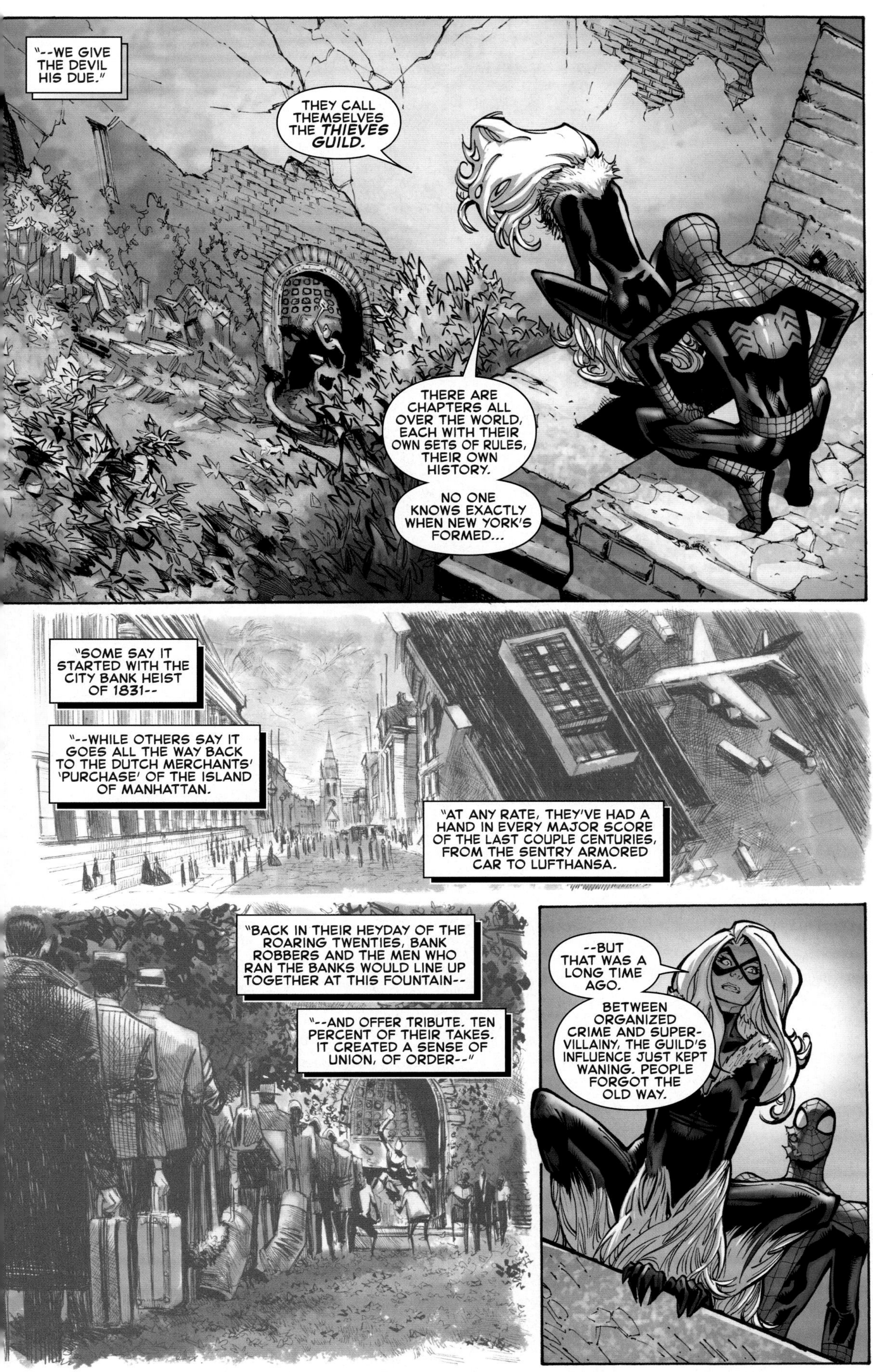
"--WE GIVE THE DEVIL HIS DUE."
THEY CALL THEMSELVES THE THIEVES GUILD.
THERE ARE CHAPTERS ALL OVER THE WORLD, EACH WITH THEIR OWN SETS OF RULES, THEIR OWN HISTORY.
NO ONE KNOWS EXACTLY WHEN NEW YORK'S FORMED...
"SOME SAY IT STARTED WITH THE CITY BANK HEIST OF 1831--
"--WHILE OTHERS SAY IT GOES ALL THE WAY BACK TO THE DUTCH MERCHANTS' 'PURCHASE' OF THE ISLAND OF MANHATTAN.
"AT ANY RATE, THEY'VE HAD A HAND IN EVERY MAJOR SCORE OF THE LAST COUPLE CENTURIES, FROM THE SENTRY ARMORED CAR TO LUFTHANSA.
"BACK IN THEIR HEYDAY OF THE ROARING TWENTIES, BANK ROBBERS AND THE MEN WHO RAN THE BANKS WOULD LINE UP TOGETHER AT THIS FOUNTAIN--
"--AND OFFER TRIBUTE. TEN PERCENT OF THEIR TAKES. IT CREATED A SENSE OF UNION, OF ORDER--"
--BUT THAT WAS A LONG TIME AGO.
BETWEEN ORGANIZED CRIME AND SUPER-VILLAINY, THE GUILD'S INFLUENCE JUST KEPT WANING. PEOPLE FORGOT THE OLD WAY.

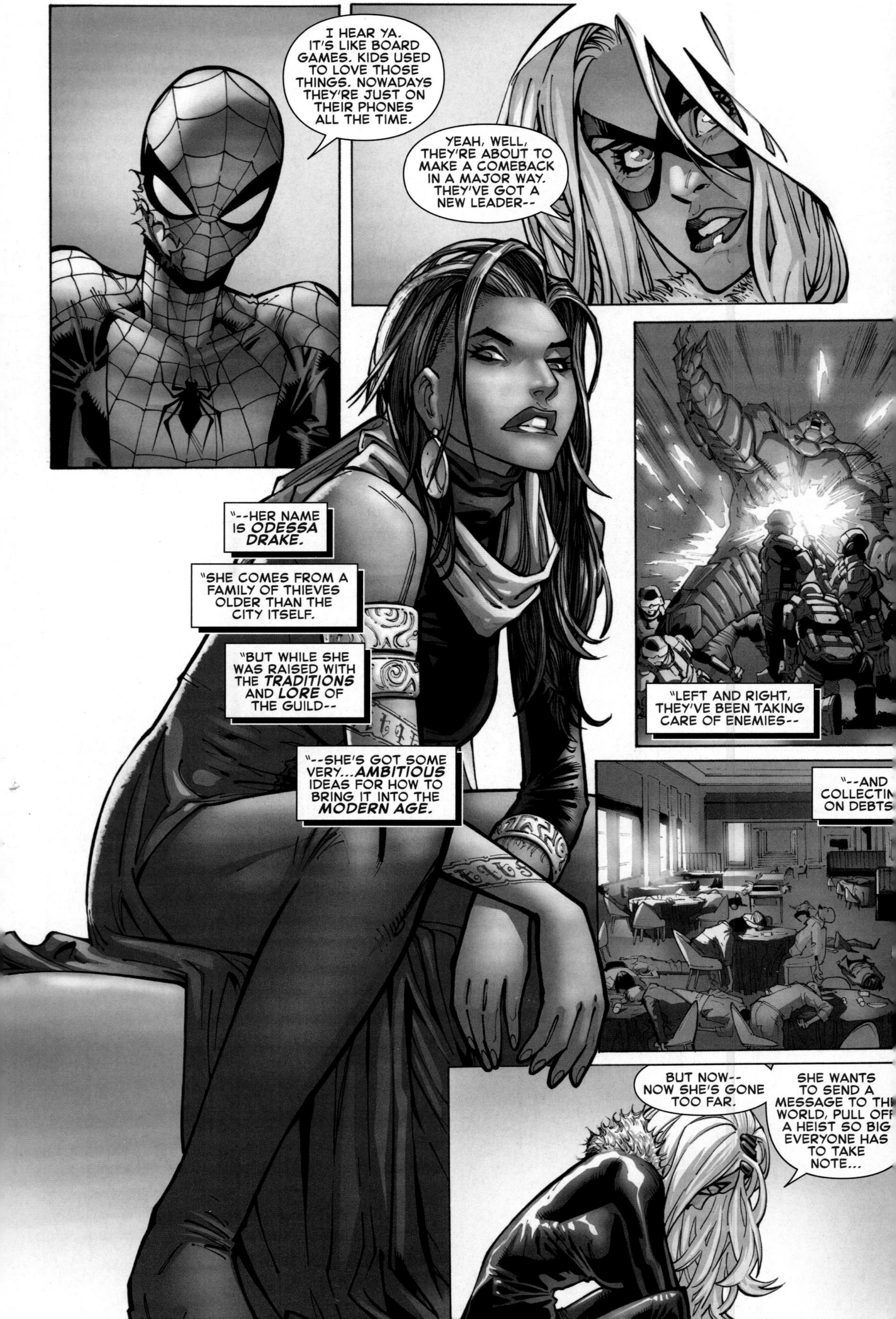

I HEAR YA. IT'S LIKE BOARD GAMES. KIDS USED TO LOVE THOSE THINGS. NOWADAYS THEY'RE JUST ON THEIR PHONES ALL THE TIME.
YEAH, WELL, THEY'RE ABOUT TO MAKE A COMEBACK IN A MAJOR WAY. THEY'VE GOT A NEW LEADER--
"--HER NAME IS ODESSA DRAKE.
"SHE COMES FROM A FAMILY OF THIEVES OLDER THAN THE CITY ITSELF.
"BUT WHILE SHE WAS RAISED WITH THE TRADITIONS AND LORE OF THE GUILD--
"--SHE'S GOT SOME VERY...AMBITIOUS IDEAS FOR HOW TO BRING IT INTO THE MODERN AGE.
"LEFT AND RIGHT, THEY'VE BEEN TAKING CARE OF ENEMIES--
"--AND COLLECTIN ON DEBTS
BUT NOW-- NOW SHE'S GONE TOO FAR.
SHE WANTS TO SEND A MESSAGE TO TH WORLD, PULL OFF A HEIST SO BIG EVERYONE HAS TO TAKE NOTE...

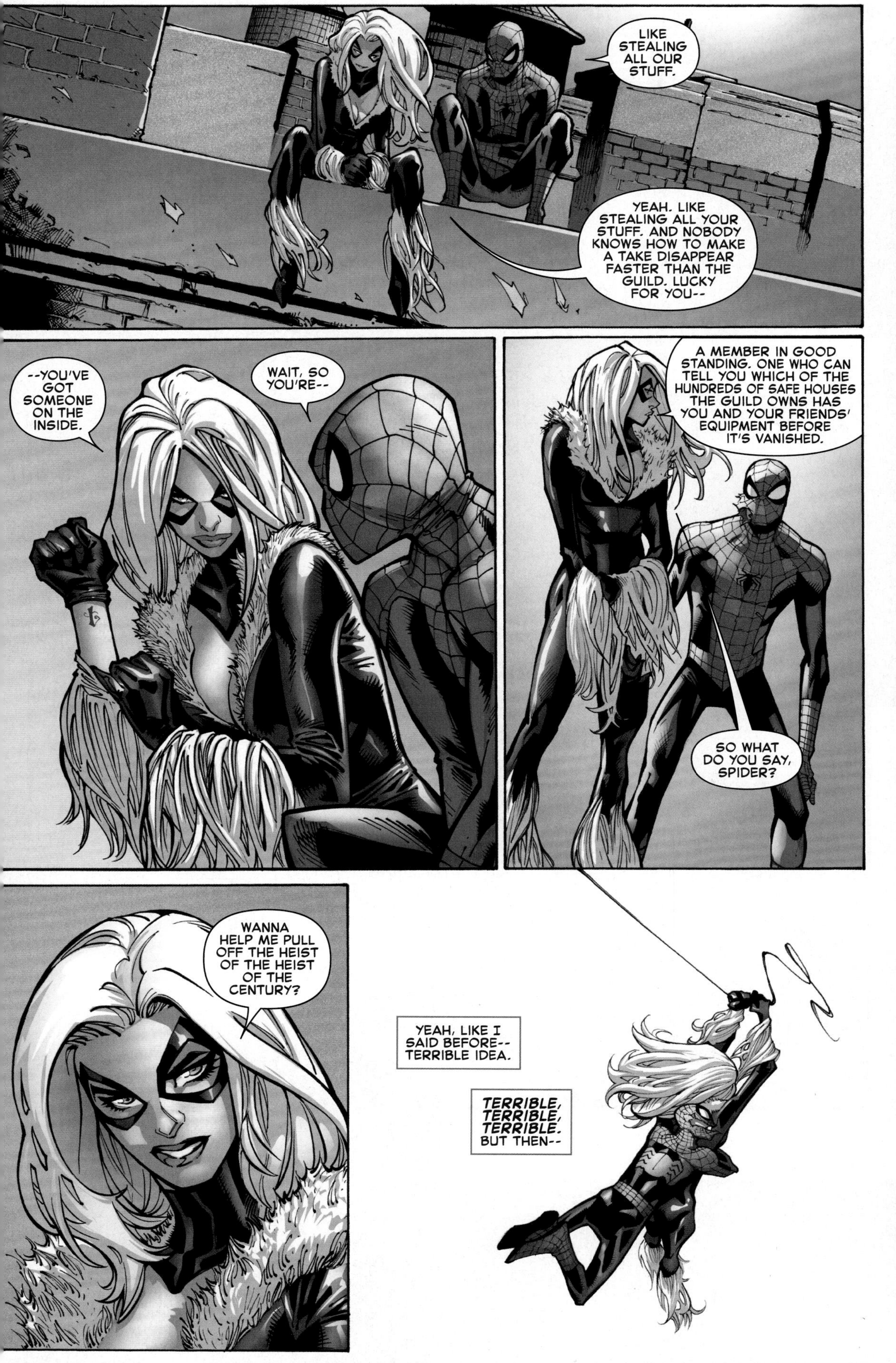

LIKE STEALING ALL OUR STUFF.
YEAH. LIKE STEALING ALL YOUR STUFF. AND NOBODY KNOWS HOW TO MAKE A TAKE DISAPPEAR FASTER THAN THE GUILD. LUCKY FOR YOU--
--YOU'VE GOT SOMEONE ON THE INSIDE.
WAIT, SO YOU'RE--
A MEMBER IN GOOD STANDING. ONE WHO CAN TELL YOU WHICH OF THE HUNDREDS OF SAFE HOUSES THE GUILD OWNS HAS YOU AND YOUR FRIENDS' EQUIPMENT BEFORE IT'S VANISHED.
SO WHAT DO YOU SAY, SPIDER?
WANNA HELP ME PULL OFF THE HEIST OF THE HEIST OF THE CENTURY?
YEAH, LIKE I SAID BEFORE-- TERRIBLE IDEA.
TERRIBLE, TERRIBLE, TERRIBLE. BUT THEN--

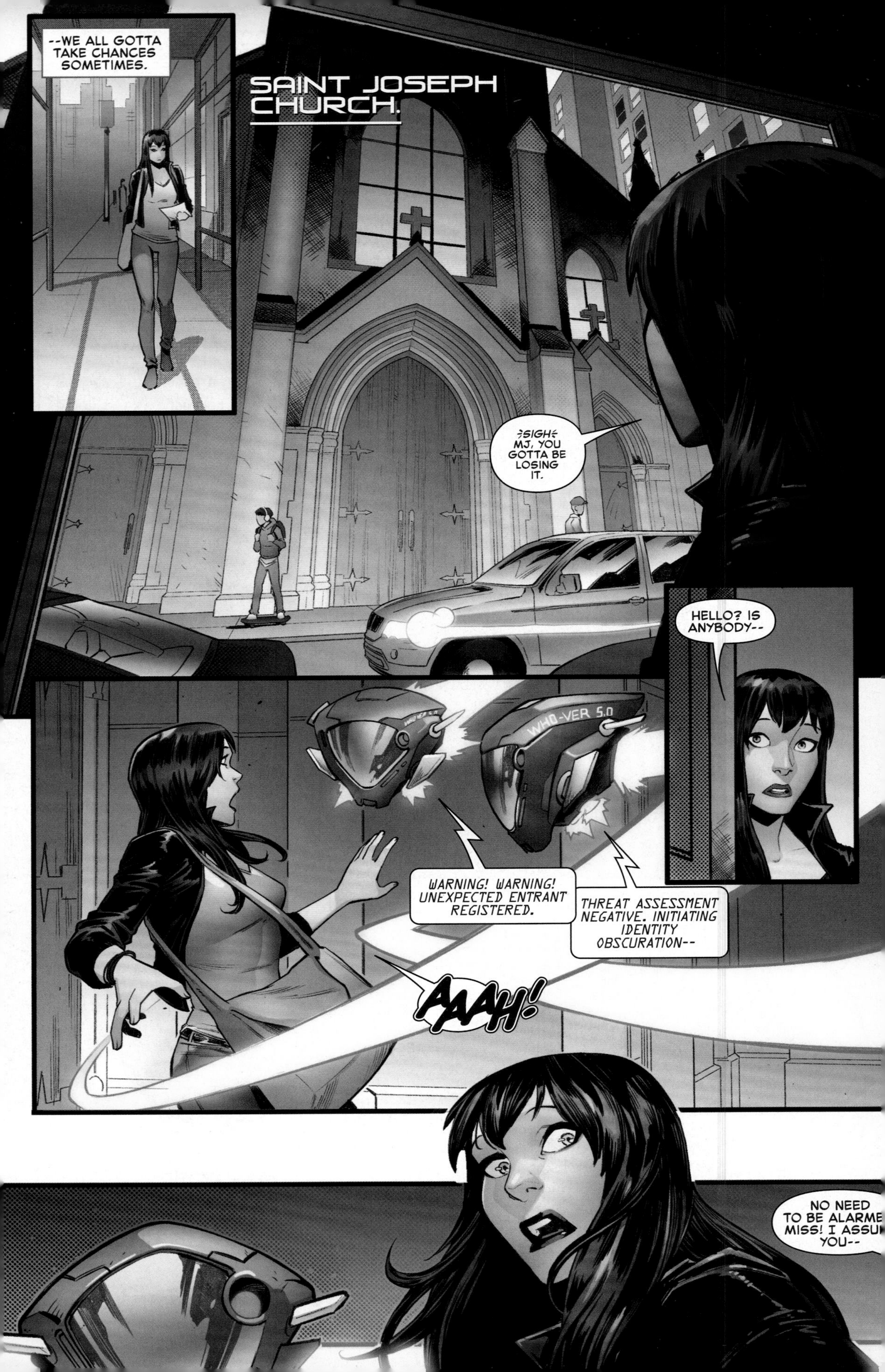
--WE ALL GOTTA TAKE CHANCES SOMETIMES.
SAINT JOSEPH CHURCH.
SIGH MJ, YOU GOTTA BE LOSING IT.
HELLO? IS ANYBODY--
WHO-VER 5.0
WARNING! WARNING! UNEXPECTED ENTRANT REGISTERED.
THREAT ASSESSMENT NEGATIVE. INITIATING IDENTITY OBSCURATION--
AAAH!
NO NEED TO BE ALARME MISS! I ASSU YOU--

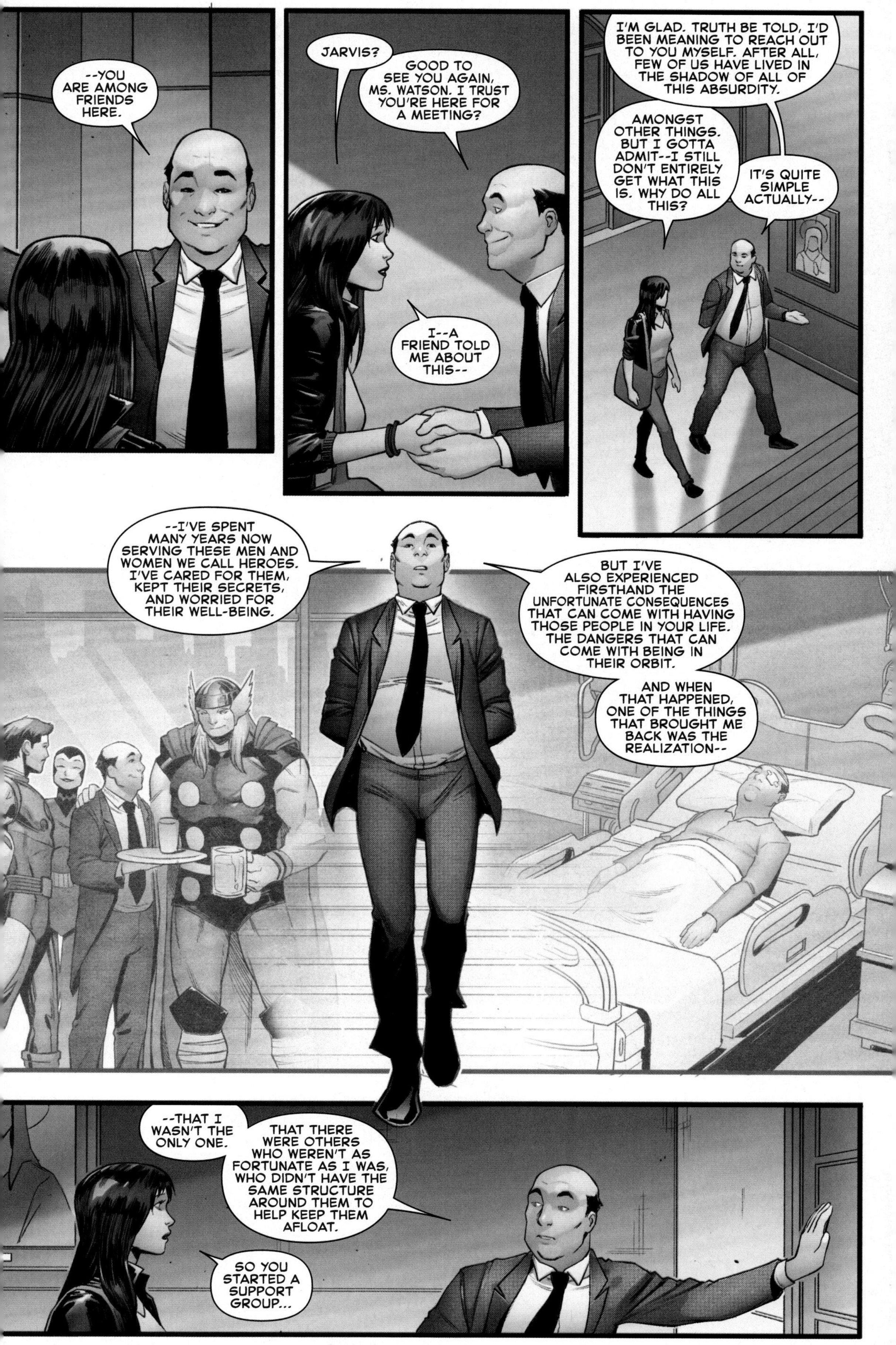
--YOU ARE AMONG FRIENDS HERE.
JARVIS?
GOOD TO SEE YOU AGAIN, MS. WATSON. I TRUST YOU'RE HERE FOR A MEETING?
I--A FRIEND TOLD ME ABOUT THIS--
I'M GLAD. TRUTH BE TOLD, I'D BEEN MEANING TO REACH OUT TO YOU MYSELF. AFTER ALL, FEW OF US HAVE LIVED IN THE SHADOW OF ALL OF THIS ABSURDITY.
AMONGST OTHER THINGS. BUT I GOTTA ADMIT--I STILL DON'T ENTIRELY GET WHAT THIS IS. WHY DO ALL THIS?
IT'S QUITE SIMPLE ACTUALLY--
--I'VE SPENT MANY YEARS NOW SERVING THESE MEN AND WOMEN WE CALL HEROES. I'VE CARED FOR THEM, KEPT THEIR SECRETS, AND WORRIED FOR THEIR WELL-BEING.
BUT I'VE ALSO EXPERIENCED FIRSTHAND THE UNFORTUNATE CONSEQUENCES THAT CAN COME WITH HAVING THOSE PEOPLE IN YOUR LIFE. THE DANGERS THAT CAN COME WITH BEING IN THEIR ORBIT.
AND WHEN THAT HAPPENED, ONE OF THE THINGS THAT BROUGHT ME BACK WAS THE REALIZATION--
--THAT I WASN'T THE ONLY ONE.
THAT THERE WERE OTHERS WHO WEREN'T AS FORTUNATE AS I WAS, WHO DIDN'T HAVE THE SAME STRUCTURE AROUND THEM TO HELP KEEP THEM AFLOAT.
SO YOU STARTED A SUPPORT GROUP...

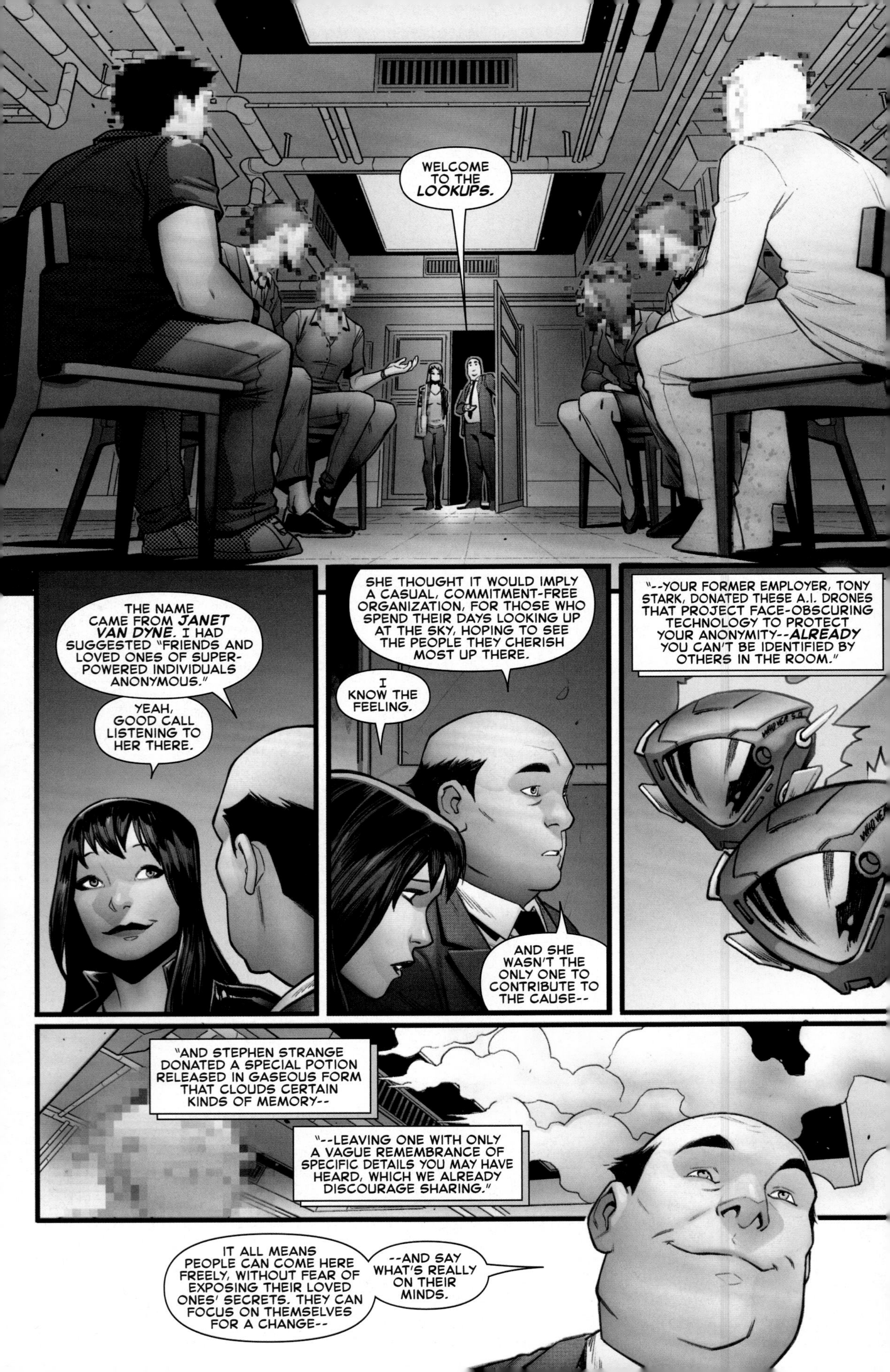
WELCOME TO THE *LOOKUPS.*
THE NAME CAME FROM ***JANET VAN DYNE.*** I HAD SUGGESTED "FRIENDS AND LOVED ONES OF SUPER-POWERED INDIVIDUALS ANONYMOUS."
YEAH, GOOD CALL LISTENING TO HER THERE.
SHE THOUGHT IT WOULD IMPLY A CASUAL, COMMITMENT-FREE ORGANIZATION, FOR THOSE WHO SPEND THEIR DAYS LOOKING UP AT THE SKY, HOPING TO SEE THE PEOPLE THEY CHERISH MOST UP THERE.
I KNOW THE FEELING.
AND SHE WASN'T THE ONLY ONE TO CONTRIBUTE TO THE CAUSE--
"--YOUR FORMER EMPLOYER, TONY STARK, DONATED THESE A.I. DRONES THAT PROJECT FACE-OBSCURING TECHNOLOGY TO PROTECT YOUR ANONYMITY--***ALREADY*** YOU CAN'T BE IDENTIFIED BY OTHERS IN THE ROOM."
"AND STEPHEN STRANGE DONATED A SPECIAL POTION RELEASED IN GASEOUS FORM THAT CLOUDS CERTAIN KINDS OF MEMORY--
"--LEAVING ONE WITH ONLY A VAGUE REMEMBRANCE OF SPECIFIC DETAILS YOU MAY HAVE HEARD, WHICH WE ALREADY DISCOURAGE SHARING."
IT ALL MEANS PEOPLE CAN COME HERE FREELY, WITHOUT FEAR OF EXPOSING THEIR LOVED ONES' SECRETS. THEY CAN FOCUS ON THEMSELVES FOR A CHANGE--
--AND SAY WHAT'S REALLY ON THEIR MINDS.

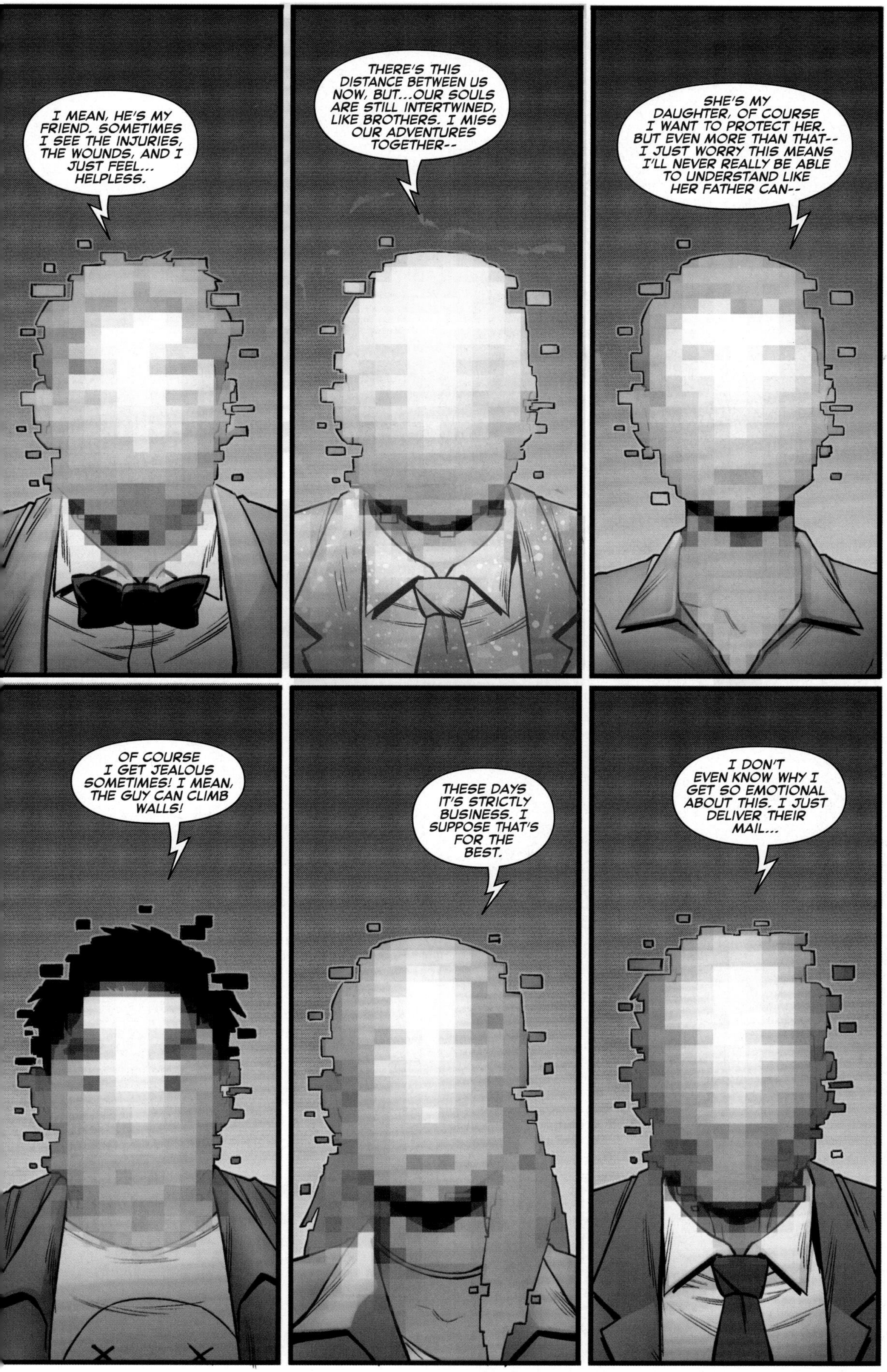
I MEAN, HE'S MY FRIEND. SOMETIMES I SEE THE INJURIES, THE WOUNDS, AND I JUST FEEL... HELPLESS.
THERE'S THIS DISTANCE BETWEEN US NOW, BUT...OUR SOULS ARE STILL INTERTWINED, LIKE BROTHERS. I MISS OUR ADVENTURES TOGETHER--
SHE'S MY DAUGHTER, OF COURSE I WANT TO PROTECT HER. BUT EVEN MORE THAN THAT-- I JUST WORRY THIS MEANS I'LL NEVER REALLY BE ABLE TO UNDERSTAND LIKE HER FATHER CAN--
OF COURSE I GET JEALOUS SOMETIMES! I MEAN, THE GUY CAN CLIMB WALLS!
THESE DAYS IT'S STRICTLY BUSINESS. I SUPPOSE THAT'S FOR THE BEST.
I DON'T EVEN KNOW WHY I GET SO EMOTIONAL ABOUT THIS. I JUST DELIVER THEIR MAIL...

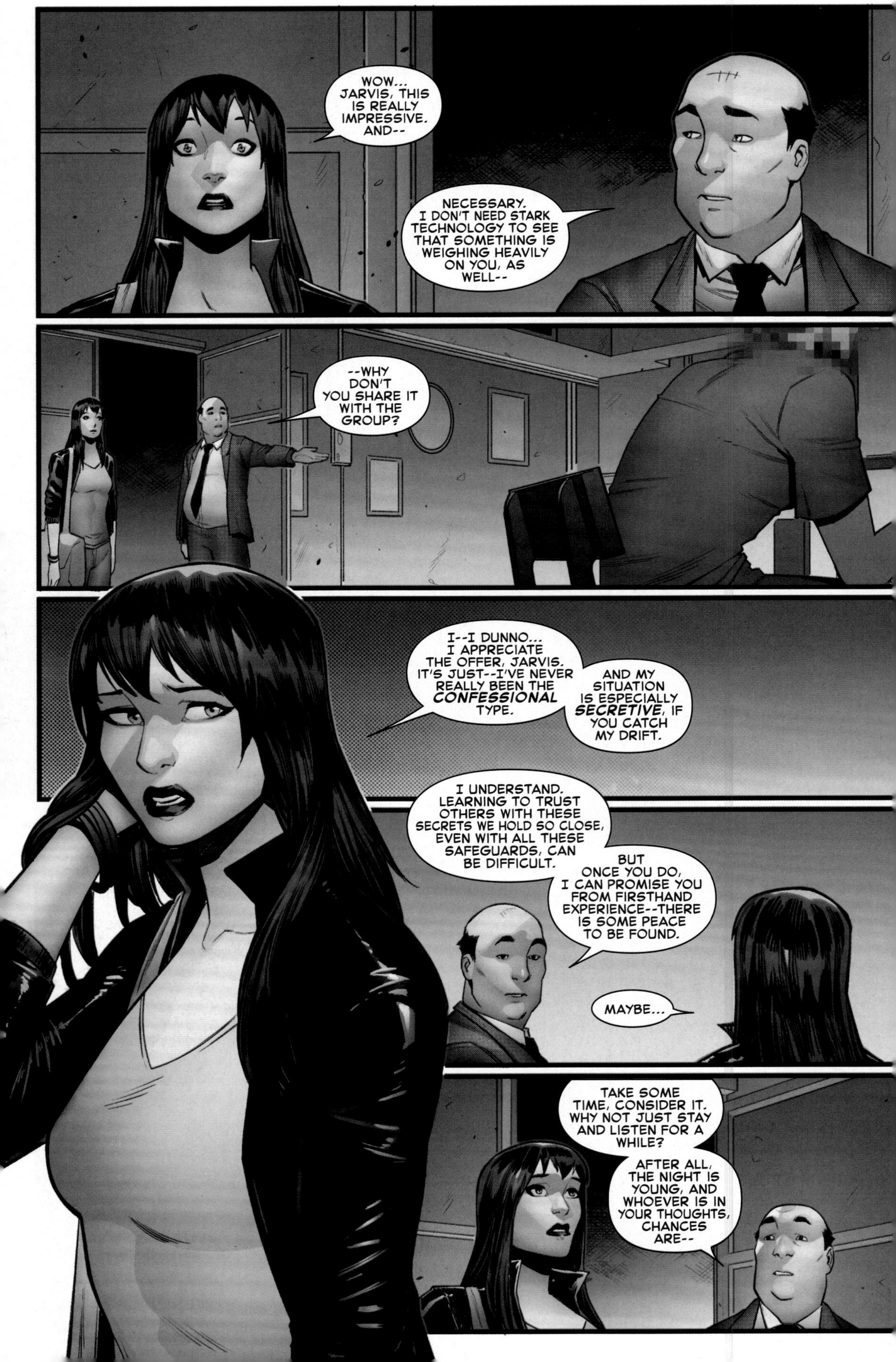
WOW... JARVIS, THIS IS REALLY IMPRESSIVE. AND--
NECESSARY. I DON'T NEED STARK TECHNOLOGY TO SEE THAT SOMETHING IS WEIGHING HEAVILY ON YOU, AS WELL--
--WHY DON'T YOU SHARE IT WITH THE GROUP?
I--I DUNNO... I APPRECIATE THE OFFER, JARVIS. IT'S JUST--I'VE NEVER REALLY BEEN THE CONFESSIONAL TYPE.
AND MY SITUATION IS ESPECIALLY SECRETIVE, IF YOU CATCH MY DRIFT.
I UNDERSTAND. LEARNING TO TRUST OTHERS WITH THESE SECRETS WE HOLD SO CLOSE, EVEN WITH ALL THESE SAFEGUARDS, CAN BE DIFFICULT.
BUT ONCE YOU DO, I CAN PROMISE YOU FROM FIRSTHAND EXPERIENCE--THERE IS SOME PEACE TO BE FOUND.
MAYBE...
TAKE SOME TIME, CONSIDER IT. WHY NOT JUST STAY AND LISTEN FOR A WHILE?
AFTER ALL, THE NIGHT IS YOUNG, AND WHOEVER IS IN YOUR THOUGHTS, CHANCES ARE--

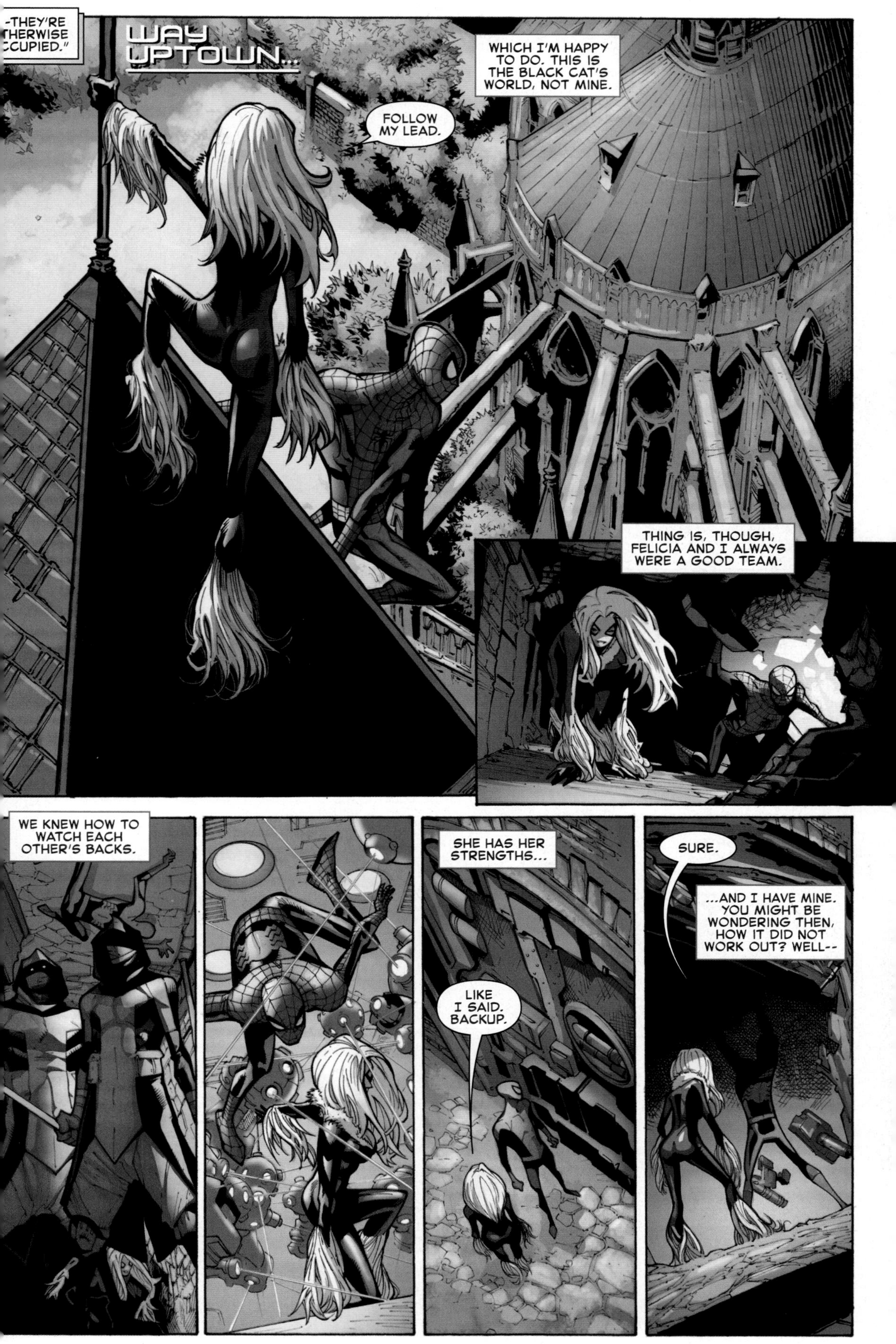
-THEY'RE
THERWISE
CCUPIED."
WAY UPTOWN...
WHICH I'M HAPPY TO DO. THIS IS THE BLACK CAT'S WORLD, NOT MINE.
FOLLOW MY LEAD.
THING IS, THOUGH, FELICIA AND I ALWAYS WERE A GOOD TEAM.
WE KNEW HOW TO WATCH EACH OTHER'S BACKS.
SHE HAS HER STRENGTHS...
LIKE I SAID. BACKUP.
SURE.
...AND I HAVE MINE. YOU MIGHT BE WONDERING THEN, HOW IT DID NOT WORK OUT? WELL--

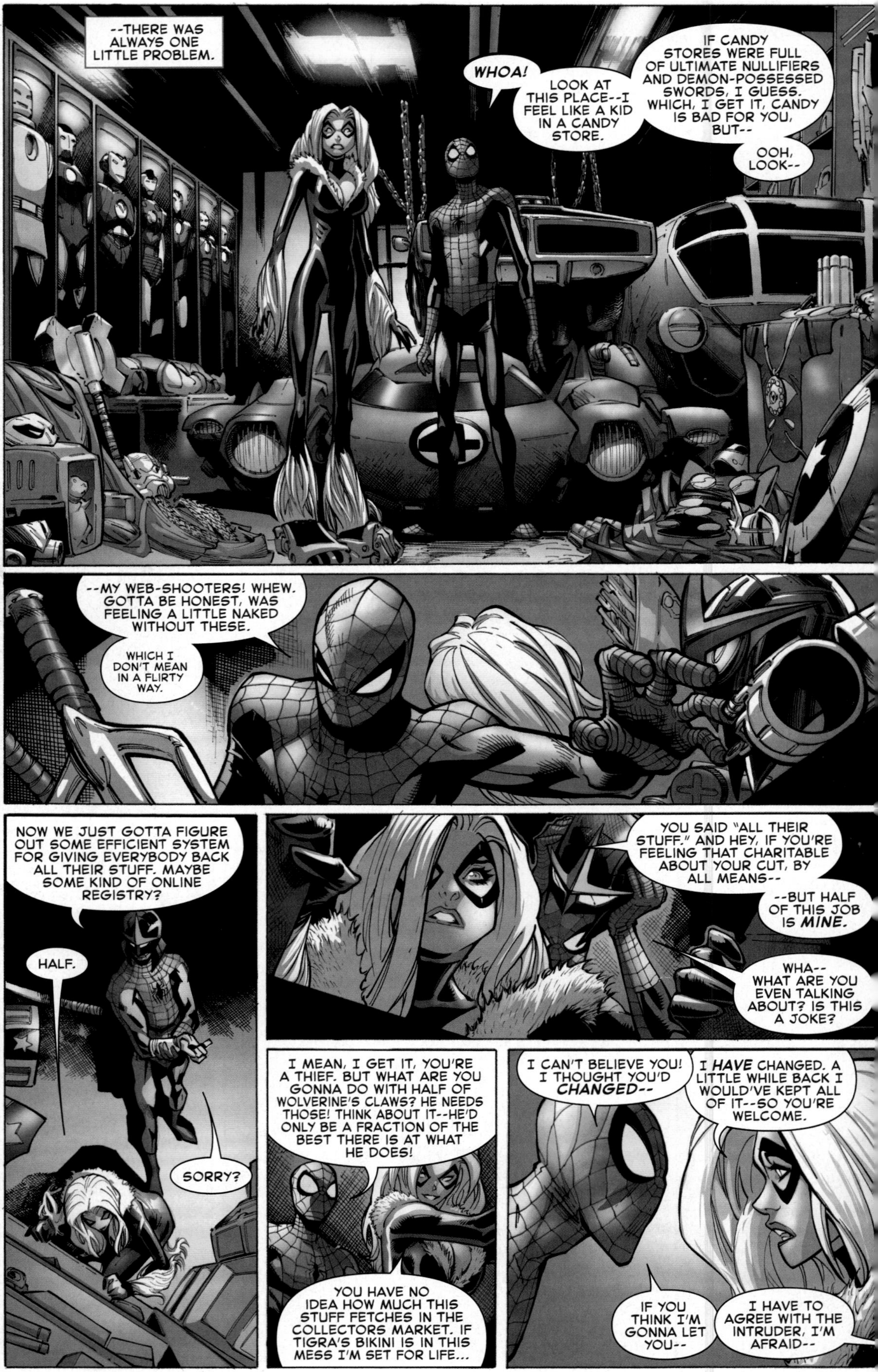
--THERE WAS ALWAYS ONE LITTLE PROBLEM.
WHOA!
LOOK AT THIS PLACE--I FEEL LIKE A KID IN A CANDY STORE.
IF CANDY STORES WERE FULL OF ULTIMATE NULLIFIERS AND DEMON-POSSESSED SWORDS, I GUESS. WHICH, I GET IT, CANDY IS BAD FOR YOU, BUT--
OOH, LOOK--
--MY WEB-SHOOTERS! WHEW. GOTTA BE HONEST, WAS FEELING A LITTLE NAKED WITHOUT THESE.
WHICH I DON'T MEAN IN A FLIRTY WAY.
NOW WE JUST GOTTA FIGURE OUT SOME EFFICIENT SYSTEM FOR GIVING EVERYBODY BACK ALL THEIR STUFF. MAYBE SOME KIND OF ONLINE REGISTRY?
HALF.
SORRY?
YOU SAID "ALL THEIR STUFF." AND HEY, IF YOU'RE FEELING THAT CHARITABLE ABOUT YOUR CUT, BY ALL MEANS--
--BUT HALF OF THIS JOB IS MINE.
WHA--WHAT ARE YOU EVEN TALKING ABOUT? IS THIS A JOKE?
I MEAN, I GET IT, YOU'RE A THIEF. BUT WHAT ARE YOU GONNA DO WITH HALF OF WOLVERINE'S CLAWS? HE NEEDS THOSE! THINK ABOUT IT--HE'D ONLY BE A FRACTION OF THE BEST THERE IS AT WHAT HE DOES!
YOU HAVE NO IDEA HOW MUCH THIS STUFF FETCHES IN THE COLLECTORS MARKET. IF TIGRA'S BIKINI IS IN THIS MESS I'M SET FOR LIFE...
I CAN'T BELIEVE YOU! I THOUGHT YOU'D CHANGED--
I HAVE CHANGED. A LITTLE WHILE BACK I WOULD'VE KEPT ALL OF IT--SO YOU'RE WELCOME.
IF YOU THINK I'M GONNA LET YOU--
I HAVE TO AGREE WITH THE INTRUDER, I'M AFRAID--

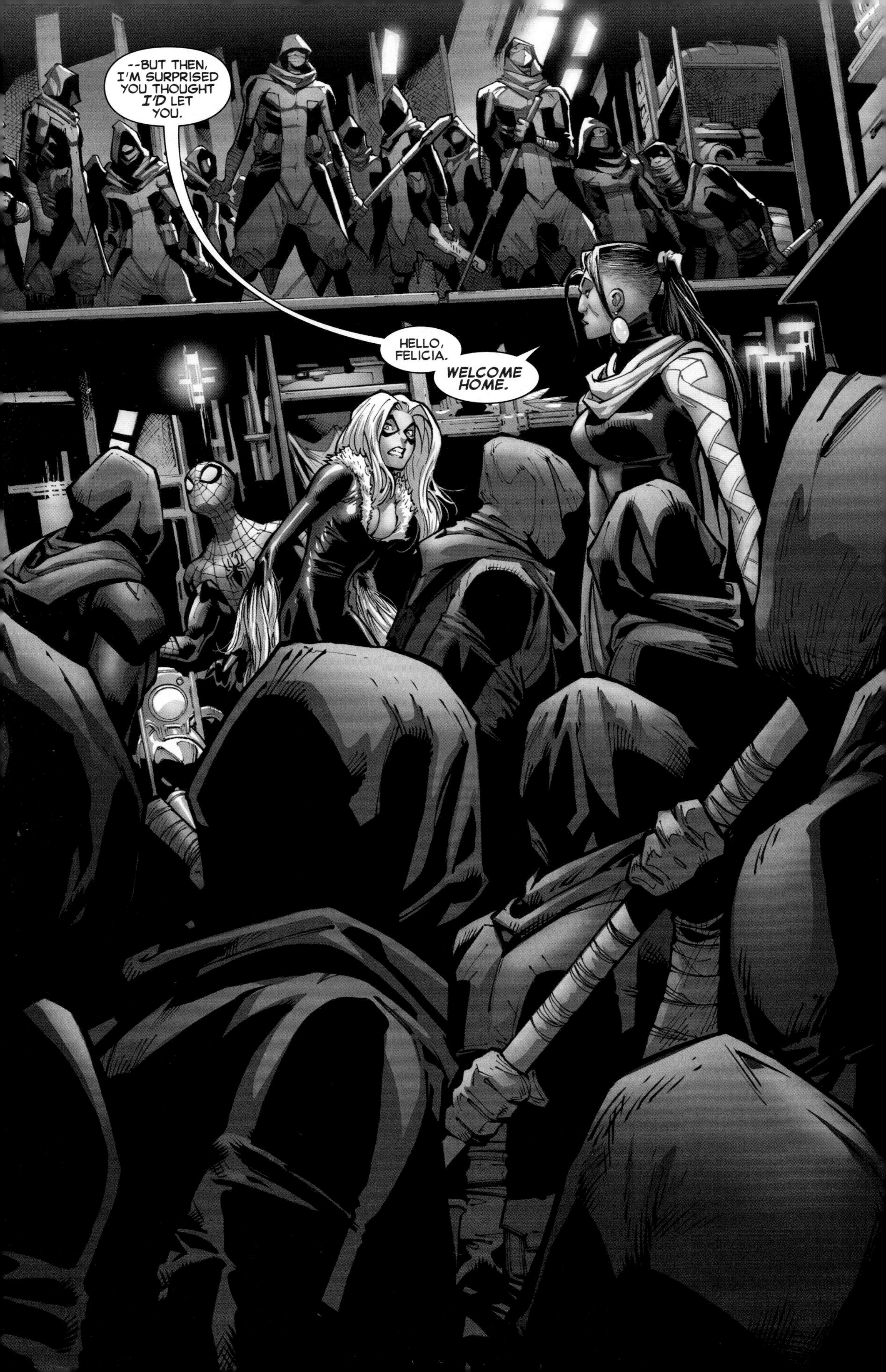
--BUT THEN, I'M SURPRISED YOU THOUGHT *I'D* LET YOU.
HELLO, FELICIA.
WELCOME HOME.

10

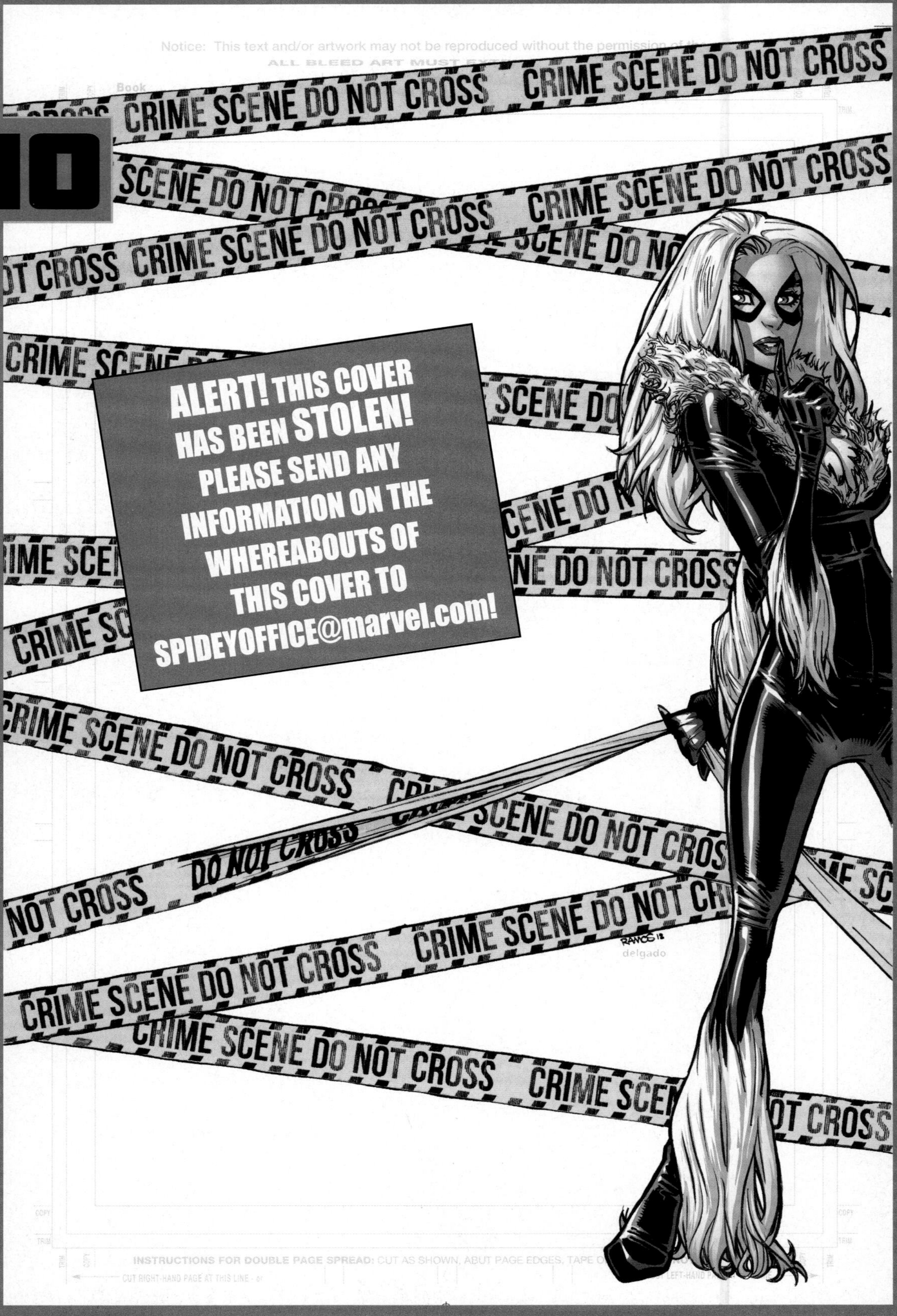
Notice: This text and/or artwork may not be reproduced without the permission of the
ALL BLEED ART MUST EXT
Book
CRIME SCENE DO NOT CROSS
ALERT! THIS COVER HAS BEEN STOLEN! PLEASE SEND ANY INFORMATION ON THE WHEREABOUTS OF THIS COVER TO SPIDEYOFFICE@marvel.com!
RAMOS 18
delgado
INSTRUCTIONS FOR DOUBLE PAGE SPREAD: CUT AS SHOWN, ABUT PAGE EDGES, TAPE O
CUT RIGHT-HAND PAGE AT THIS LINE

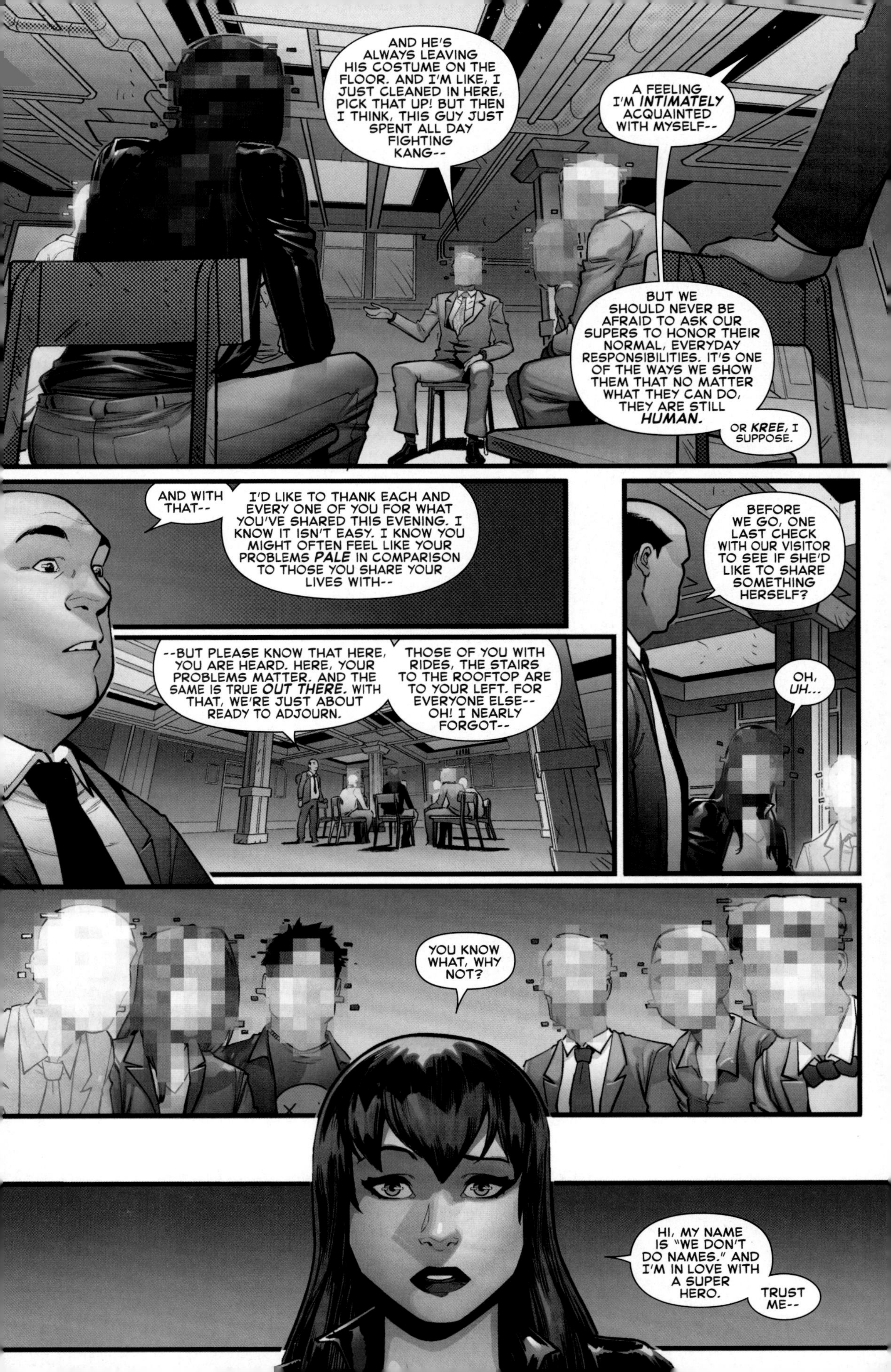
AND HE'S ALWAYS LEAVING HIS COSTUME ON THE FLOOR. AND I'M LIKE, I JUST CLEANED IN HERE, PICK THAT UP! BUT THEN I THINK, THIS GUY JUST SPENT ALL DAY FIGHTING KANG--
A FEELING I'M *INTIMATELY* ACQUAINTED WITH MYSELF--
BUT WE SHOULD NEVER BE AFRAID TO ASK OUR SUPERS TO HONOR THEIR NORMAL, EVERYDAY RESPONSIBILITIES. IT'S ONE OF THE WAYS WE SHOW THEM THAT NO MATTER WHAT THEY CAN DO, THEY ARE STILL ***HUMAN.***
OR *KREE*, I SUPPOSE.
AND WITH THAT--
I'D LIKE TO THANK EACH AND EVERY ONE OF YOU FOR WHAT YOU'VE SHARED THIS EVENING. I KNOW IT ISN'T EASY. I KNOW YOU MIGHT OFTEN FEEL LIKE YOUR PROBLEMS *PALE* IN COMPARISON TO THOSE YOU SHARE YOUR LIVES WITH--
--BUT PLEASE KNOW THAT HERE, YOU ARE HEARD. HERE, YOUR PROBLEMS MATTER. AND THE SAME IS TRUE *OUT THERE.* WITH THAT, WE'RE JUST ABOUT READY TO ADJOURN.
THOSE OF YOU WITH RIDES, THE STAIRS TO THE ROOFTOP ARE TO YOUR LEFT. FOR EVERYONE ELSE-- OH! I NEARLY FORGOT--
BEFORE WE GO, ONE LAST CHECK WITH OUR VISITOR TO SEE IF SHE'D LIKE TO SHARE SOMETHING HERSELF?
OH, *UH...*
YOU KNOW WHAT, WHY NOT?
HI, MY NAME IS "WE DON'T DO NAMES." AND I'M IN LOVE WITH A SUPER HERO.
TRUST ME--

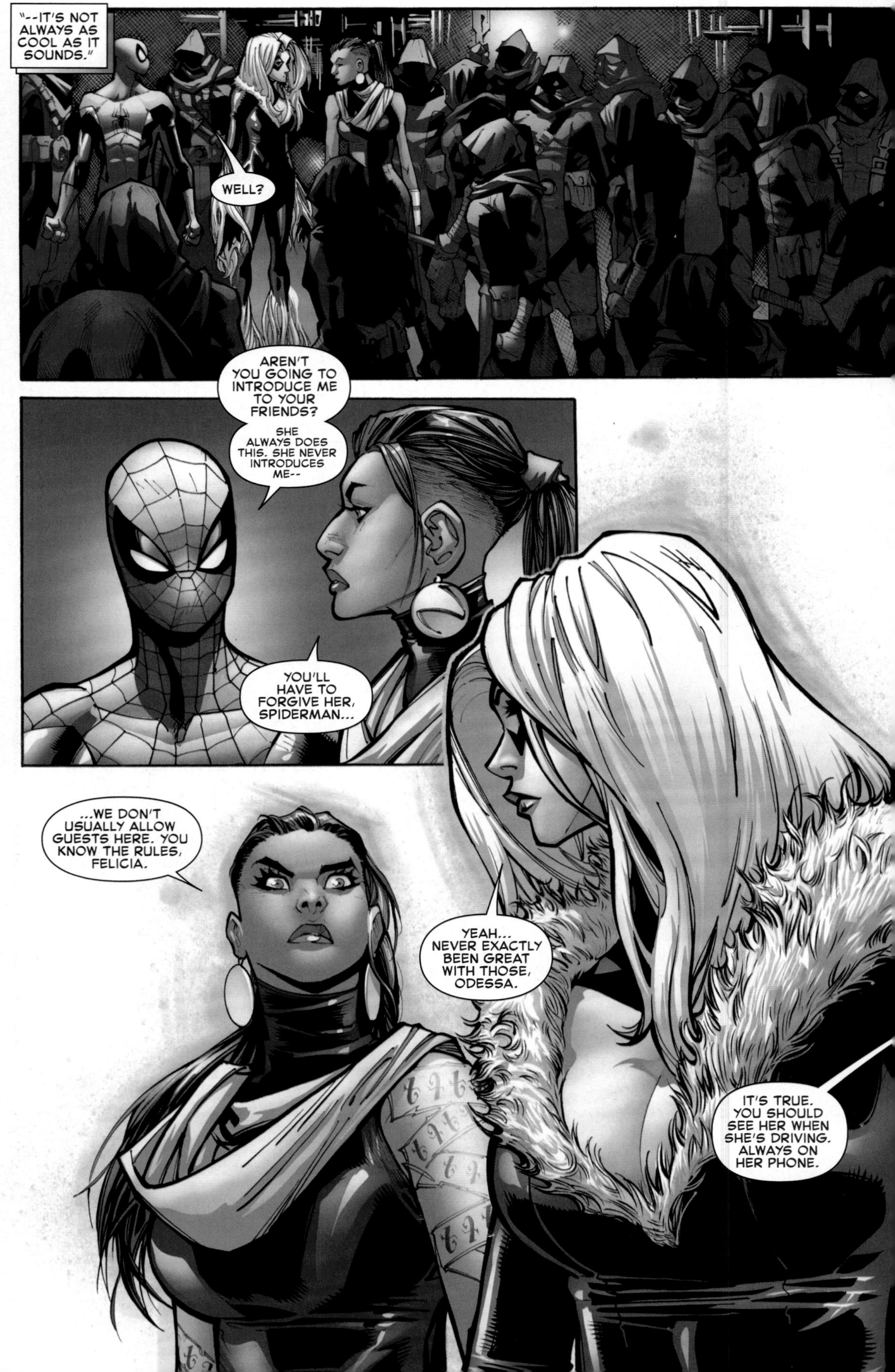
"--IT'S NOT ALWAYS AS COOL AS IT SOUNDS."
WELL?
AREN'T YOU GOING TO INTRODUCE ME TO YOUR FRIENDS?
SHE ALWAYS DOES THIS. SHE NEVER INTRODUCES ME--
YOU'LL HAVE TO FORGIVE HER, SPIDERMAN...
...WE DON'T USUALLY ALLOW GUESTS HERE. YOU KNOW THE RULES, FELICIA.
YEAH... NEVER EXACTLY BEEN GREAT WITH THOSE, ODESSA.
IT'S TRUE. YOU SHOULD SEE HER WHEN SHE'S DRIVING. ALWAYS ON HER PHONE.

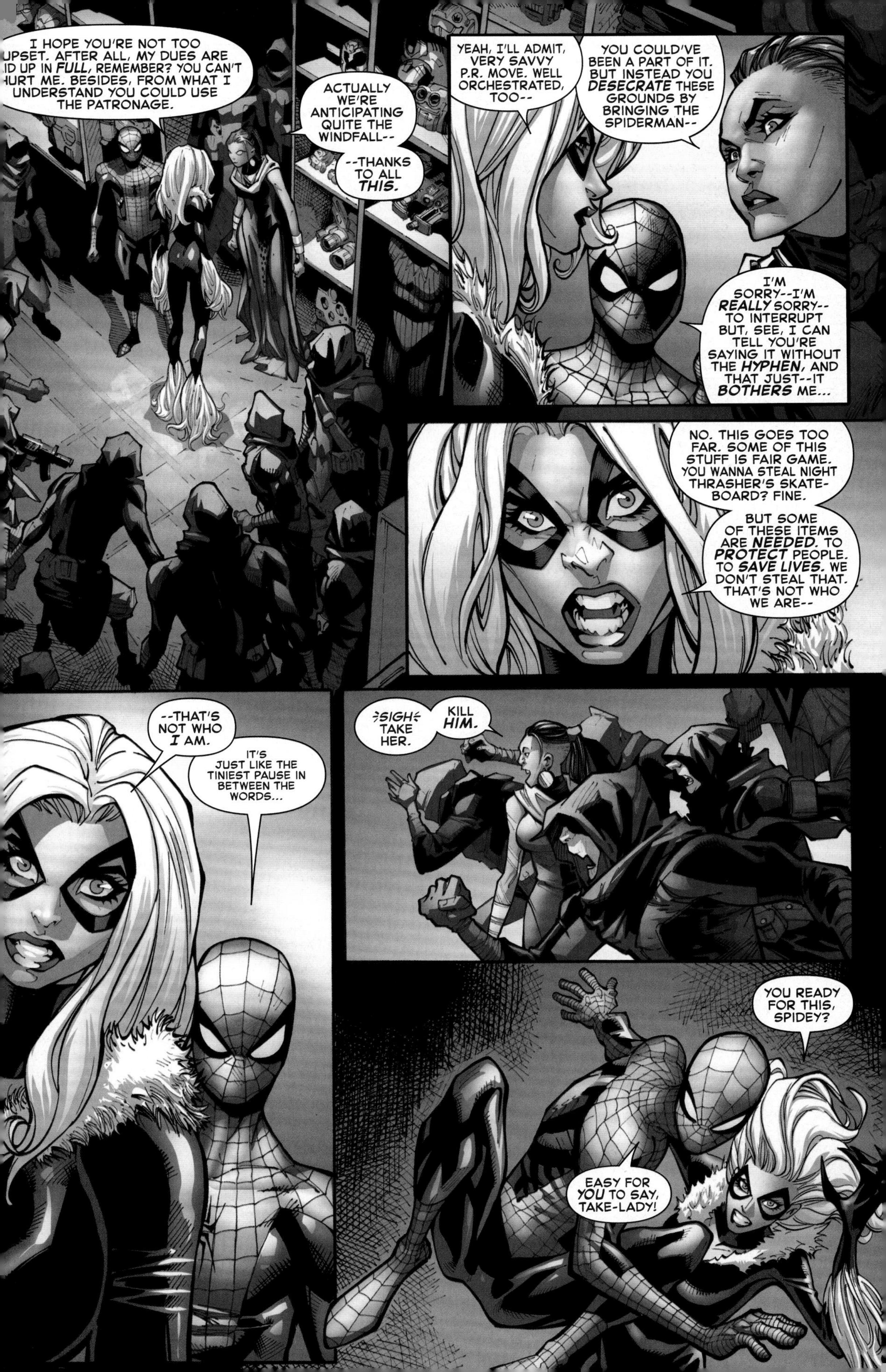
I HOPE YOU'RE NOT TOO UPSET. AFTER ALL, MY DUES ARE PAID UP IN FULL, REMEMBER? YOU CAN'T HURT ME. BESIDES, FROM WHAT I UNDERSTAND YOU COULD USE THE PATRONAGE.
ACTUALLY WE'RE ANTICIPATING QUITE THE WINDFALL--
--THANKS TO ALL THIS.
YEAH, I'LL ADMIT, VERY SAVVY P.R. MOVE. WELL ORCHESTRATED, TOO--
YOU COULD'VE BEEN A PART OF IT. BUT INSTEAD YOU DESECRATE THESE GROUNDS BY BRINGING THE SPIDERMAN--
I'M SORRY--I'M REALLY SORRY--TO INTERRUPT BUT, SEE, I CAN TELL YOU'RE SAYING IT WITHOUT THE HYPHEN, AND THAT JUST--IT BOTHERS ME...
NO. THIS GOES TOO FAR. SOME OF THIS STUFF IS FAIR GAME. YOU WANNA STEAL NIGHT THRASHER'S SKATE-BOARD? FINE.
BUT SOME OF THESE ITEMS ARE NEEDED. TO PROTECT PEOPLE. TO SAVE LIVES. WE DON'T STEAL THAT. THAT'S NOT WHO WE ARE--
--THAT'S NOT WHO I AM.
IT'S JUST LIKE THE TINIEST PAUSE IN BETWEEN THE WORDS...
SIGH TAKE HER.
KILL HIM.
YOU READY FOR THIS, SPIDEY?
EASY FOR YOU TO SAY, TAKE-LADY!

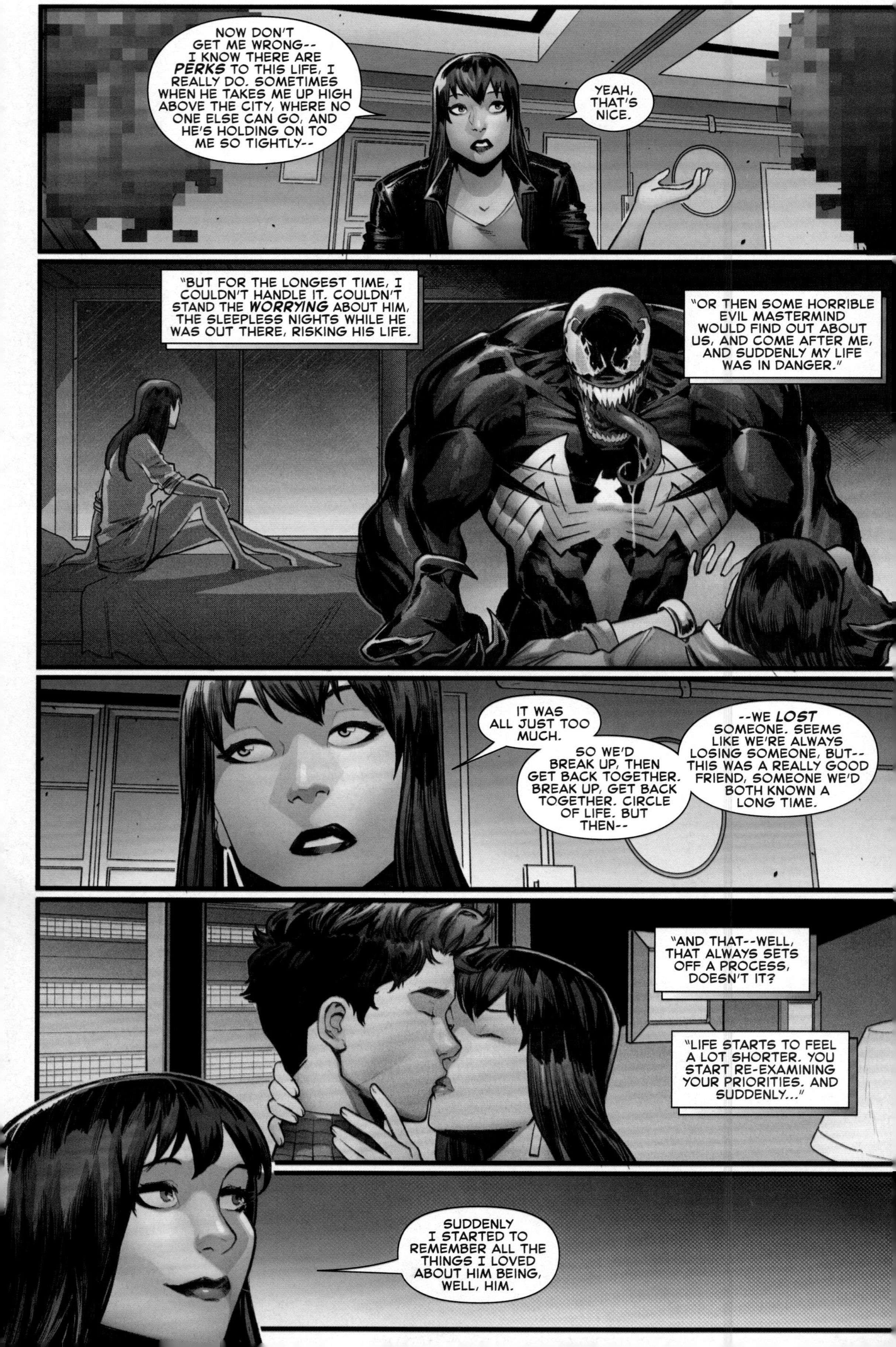
NOW DON'T GET ME WRONG-- I KNOW THERE ARE PERKS TO THIS LIFE, I REALLY DO. SOMETIMES WHEN HE TAKES ME UP HIGH ABOVE THE CITY, WHERE NO ONE ELSE CAN GO, AND HE'S HOLDING ON TO ME SO TIGHTLY--
YEAH, THAT'S NICE.
"BUT FOR THE LONGEST TIME, I COULDN'T HANDLE IT. COULDN'T STAND THE WORRYING ABOUT HIM, THE SLEEPLESS NIGHTS WHILE HE WAS OUT THERE, RISKING HIS LIFE.
"OR THEN SOME HORRIBLE EVIL MASTERMIND WOULD FIND OUT ABOUT US, AND COME AFTER ME, AND SUDDENLY MY LIFE WAS IN DANGER."
IT WAS ALL JUST TOO MUCH.
SO WE'D BREAK UP, THEN GET BACK TOGETHER. BREAK UP, GET BACK TOGETHER. CIRCLE OF LIFE. BUT THEN--
--WE LOST SOMEONE. SEEMS LIKE WE'RE ALWAYS LOSING SOMEONE, BUT-- THIS WAS A REALLY GOOD FRIEND, SOMEONE WE'D BOTH KNOWN A LONG TIME.
"AND THAT--WELL, THAT ALWAYS SETS OFF A PROCESS, DOESN'T IT?
"LIFE STARTS TO FEEL A LOT SHORTER. YOU START RE-EXAMINING YOUR PRIORITIES. AND SUDDENLY..."
SUDDENLY I STARTED TO REMEMBER ALL THE THINGS I LOVED ABOUT HIM BEING, WELL, HIM.

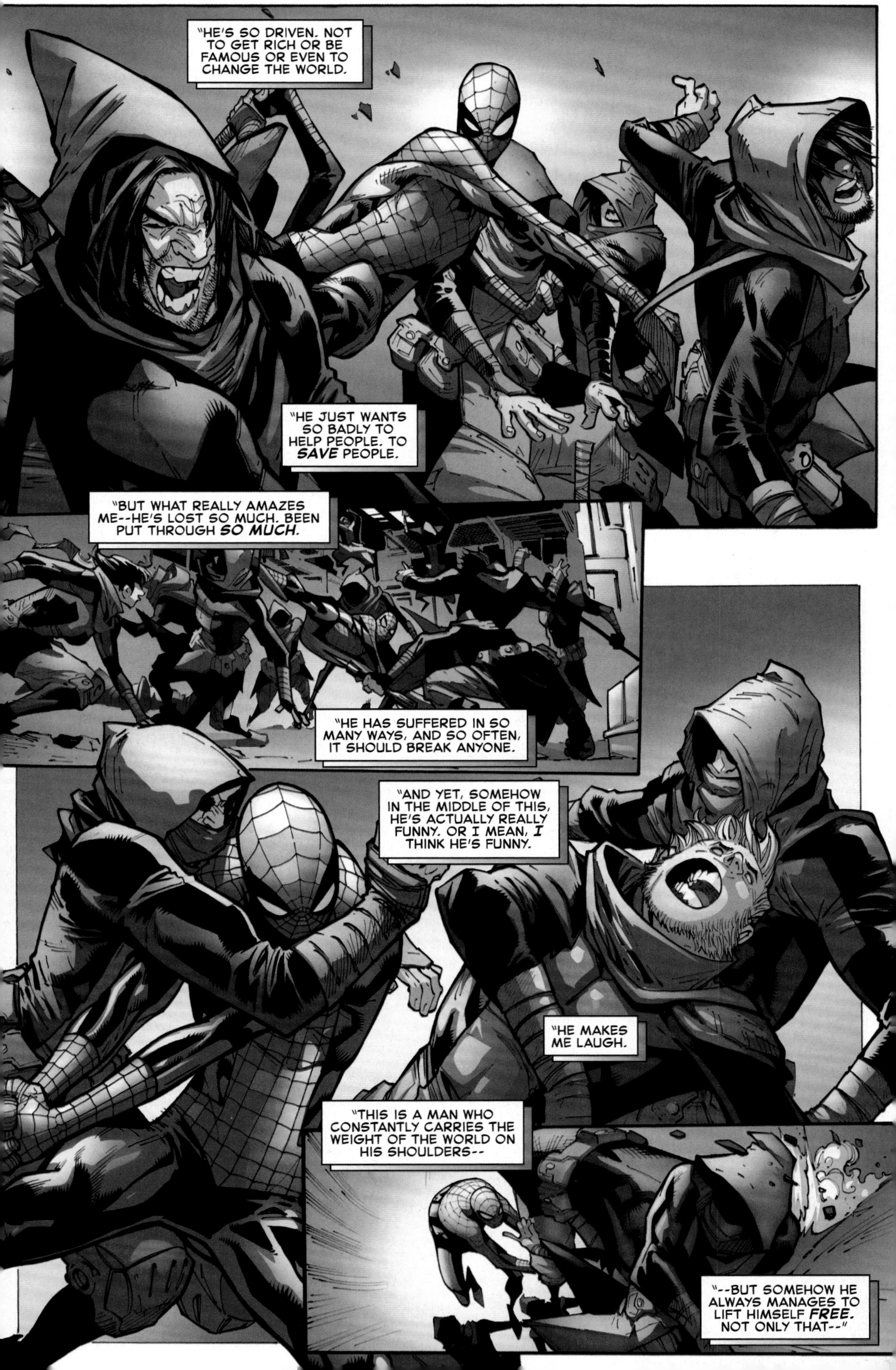
"HE'S SO DRIVEN. NOT TO GET RICH OR BE FAMOUS OR EVEN TO CHANGE THE WORLD.
"HE JUST WANTS SO BADLY TO HELP PEOPLE. TO SAVE PEOPLE.
"BUT WHAT REALLY AMAZES ME--HE'S LOST SO MUCH. BEEN PUT THROUGH SO MUCH.
"HE HAS SUFFERED IN SO MANY WAYS, AND SO OFTEN, IT SHOULD BREAK ANYONE.
"AND YET, SOMEHOW IN THE MIDDLE OF THIS, HE'S ACTUALLY REALLY FUNNY. OR I MEAN, I THINK HE'S FUNNY.
"HE MAKES ME LAUGH.
"THIS IS A MAN WHO CONSTANTLY CARRIES THE WEIGHT OF THE WORLD ON HIS SHOULDERS--
"--BUT SOMEHOW HE ALWAYS MANAGES TO LIFT HIMSELF FREE. NOT ONLY THAT--"

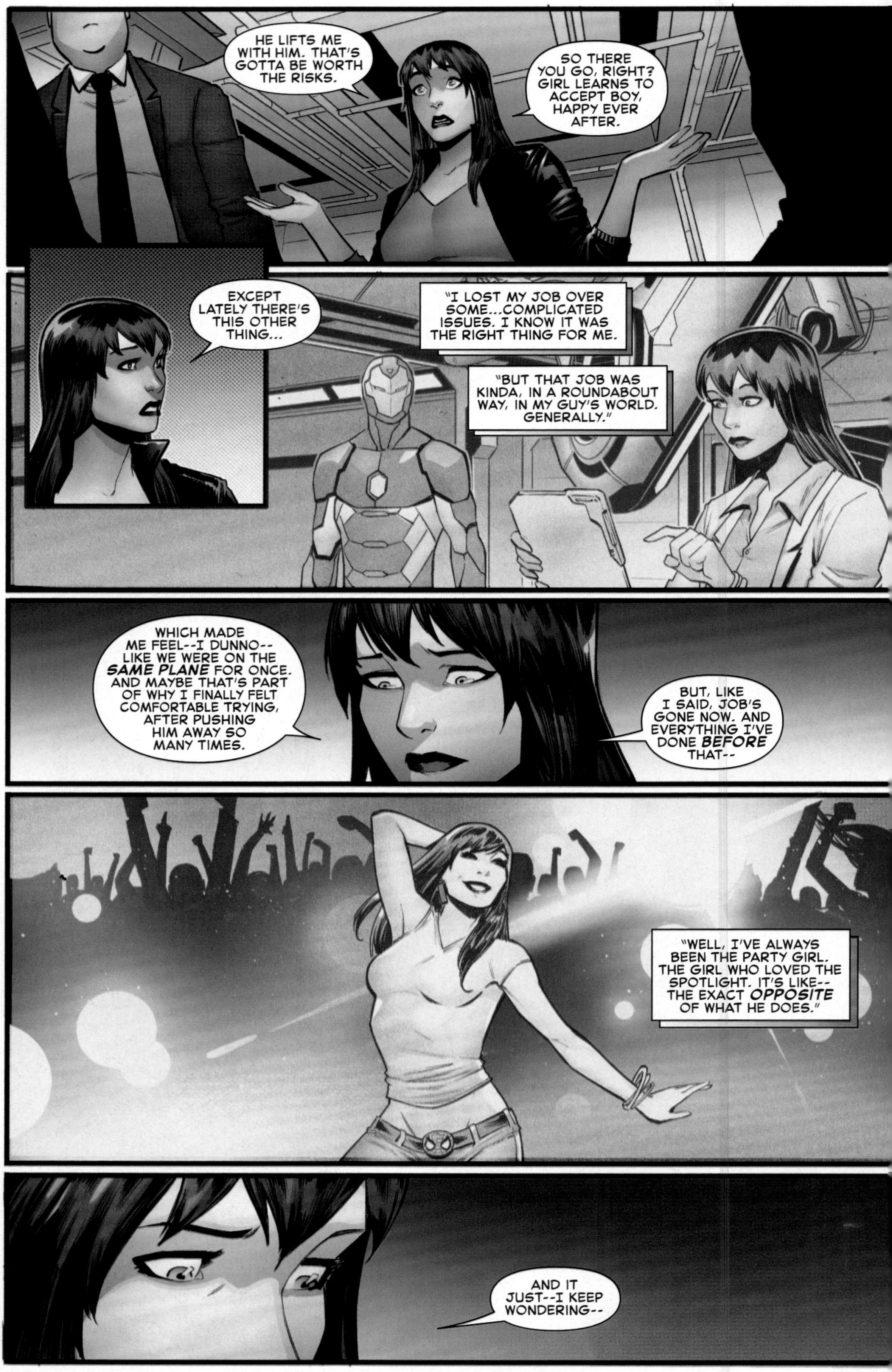
HE LIFTS ME WITH HIM. THAT'S GOTTA BE WORTH THE RISKS.
SO THERE YOU GO, RIGHT? GIRL LEARNS TO ACCEPT BOY, HAPPY EVER AFTER.
EXCEPT LATELY THERE'S THIS OTHER THING...
"I LOST MY JOB OVER SOME...COMPLICATED ISSUES. I KNOW IT WAS THE RIGHT THING FOR ME.
"BUT THAT JOB WAS KINDA, IN A ROUNDABOUT WAY, IN MY GUY'S WORLD. GENERALLY."
WHICH MADE ME FEEL--I DUNNO--LIKE WE WERE ON THE SAME PLANE FOR ONCE. AND MAYBE THAT'S PART OF WHY I FINALLY FELT COMFORTABLE TRYING, AFTER PUSHING HIM AWAY SO MANY TIMES.
BUT, LIKE I SAID, JOB'S GONE NOW. AND EVERYTHING I'VE DONE BEFORE THAT--
"WELL, I'VE ALWAYS BEEN THE PARTY GIRL. THE GIRL WHO LOVED THE SPOTLIGHT. IT'S LIKE--THE EXACT OPPOSITE OF WHAT HE DOES."
AND IT JUST--I KEEP WONDERING--

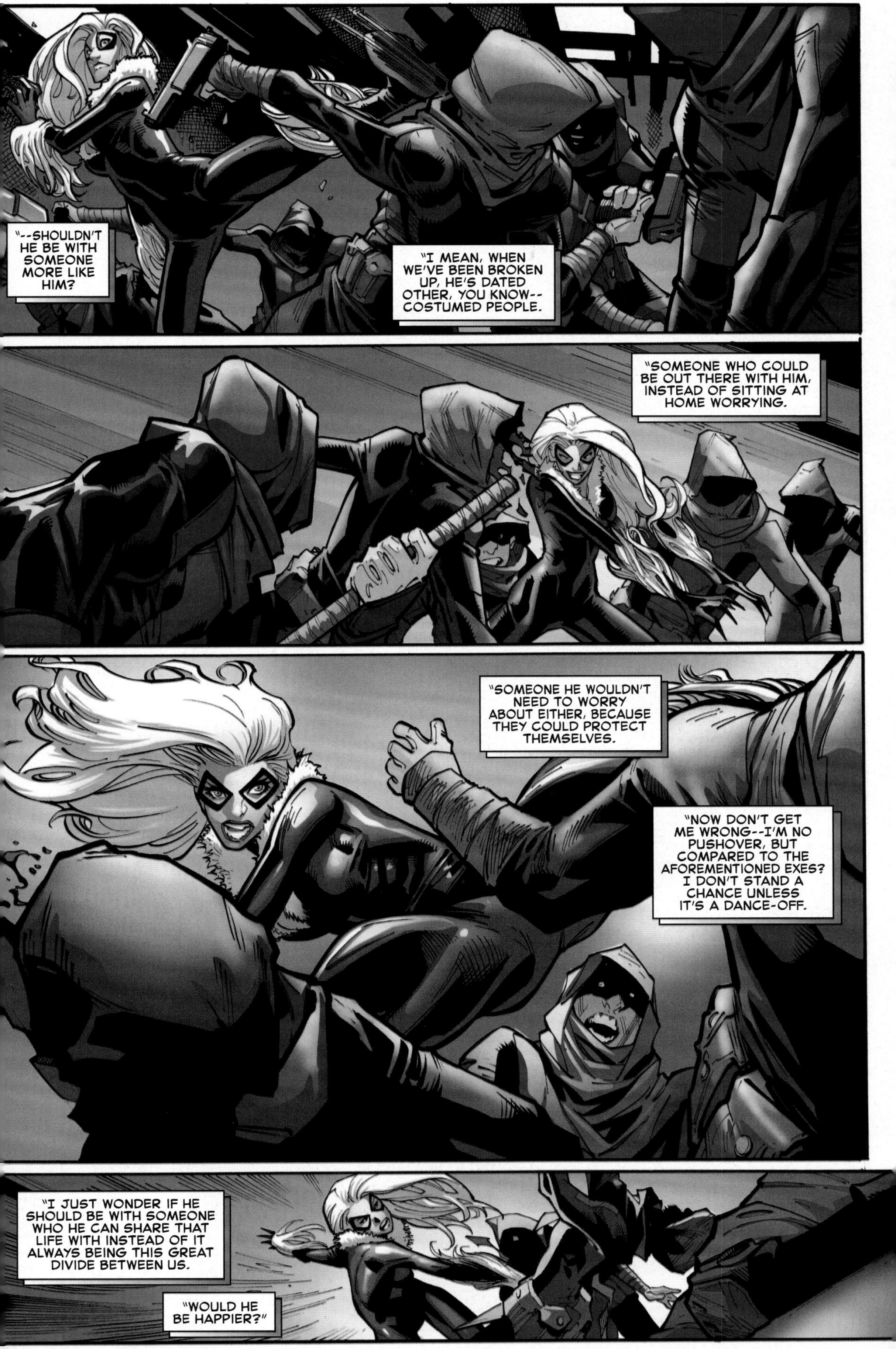
"--SHOULDN'T HE BE WITH SOMEONE MORE LIKE HIM?
"I MEAN, WHEN WE'VE BEEN BROKEN UP, HE'S DATED OTHER, YOU KNOW-- COSTUMED PEOPLE.
"SOMEONE WHO COULD BE OUT THERE WITH HIM, INSTEAD OF SITTING AT HOME WORRYING.
"SOMEONE HE WOULDN'T NEED TO WORRY ABOUT EITHER, BECAUSE THEY COULD PROTECT THEMSELVES.
"NOW DON'T GET ME WRONG--I'M NO PUSHOVER, BUT COMPARED TO THE AFOREMENTIONED EXES? I DON'T STAND A CHANCE UNLESS IT'S A DANCE-OFF.
"I JUST WONDER IF HE SHOULD BE WITH SOMEONE WHO HE CAN SHARE THAT LIFE WITH INSTEAD OF IT ALWAYS BEING THIS GREAT DIVIDE BETWEEN US.
"WOULD HE BE HAPPIER?"

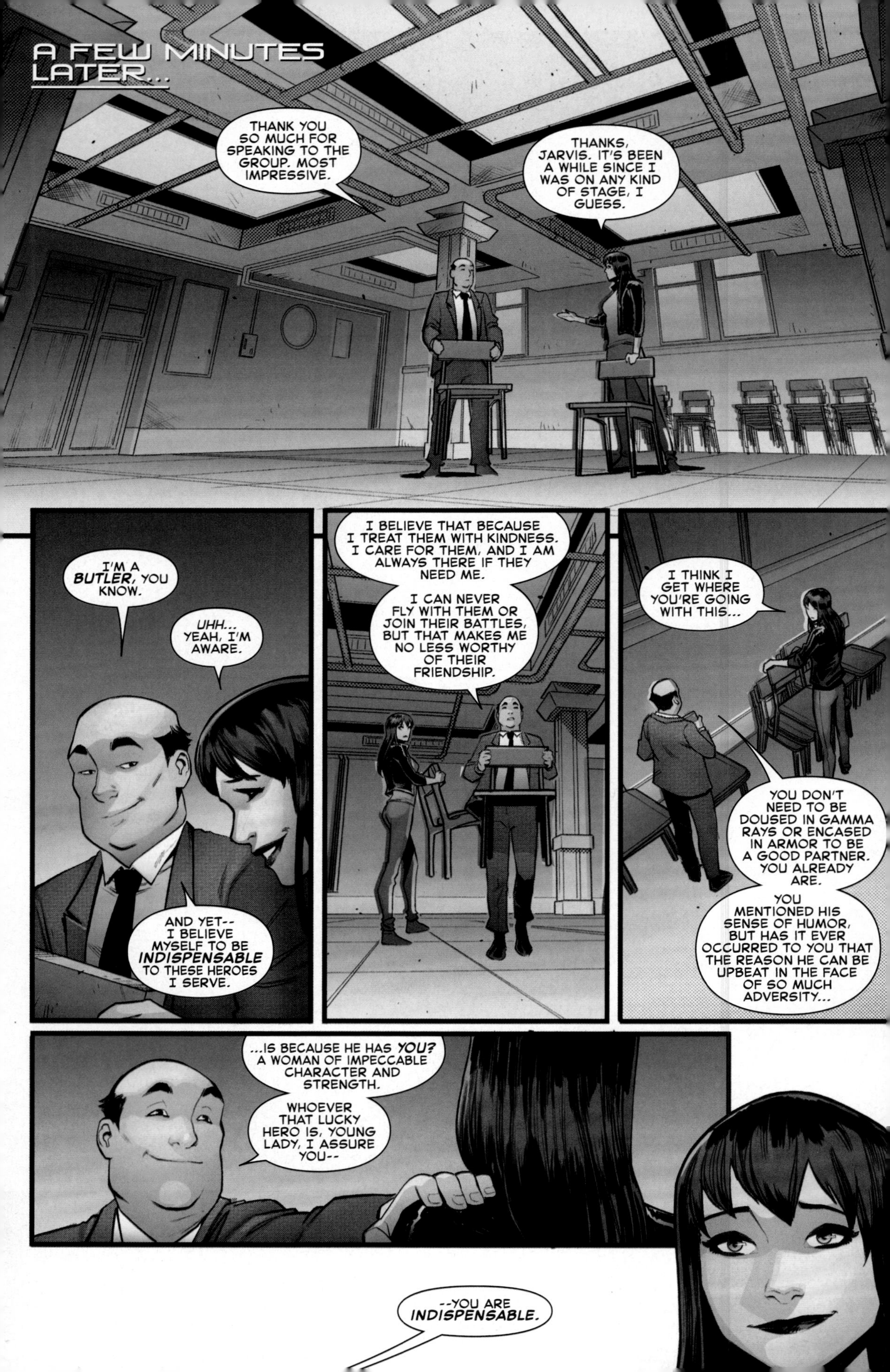
A FEW MINUTES LATER...
THANK YOU SO MUCH FOR SPEAKING TO THE GROUP. MOST IMPRESSIVE.
THANKS, JARVIS. IT'S BEEN A WHILE SINCE I WAS ON ANY KIND OF STAGE, I GUESS.
I'M A BUTLER, YOU KNOW.
UHH... YEAH, I'M AWARE.
AND YET-- I BELIEVE MYSELF TO BE INDISPENSABLE TO THESE HEROES I SERVE.
I BELIEVE THAT BECAUSE I TREAT THEM WITH KINDNESS. I CARE FOR THEM, AND I AM ALWAYS THERE IF THEY NEED ME.
I CAN NEVER FLY WITH THEM OR JOIN THEIR BATTLES, BUT THAT MAKES ME NO LESS WORTHY OF THEIR FRIENDSHIP.
I THINK I GET WHERE YOU'RE GOING WITH THIS...
YOU DON'T NEED TO BE DOUSED IN GAMMA RAYS OR ENCASED IN ARMOR TO BE A GOOD PARTNER. YOU ALREADY ARE.
YOU MENTIONED HIS SENSE OF HUMOR, BUT HAS IT EVER OCCURRED TO YOU THAT THE REASON HE CAN BE UPBEAT IN THE FACE OF SO MUCH ADVERSITY...
...IS BECAUSE HE HAS YOU? A WOMAN OF IMPECCABLE CHARACTER AND STRENGTH.
WHOEVER THAT LUCKY HERO IS, YOUNG LADY, I ASSURE YOU--
--YOU ARE INDISPENSABLE.

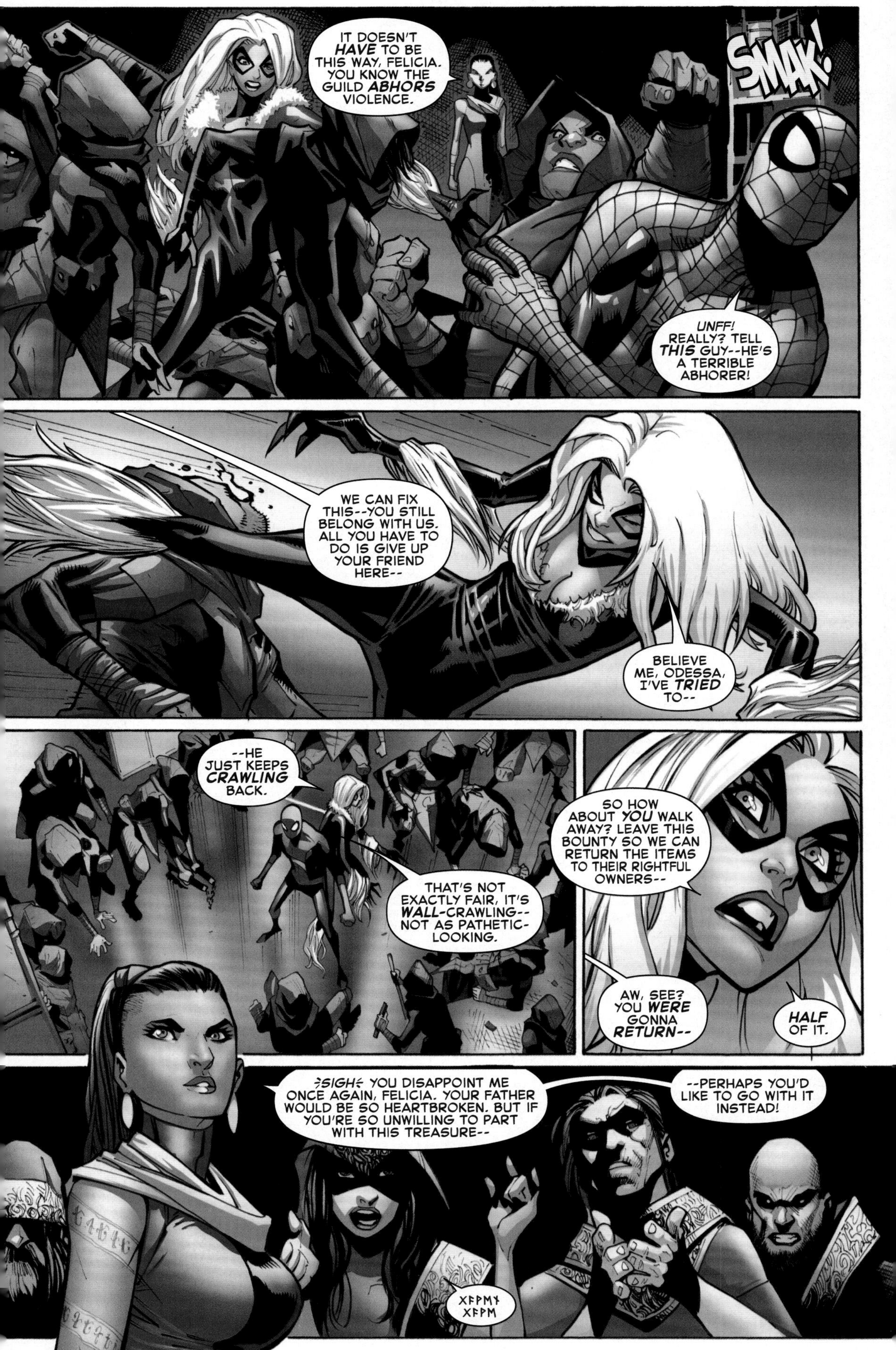
IT DOESN'T HAVE TO BE THIS WAY, FELICIA. YOU KNOW THE GUILD ABHORS VIOLENCE.
SMAK!
UNFF! REALLY? TELL THIS GUY--HE'S A TERRIBLE ABHORER!
WE CAN FIX THIS--YOU STILL BELONG WITH US. ALL YOU HAVE TO DO IS GIVE UP YOUR FRIEND HERE--
BELIEVE ME, ODESSA, I'VE TRIED TO--
--HE JUST KEEPS CRAWLING BACK.
THAT'S NOT EXACTLY FAIR, IT'S WALL-CRAWLING--NOT AS PATHETIC-LOOKING.
SO HOW ABOUT YOU WALK AWAY? LEAVE THIS BOUNTY SO WE CAN RETURN THE ITEMS TO THEIR RIGHTFUL OWNERS--
AW, SEE? YOU WERE GONNA RETURN--
HALF OF IT.
SIGH YOU DISAPPOINT ME ONCE AGAIN, FELICIA. YOUR FATHER WOULD BE SO HEARTBROKEN. BUT IF YOU'RE SO UNWILLING TO PART WITH THIS TREASURE--
--PERHAPS YOU'D LIKE TO GO WITH IT INSTEAD!

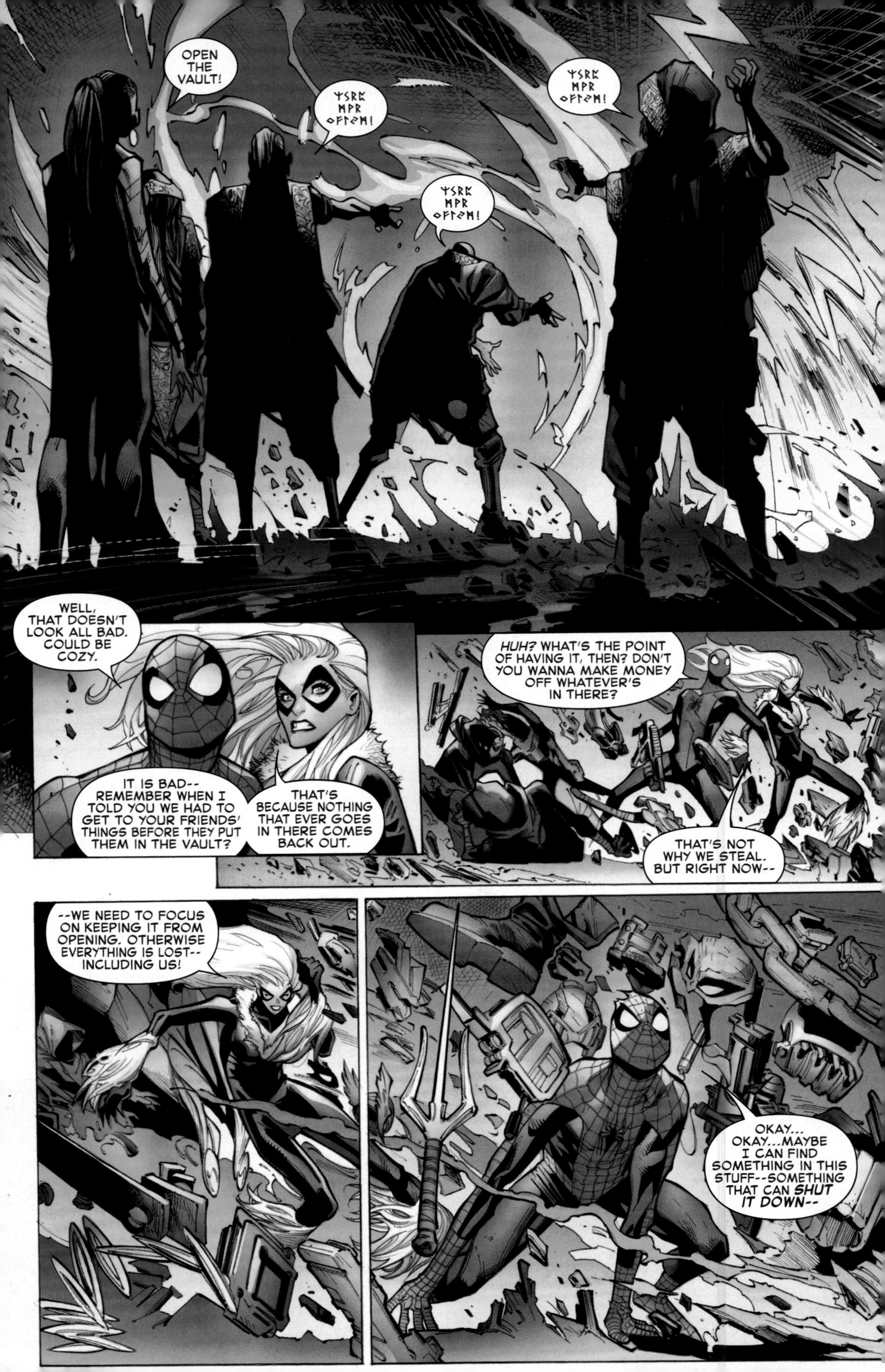
OPEN THE VAULT!
WELL, THAT DOESN'T LOOK ALL BAD. COULD BE COZY.
IT IS BAD-- REMEMBER WHEN I TOLD YOU WE HAD TO GET TO YOUR FRIENDS' THINGS BEFORE THEY PUT THEM IN THE VAULT?
THAT'S BECAUSE NOTHING THAT EVER GOES IN THERE COMES BACK OUT.
HUH? WHAT'S THE POINT OF HAVING IT, THEN? DON'T YOU WANNA MAKE MONEY OFF WHATEVER'S IN THERE?
THAT'S NOT WHY WE STEAL. BUT RIGHT NOW--
--WE NEED TO FOCUS ON KEEPING IT FROM OPENING. OTHERWISE EVERYTHING IS LOST-- INCLUDING US!
OKAY... OKAY...MAYBE I CAN FIND SOMETHING IN THIS STUFF--SOMETHING THAT CAN SHUT IT DOWN--

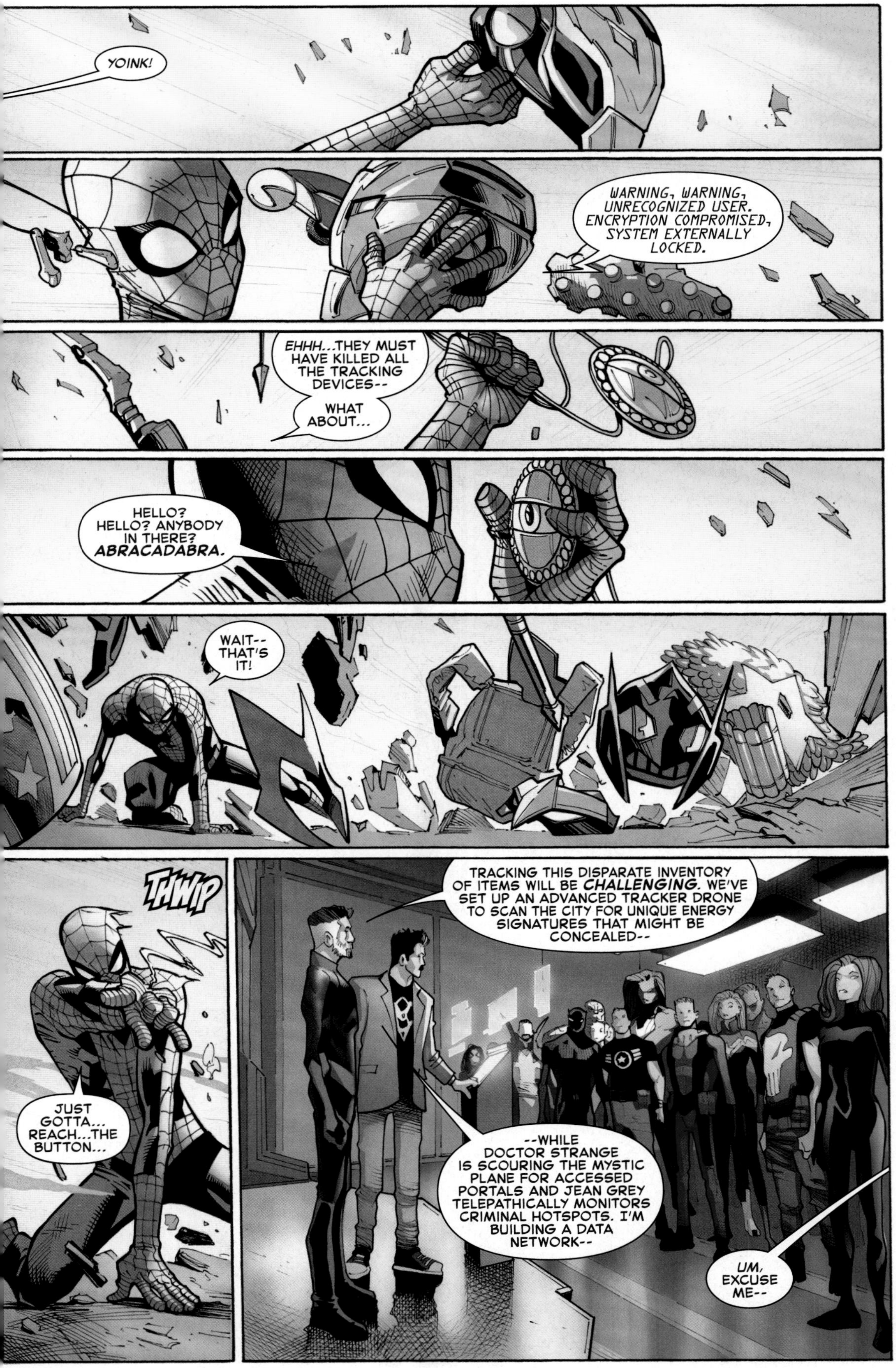

YOINK!
WARNING, WARNING, UNRECOGNIZED USER. ENCRYPTION COMPROMISED, SYSTEM EXTERNALLY LOCKED.
EHHH...THEY MUST HAVE KILLED ALL THE TRACKING DEVICES--
WHAT ABOUT...
HELLO? HELLO? ANYBODY IN THERE? ABRACADABRA.
WAIT--THAT'S IT!
THWIP
JUST GOTTA...REACH...THE BUTTON...
TRACKING THIS DISPARATE INVENTORY OF ITEMS WILL BE CHALLENGING. WE'VE SET UP AN ADVANCED TRACKER DRONE TO SCAN THE CITY FOR UNIQUE ENERGY SIGNATURES THAT MIGHT BE CONCEALED--
--WHILE DOCTOR STRANGE IS SCOURING THE MYSTIC PLANE FOR ACCESSED PORTALS AND JEAN GREY TELEPATHICALLY MONITORS CRIMINAL HOTSPOTS. I'M BUILDING A DATA NETWORK--
UM, EXCUSE ME--

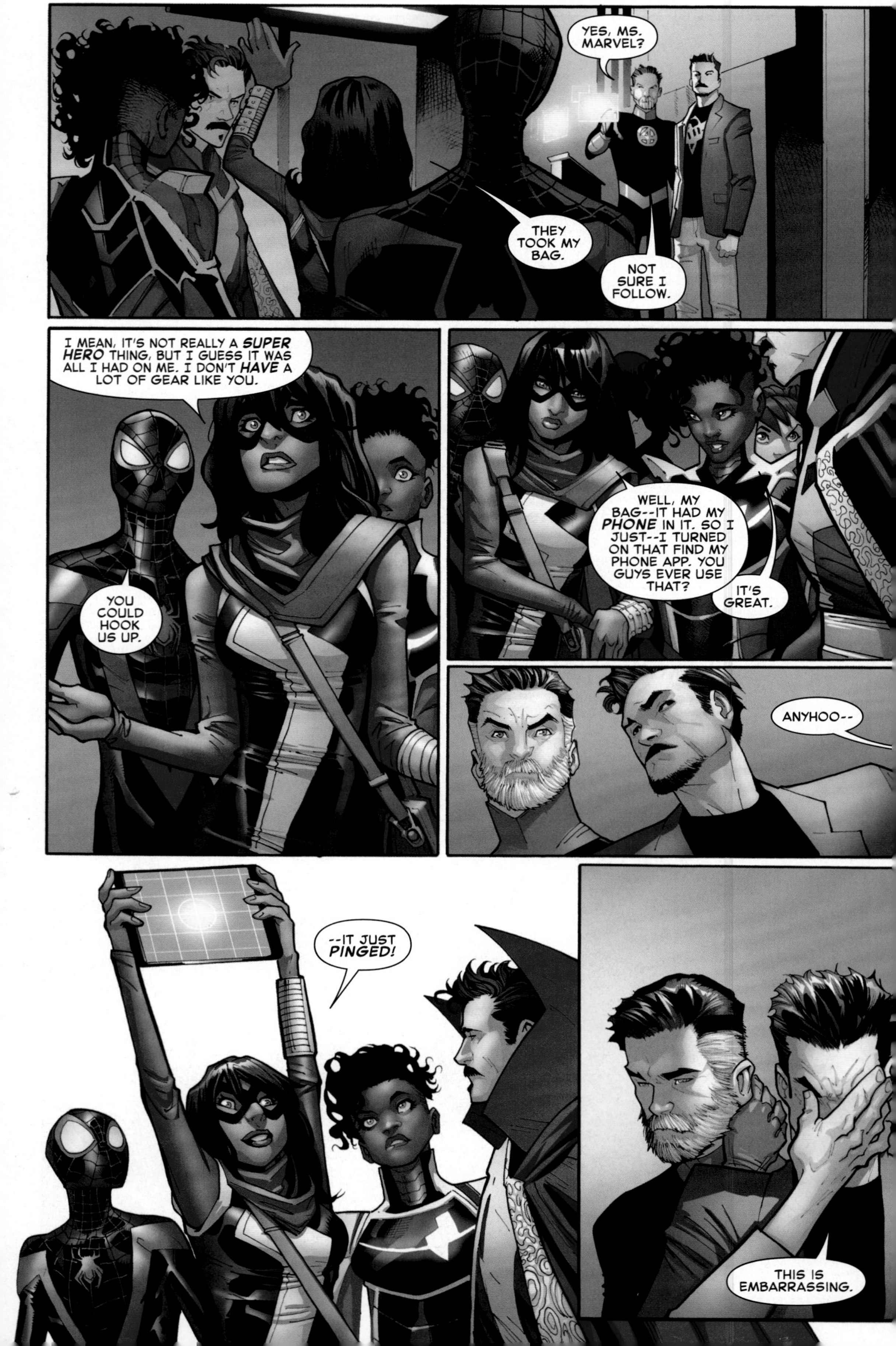
YES, MS. MARVEL?
THEY TOOK MY BAG.
NOT SURE I FOLLOW.
I MEAN, IT'S NOT REALLY A **SUPER HERO** THING, BUT I GUESS IT WAS ALL I HAD ON ME. I DON'T **HAVE** A LOT OF GEAR LIKE YOU.
YOU COULD HOOK US UP.
WELL, MY BAG--IT HAD MY **PHONE** IN IT. SO I JUST--I TURNED ON THAT FIND MY PHONE APP. YOU GUYS EVER USE THAT?
IT'S GREAT.
ANYHOO--
--IT JUST **PINGED!**
THIS IS EMBARRASSING.

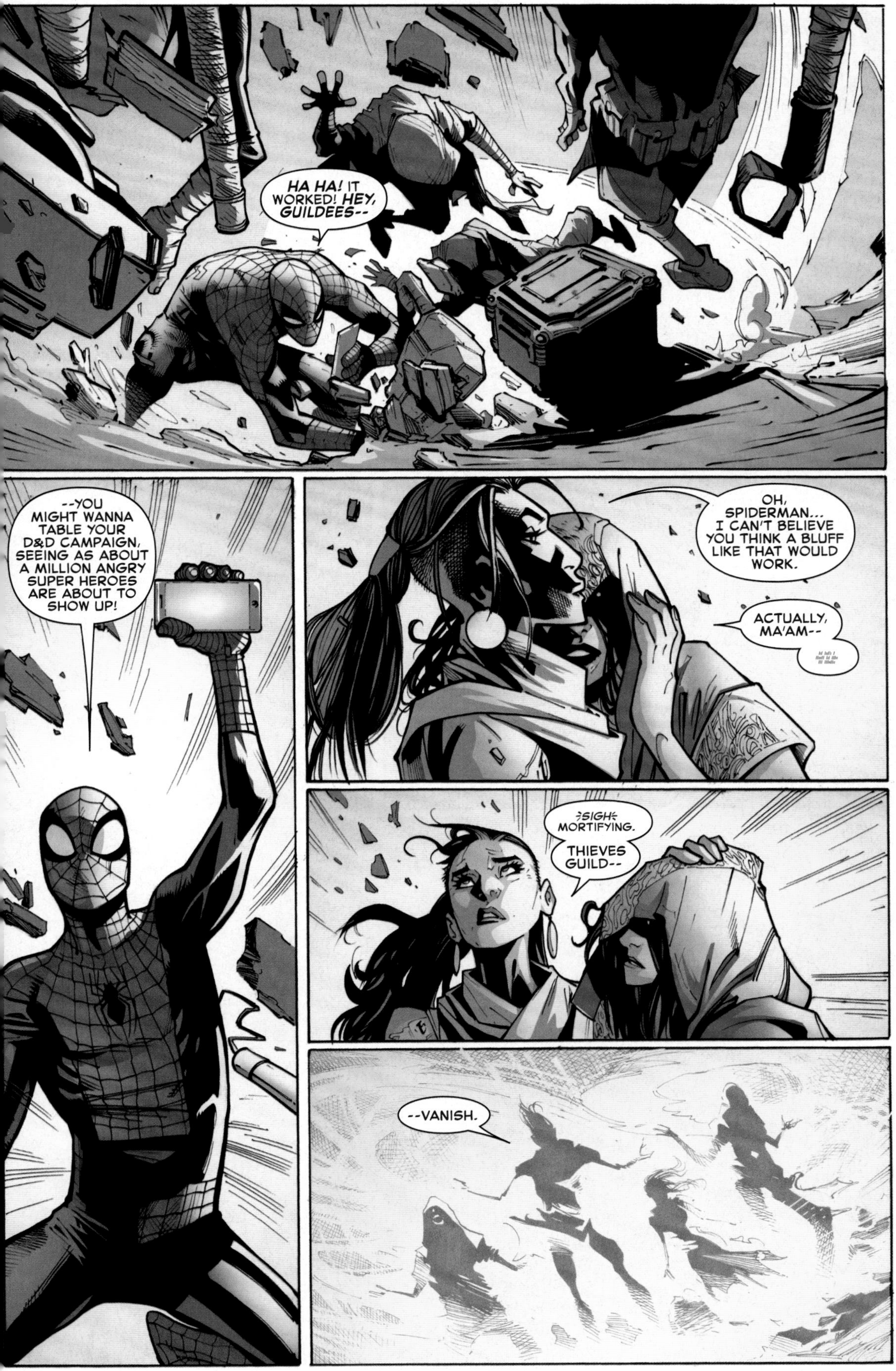
HA HA! IT WORKED! HEY, GUILDEES--
--YOU MIGHT WANNA TABLE YOUR D&D CAMPAIGN, SEEING AS ABOUT A MILLION ANGRY SUPER HEROES ARE ABOUT TO SHOW UP!
OH, SPIDERMAN... I CAN'T BELIEVE YOU THINK A BLUFF LIKE THAT WOULD WORK.
ACTUALLY, MA'AM--
SIGH MORTIFYING.
THIEVES GUILD--
--VANISH.

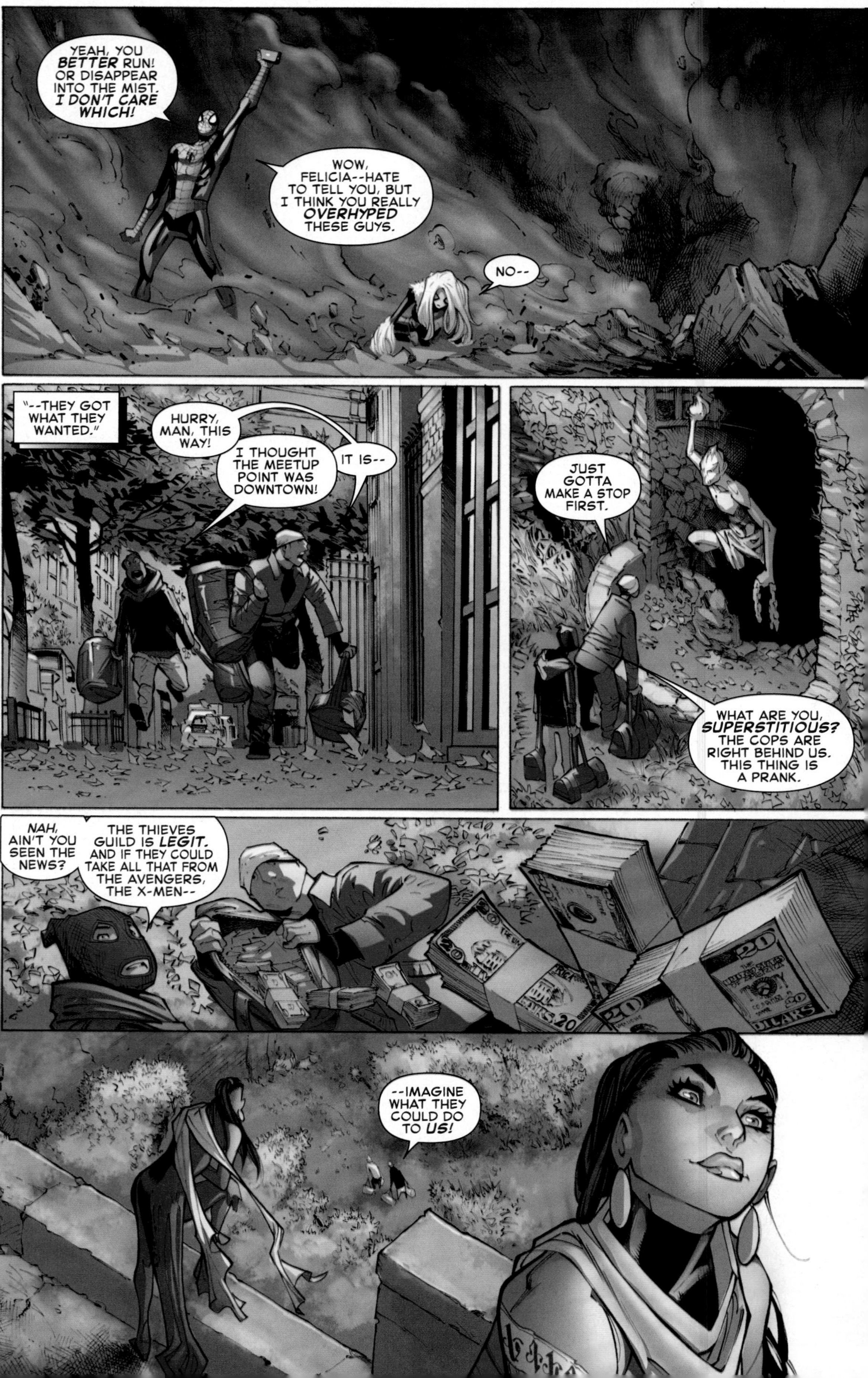
YEAH, YOU BETTER RUN! OR DISAPPEAR INTO THE MIST. I DON'T CARE WHICH!
WOW, FELICIA--HATE TO TELL YOU, BUT I THINK YOU REALLY OVERHYPED THESE GUYS.
NO--
"--THEY GOT WHAT THEY WANTED."
HURRY, MAN, THIS WAY!
I THOUGHT THE MEETUP POINT WAS DOWNTOWN!
IT IS--
JUST GOTTA MAKE A STOP FIRST.
WHAT ARE YOU, SUPERSTITIOUS? THE COPS ARE RIGHT BEHIND US. THIS THING IS A PRANK.
NAH, AIN'T YOU SEEN THE NEWS?
THE THIEVES GUILD IS LEGIT. AND IF THEY COULD TAKE ALL THAT FROM THE AVENGERS, THE X-MEN--
--IMAGINE WHAT THEY COULD DO TO US!

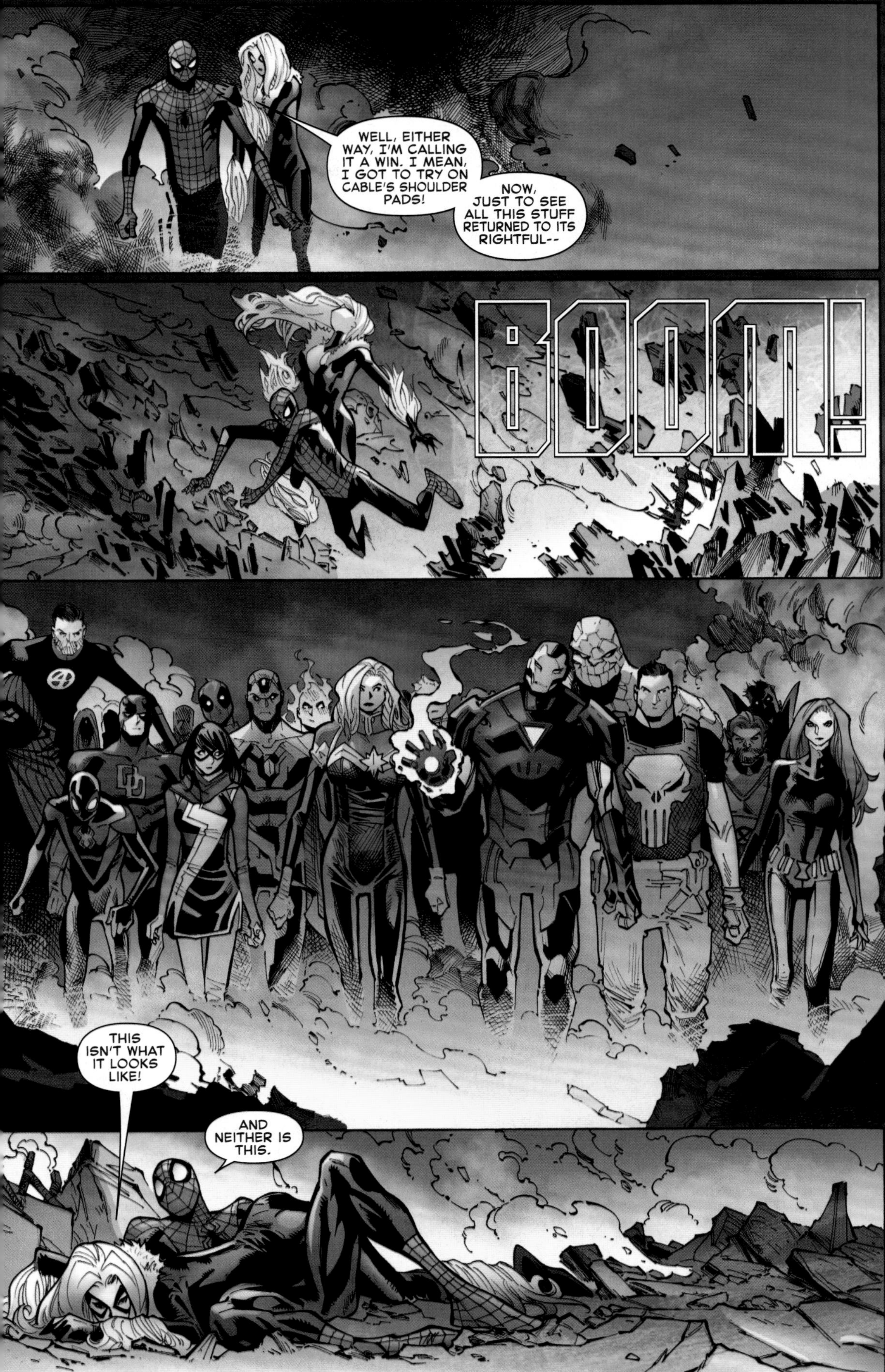
WELL, EITHER WAY, I'M CALLING IT A WIN. I MEAN, I GOT TO TRY ON CABLE'S SHOULDER PADS!
NOW, JUST TO SEE ALL THIS STUFF RETURNED TO ITS RIGHTFUL--
BOOM!
THIS ISN'T WHAT IT LOOKS LIKE!
AND NEITHER IS THIS.

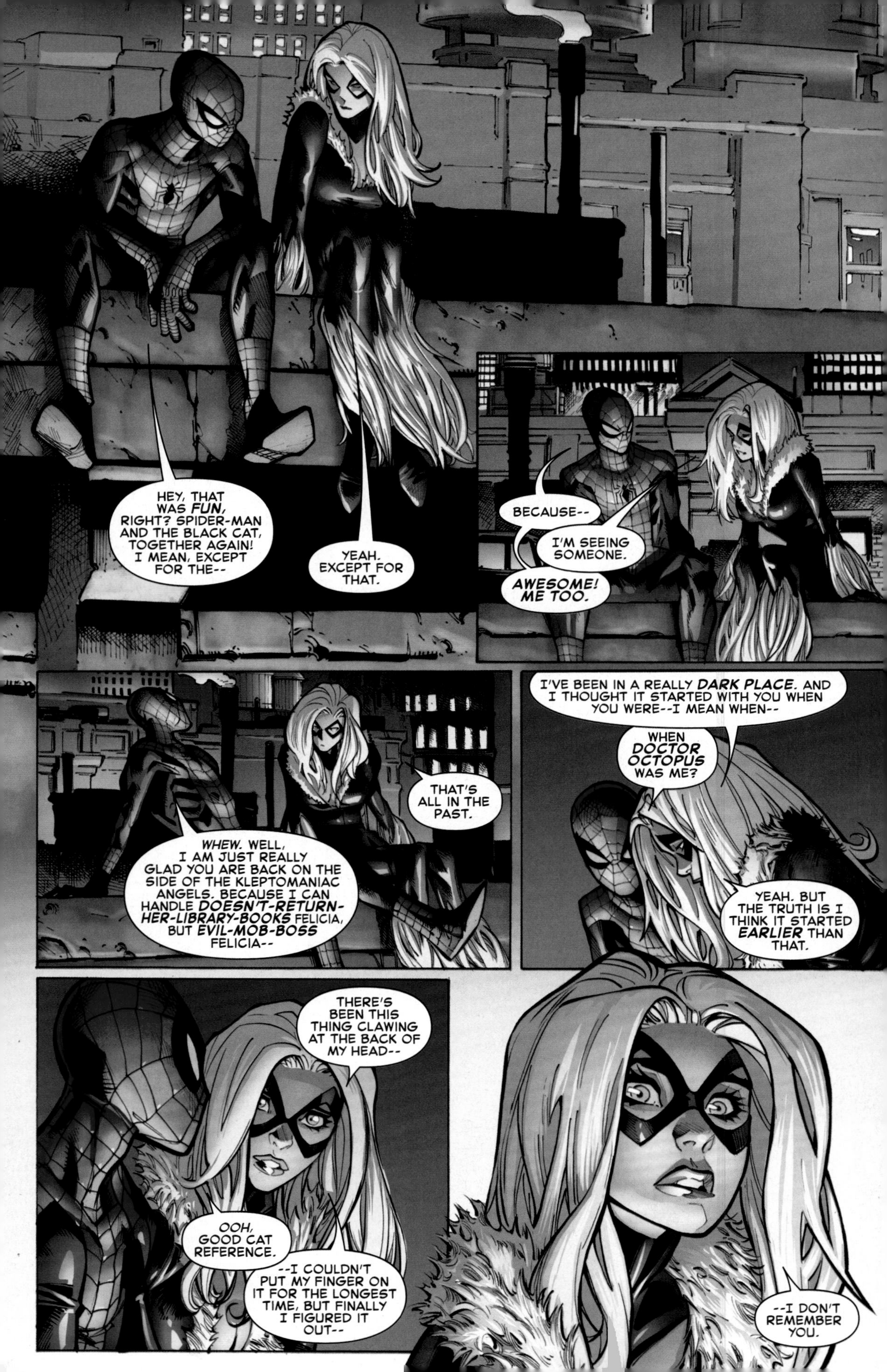
HEY, THAT WAS FUN, RIGHT? SPIDER-MAN AND THE BLACK CAT, TOGETHER AGAIN! I MEAN, EXCEPT FOR THE--
YEAH. EXCEPT FOR THAT.
BECAUSE--
I'M SEEING SOMEONE.
AWESOME! ME TOO.
THAT'S ALL IN THE PAST.
WHEW. WELL, I AM JUST REALLY GLAD YOU ARE BACK ON THE SIDE OF THE KLEPTOMANIAC ANGELS. BECAUSE I CAN HANDLE DOESN'T-RETURN-HER-LIBRARY-BOOKS FELICIA, BUT EVIL-MOB-BOSS FELICIA--
I'VE BEEN IN A REALLY DARK PLACE. AND I THOUGHT IT STARTED WITH YOU WHEN YOU WERE--I MEAN WHEN--
WHEN DOCTOR OCTOPUS WAS ME?
YEAH. BUT THE TRUTH IS I THINK IT STARTED EARLIER THAN THAT.
THERE'S BEEN THIS THING CLAWING AT THE BACK OF MY HEAD--
OOH, GOOD CAT REFERENCE.
--I COULDN'T PUT MY FINGER ON IT FOR THE LONGEST TIME, BUT FINALLY I FIGURED IT OUT--
--I DON'T REMEMBER YOU.

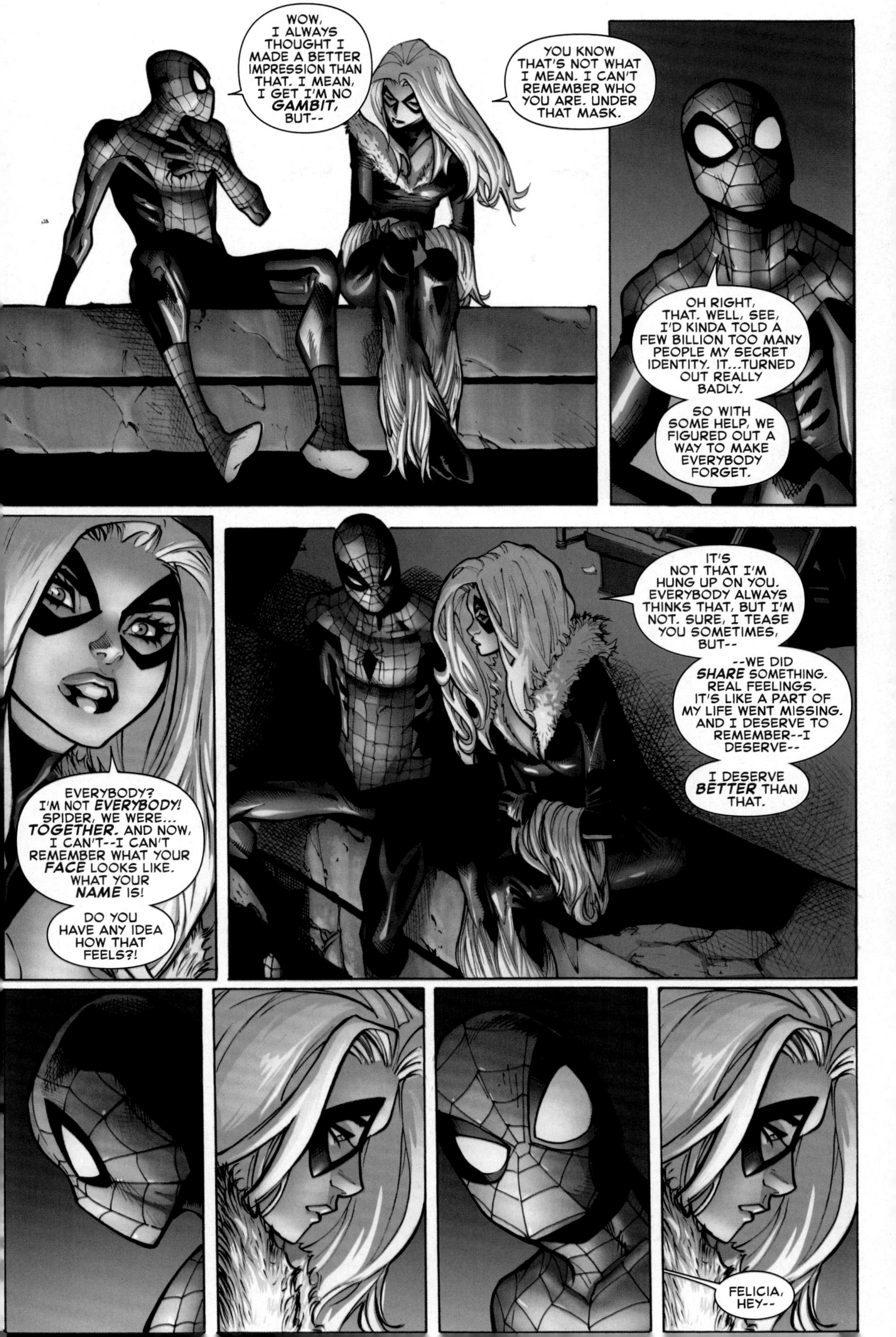

WOW, I ALWAYS THOUGHT I MADE A BETTER IMPRESSION THAN THAT. I MEAN, I GET I'M NO GAMBIT, BUT--
YOU KNOW THAT'S NOT WHAT I MEAN. I CAN'T REMEMBER WHO YOU ARE. UNDER THAT MASK.
OH RIGHT, THAT. WELL, SEE, I'D KINDA TOLD A FEW BILLION TOO MANY PEOPLE MY SECRET IDENTITY. IT...TURNED OUT REALLY BADLY.
SO WITH SOME HELP, WE FIGURED OUT A WAY TO MAKE EVERYBODY FORGET.
EVERYBODY? I'M NOT EVERYBODY! SPIDER, WE WERE... TOGETHER. AND NOW, I CAN'T--I CAN'T REMEMBER WHAT YOUR FACE LOOKS LIKE. WHAT YOUR NAME IS!
DO YOU HAVE ANY IDEA HOW THAT FEELS?!
IT'S NOT THAT I'M HUNG UP ON YOU. EVERYBODY ALWAYS THINKS THAT, BUT I'M NOT. SURE, I TEASE YOU SOMETIMES, BUT--
--WE DID SHARE SOMETHING. REAL FEELINGS. IT'S LIKE A PART OF MY LIFE WENT MISSING. AND I DESERVE TO REMEMBER--I DESERVE--
I DESERVE BETTER THAN THAT.
FELICIA, HEY--

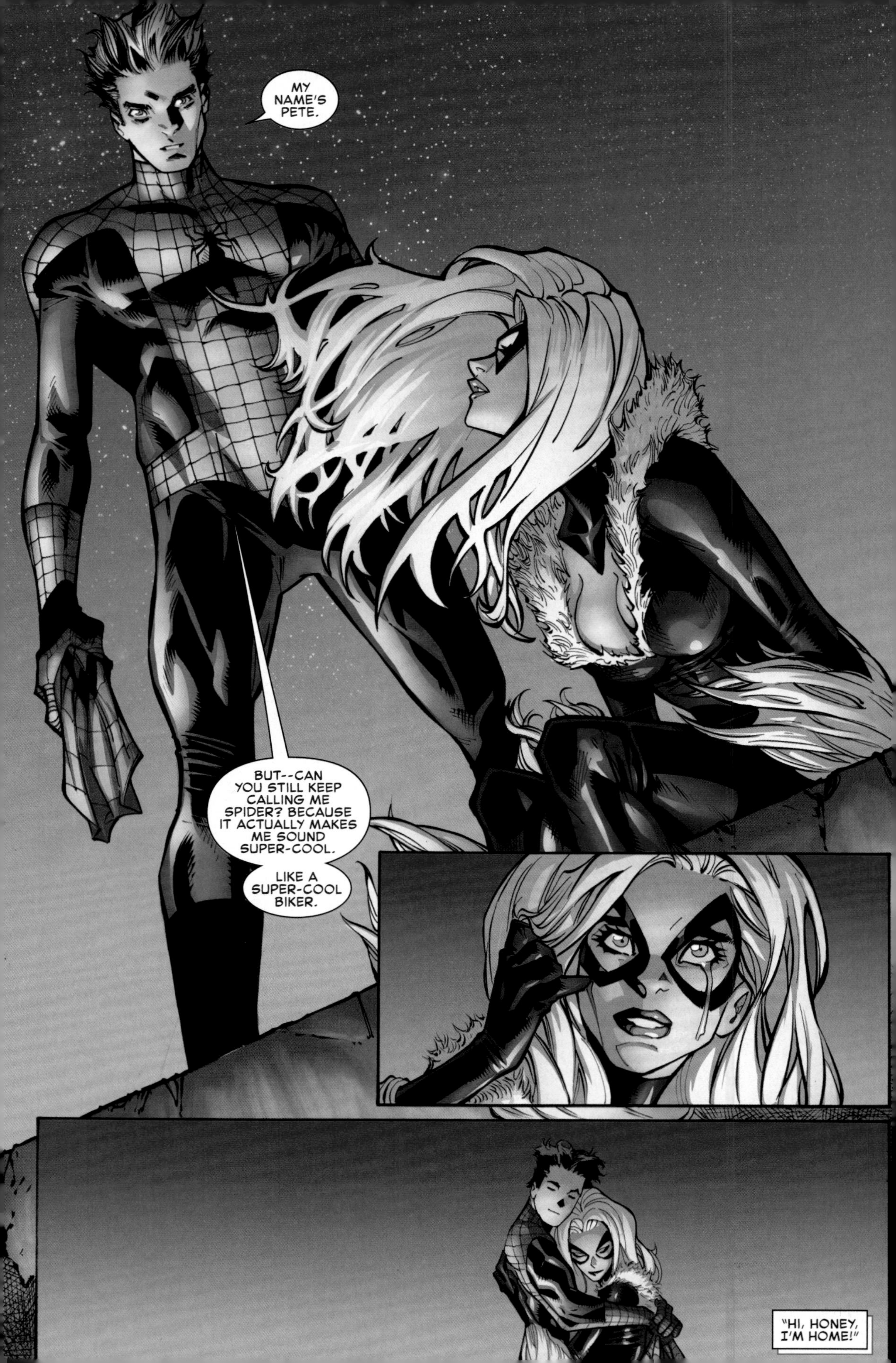
MY NAME'S PETE.
BUT--CAN YOU STILL KEEP CALLING ME SPIDER? BECAUSE IT ACTUALLY MAKES ME SOUND SUPER-COOL.
LIKE A SUPER-COOL BIKER.
"HI, HONEY, I'M HOME!"

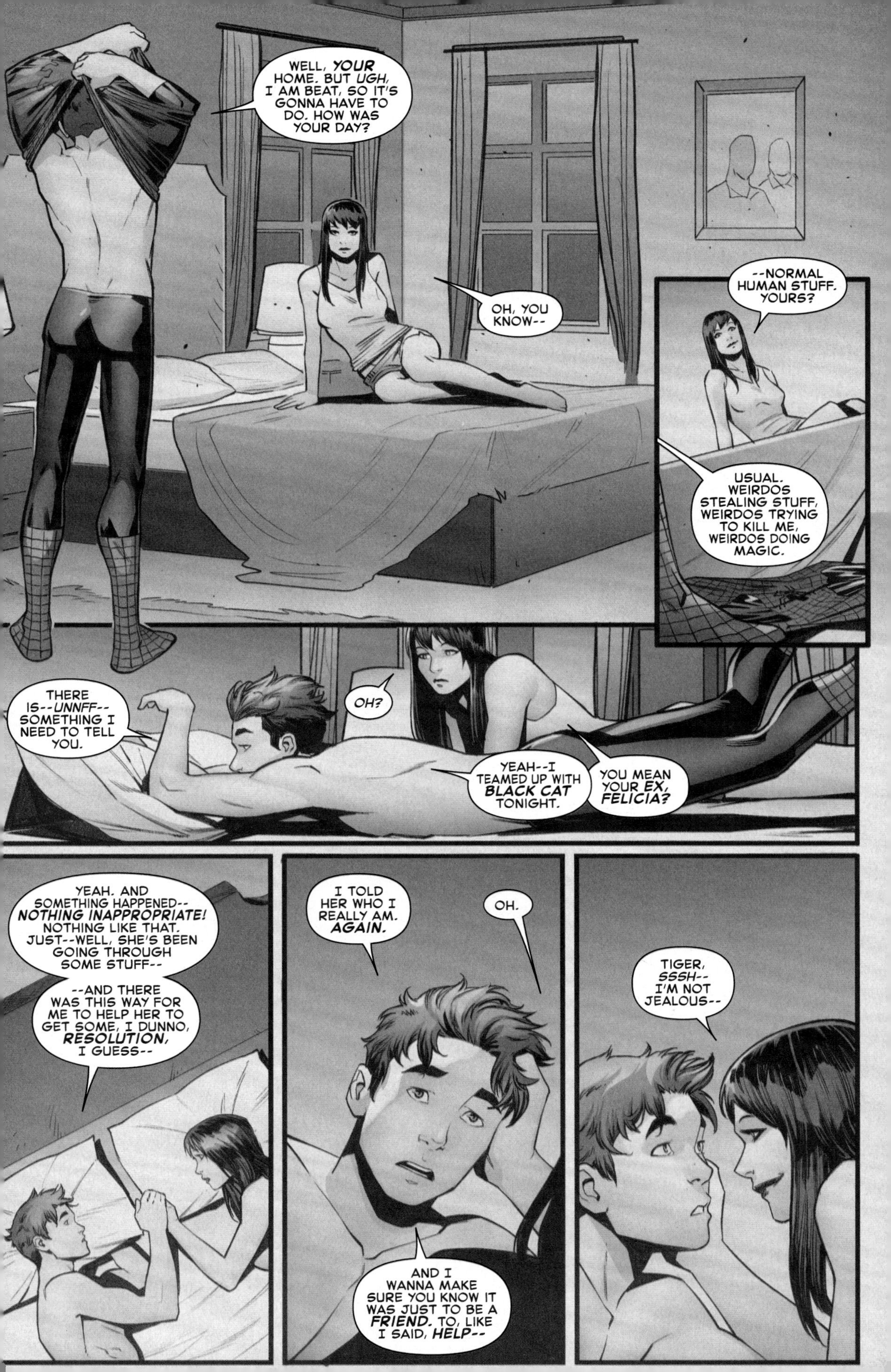

WELL, *YOUR* HOME. BUT *UGH*, I AM BEAT, SO IT'S GONNA HAVE TO DO. HOW WAS YOUR DAY?
OH, YOU KNOW--
--NORMAL HUMAN STUFF. YOURS?
USUAL. WEIRDOS STEALING STUFF, WEIRDOS TRYING TO KILL ME, WEIRDOS DOING MAGIC.
THERE IS--*UNNFF*--SOMETHING I NEED TO TELL YOU.
OH?
YEAH--I TEAMED UP WITH **BLACK CAT** TONIGHT.
YOU MEAN YOUR ***EX, FELICIA?***
YEAH. AND SOMETHING HAPPENED-- ***NOTHING INAPPROPRIATE!*** NOTHING LIKE THAT. JUST--WELL, SHE'S BEEN GOING THROUGH SOME STUFF--
--AND THERE WAS THIS WAY FOR ME TO HELP HER TO GET SOME, I DUNNO, ***RESOLUTION,*** I GUESS--
I TOLD HER WHO I REALLY AM. ***AGAIN.***
OH.
AND I WANNA MAKE SURE YOU KNOW IT WAS JUST TO BE A ***FRIEND.*** TO, LIKE I SAID, ***HELP--***
TIGER, *SSSH--* I'M NOT JEALOUS--

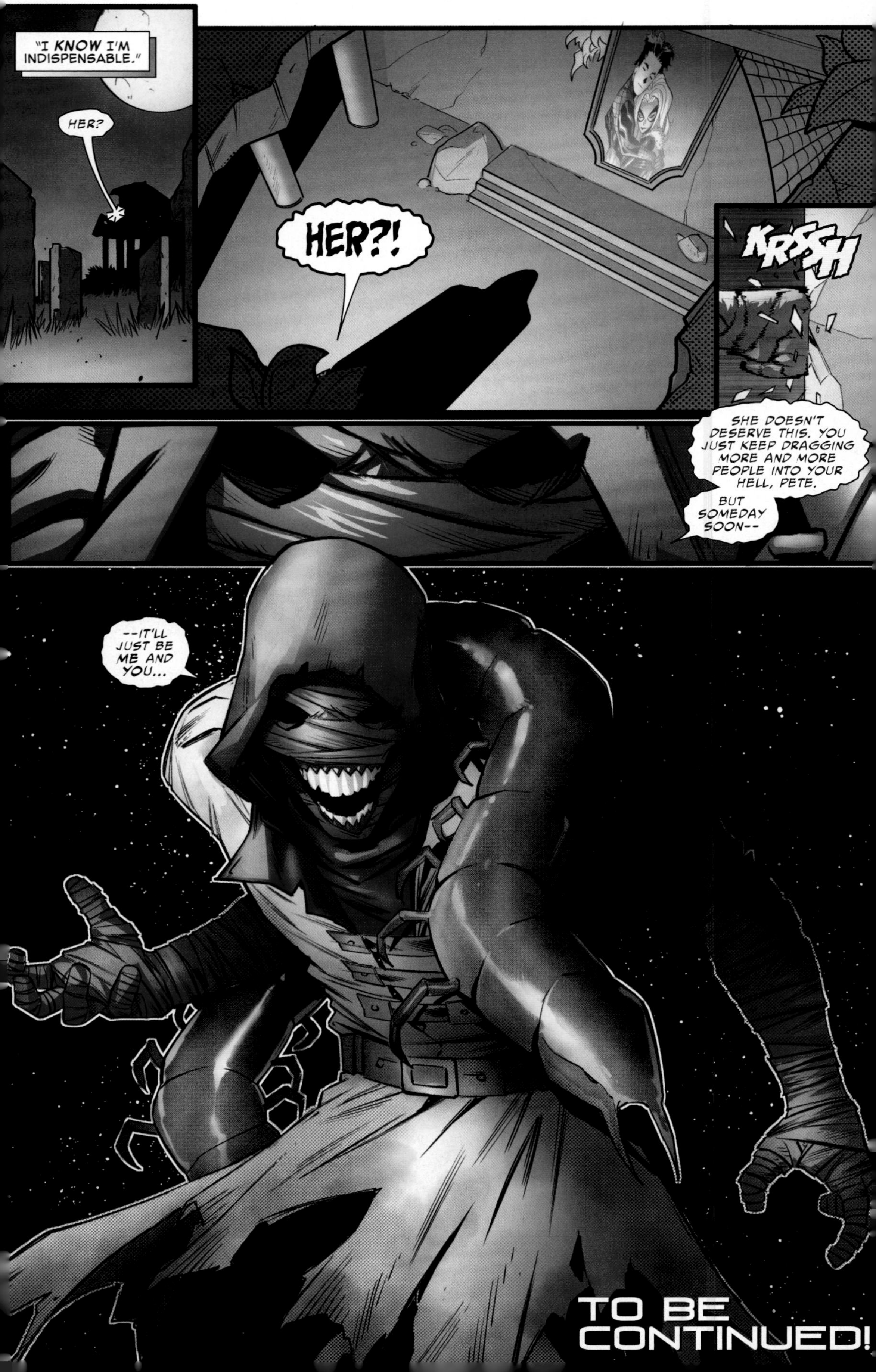
"I KNOW I'M INDISPENSABLE."
HER?
HER?!
KRSSH
SHE DOESN'T DESERVE THIS. YOU JUST KEEP DRAGGING MORE AND MORE PEOPLE INTO YOUR HELL, PETE.
BUT SOMEDAY SOON--
--IT'LL JUST BE ME AND YOU...
TO BE CONTINUED!

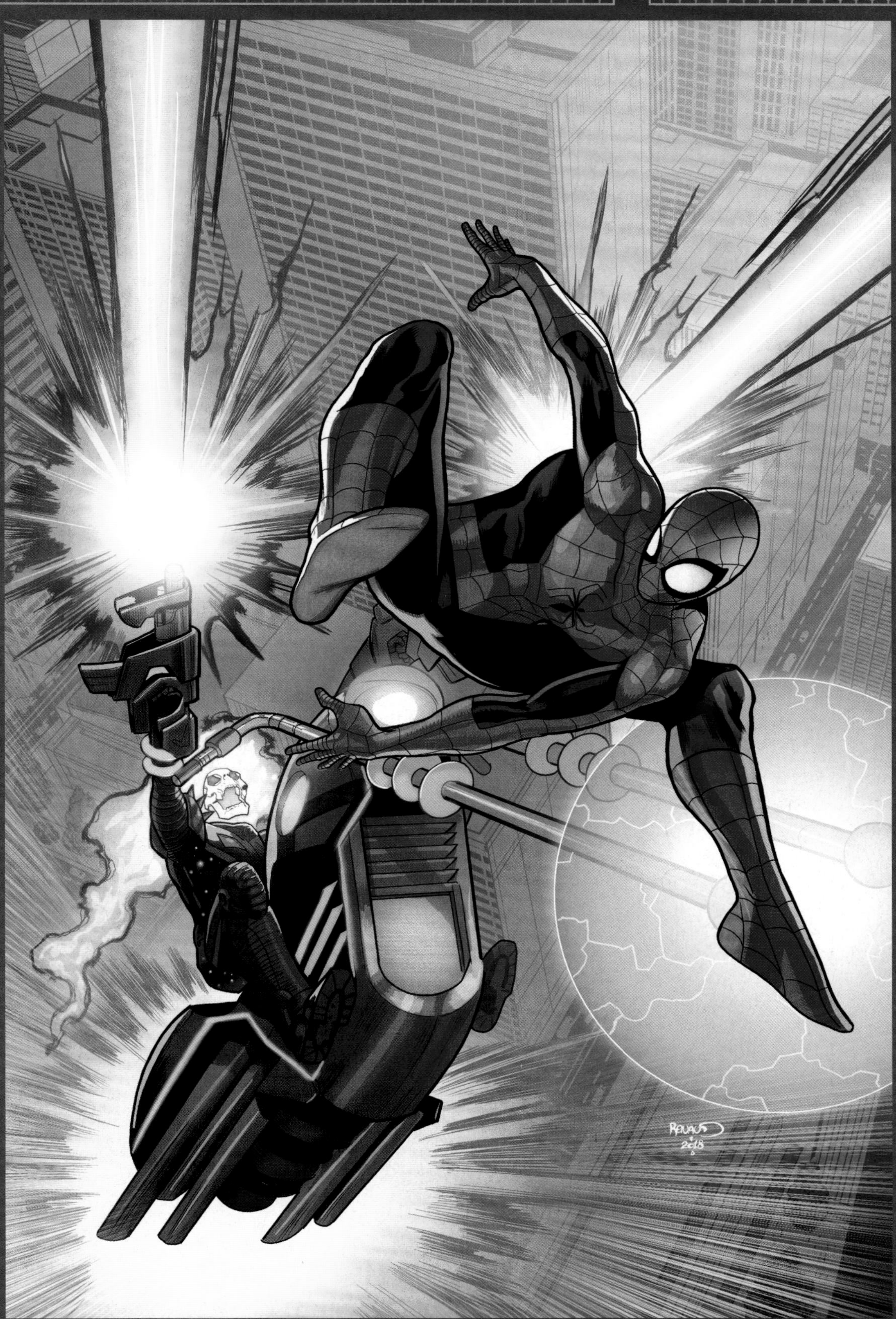
RENAUD
2018

#6 COSMIC GHOST RIDER VS. VARIANT BY PAUL RENAUD

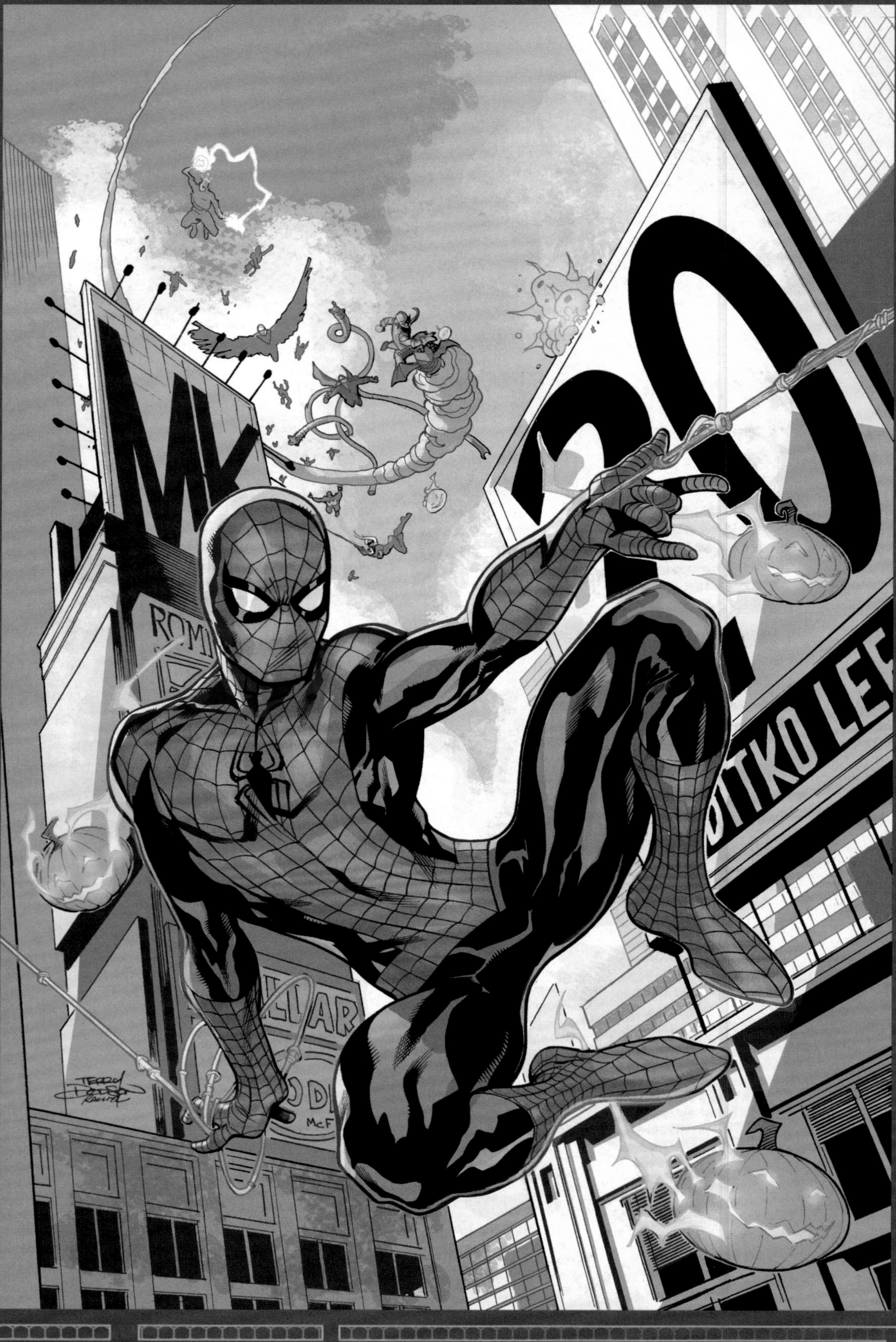
MK
20

#7 MARVEL KNIGHTS 20TH ANNIVERSARY VARIANT BY TERRY DODSON & RACHEL DODSON

#8 BLACK CAT VARIANT BY J.G. JONES & PAUL MOUNTS

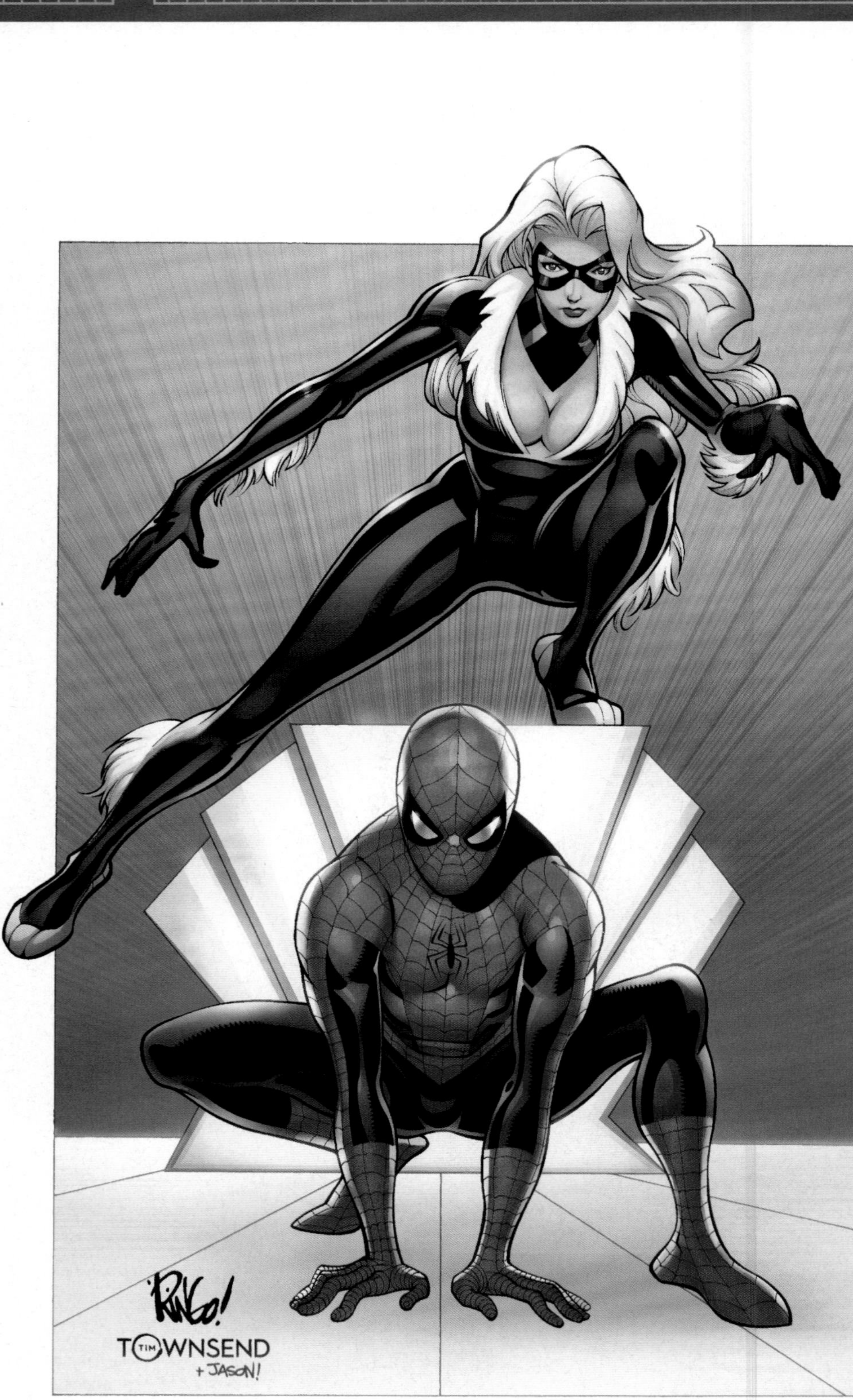
'RINGO!
TIM TOWNSEND
+ JASON!

#9 BLACK CAT VARIANT BY MIKE WIERINGO, TIM TOWNSEND & JASON KEITH

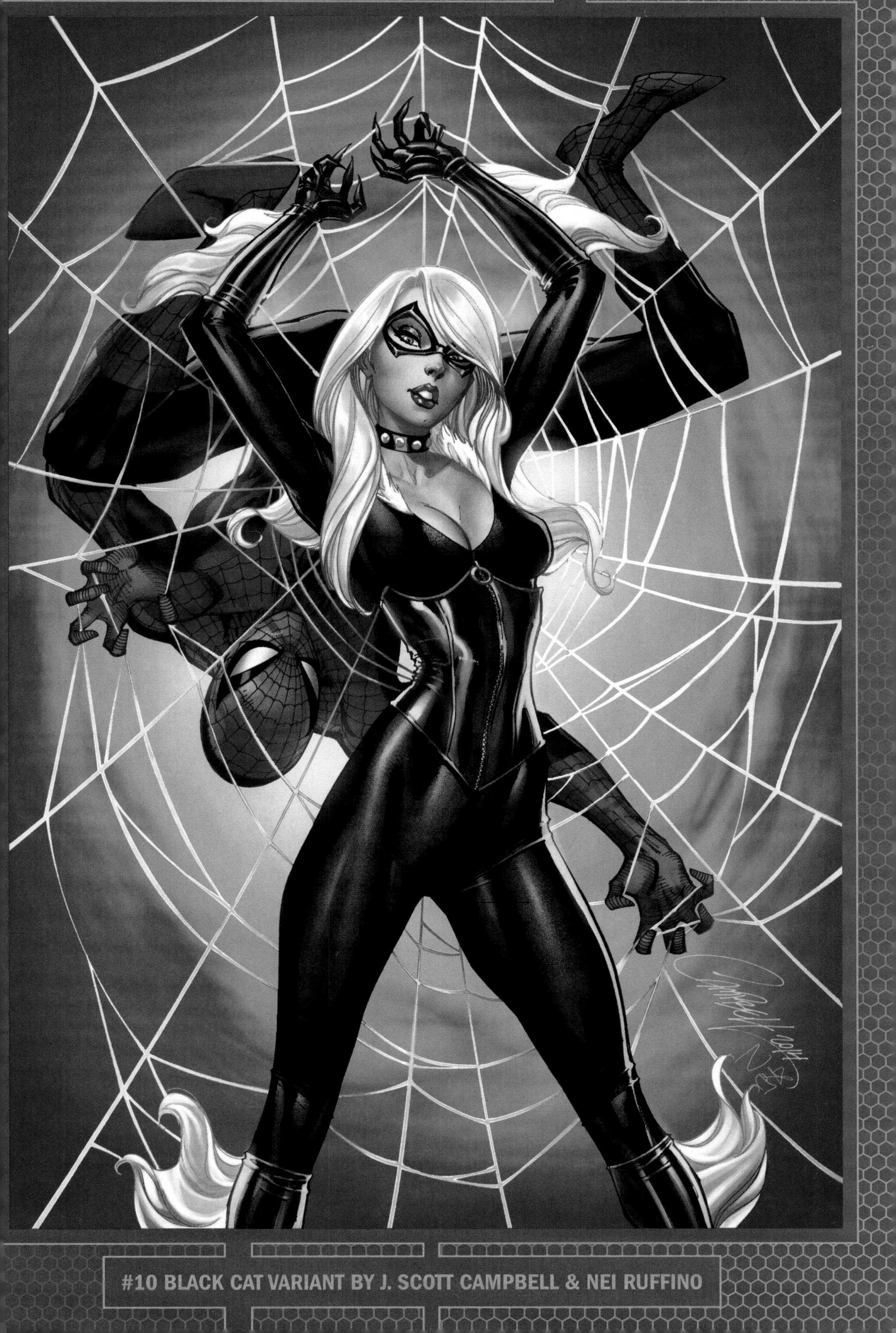

#10 BLACK CAT VARIANT BY J. SCOTT CAMPBELL & NEI RUFFINO

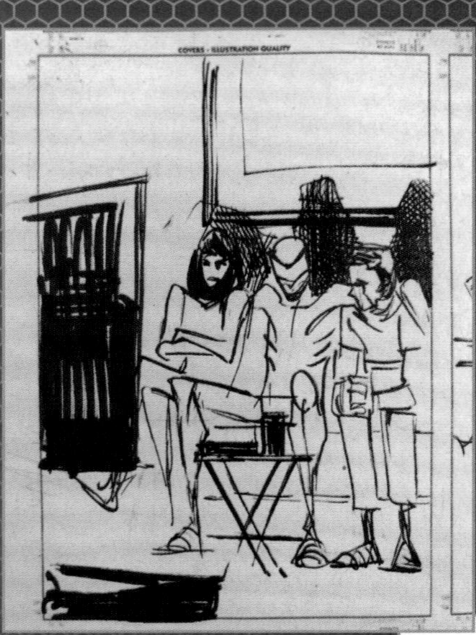

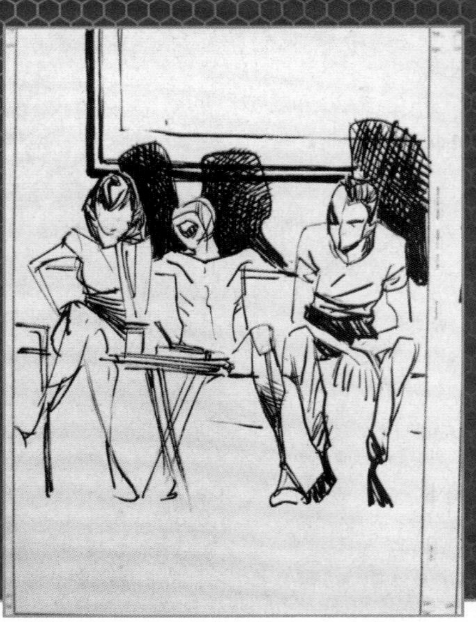

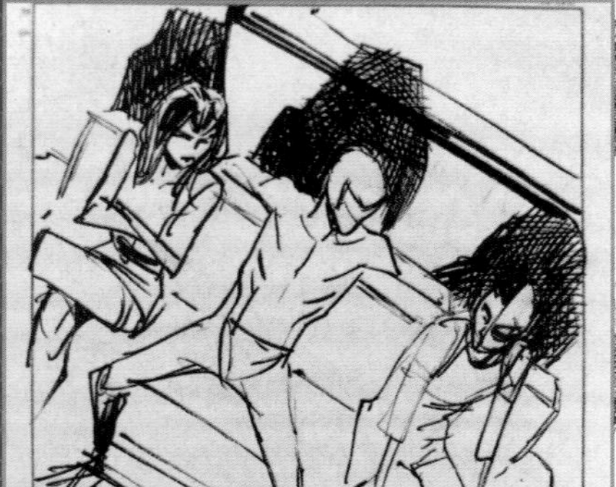

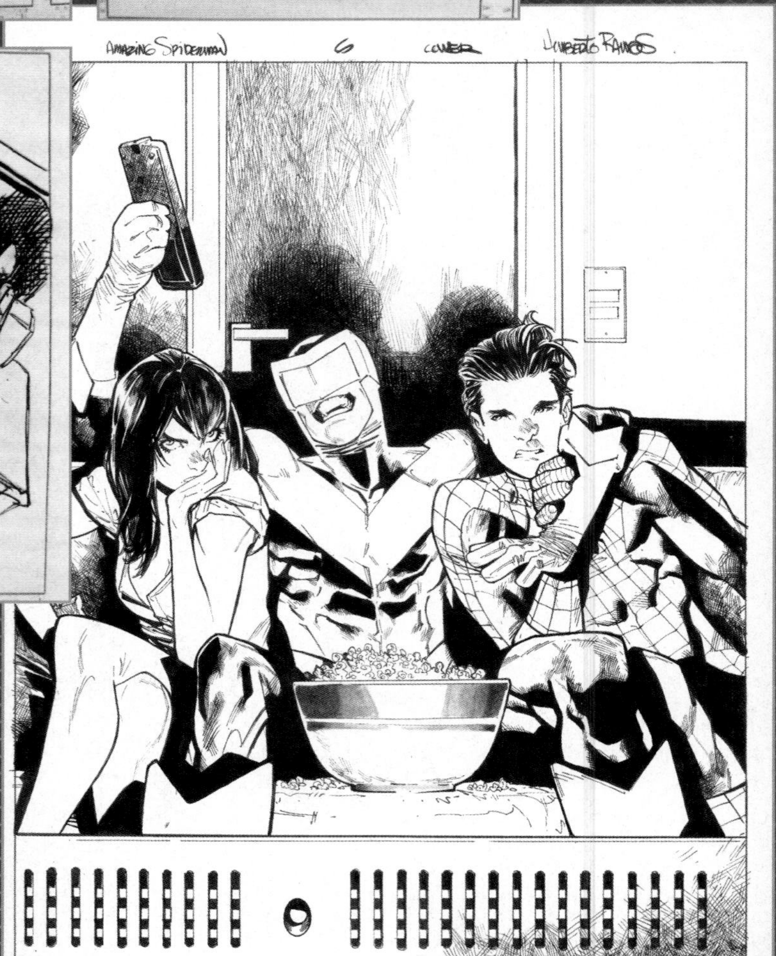
AMAZING SPIDERMAN 6 COVER HUMBERTO RAMOS

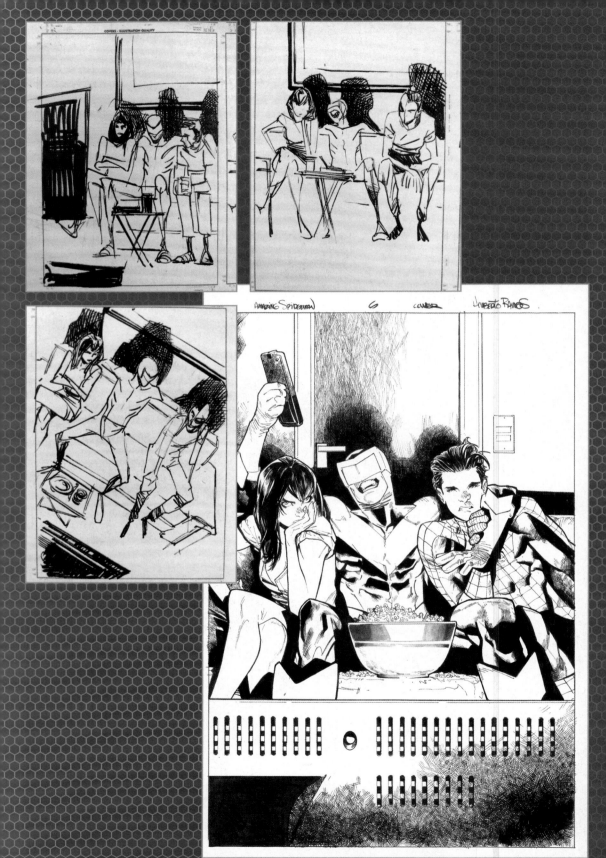

#6 COVER PROCESS BY HUMBERTO RAMOS

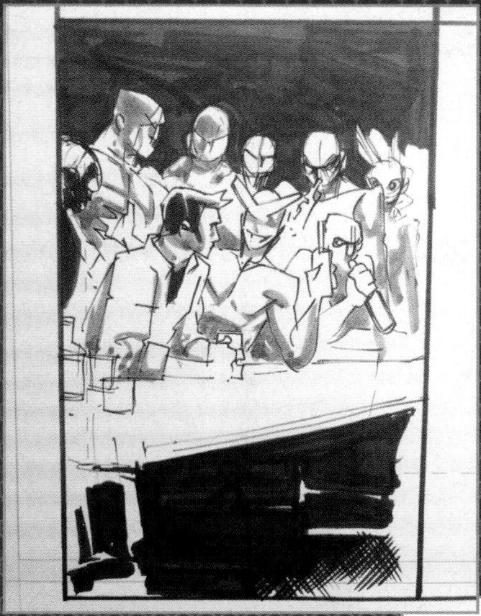
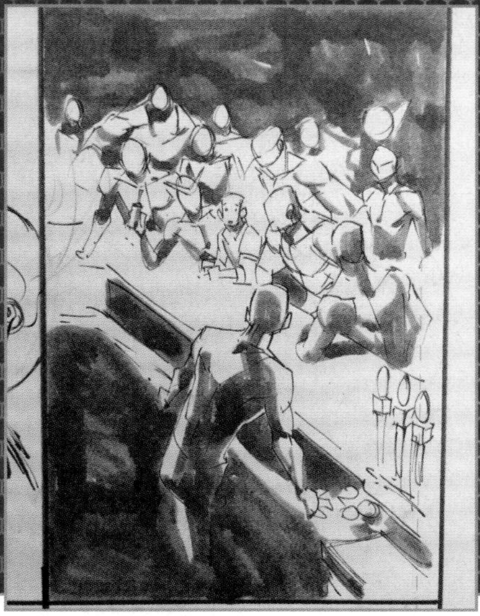
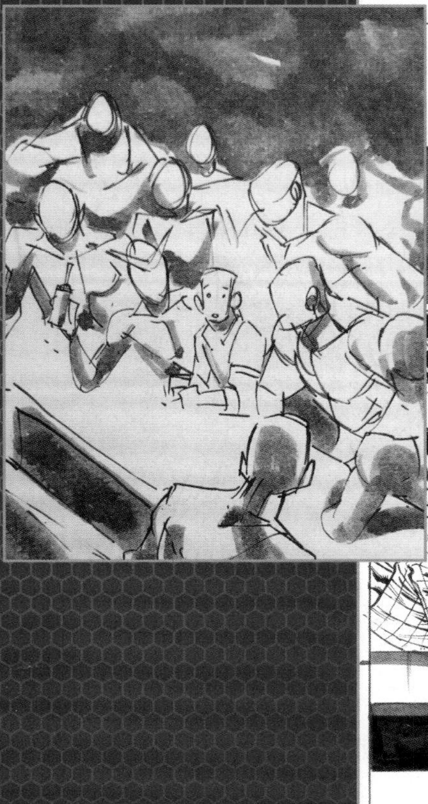
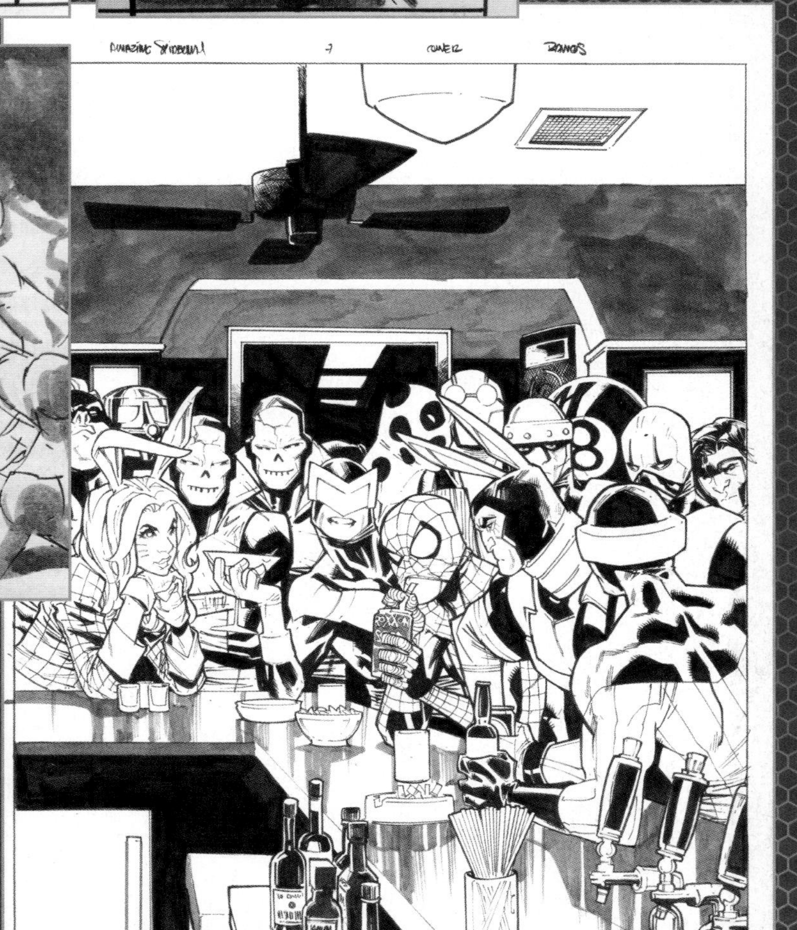

#7 COVER PROCESS BY HUMBERTO RAMOS

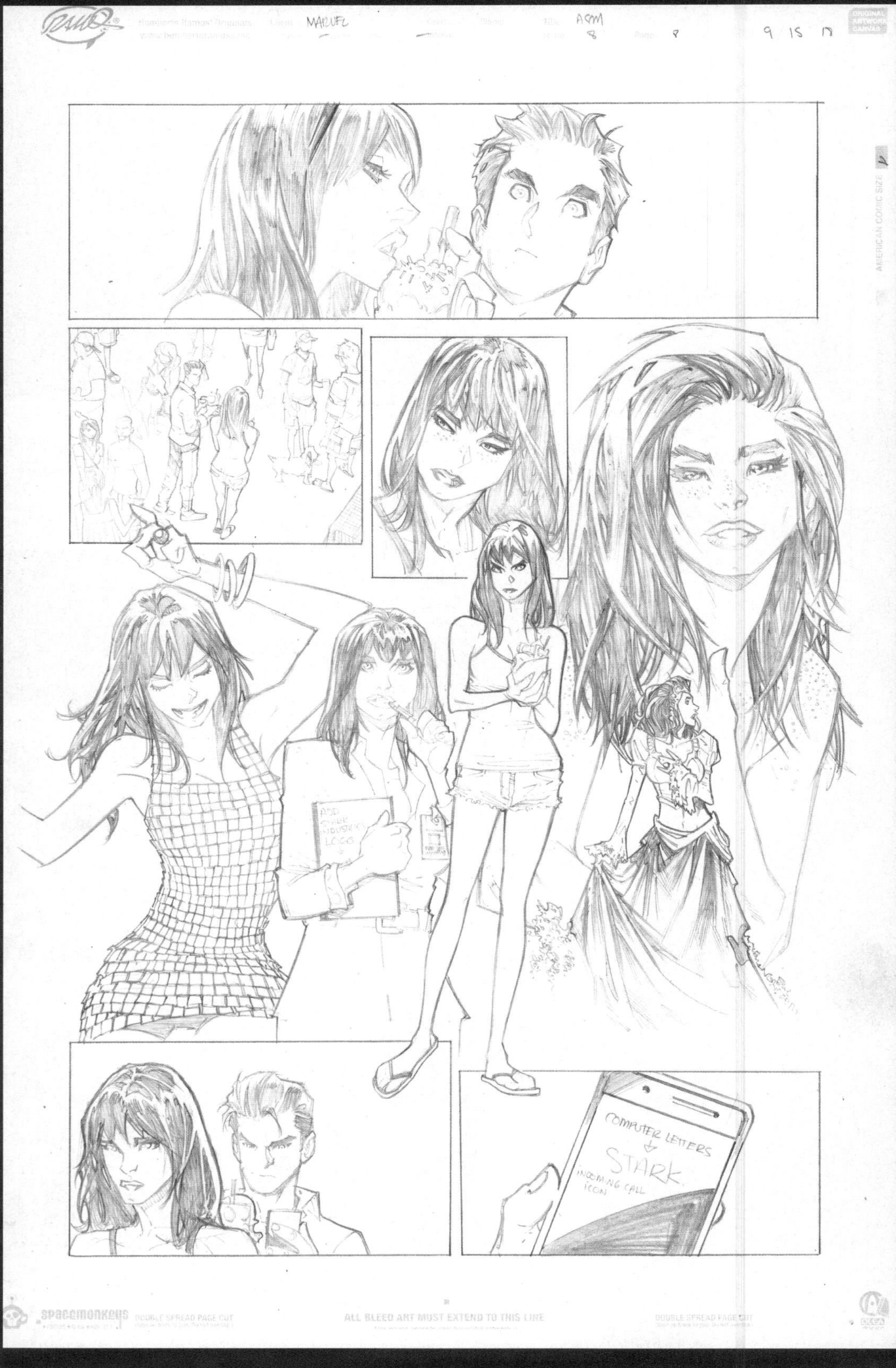
MARVEL
ASM
8
8
9 15 17
ADD STARK INDUSTRIES LOGO
COMPUTER LETTERS
STARK
INCOMING CALL ICON
ALL BLEED ART MUST EXTEND TO THIS LINE

#8, PAGE 8 PENCILS BY HUMBERTO RAMOS

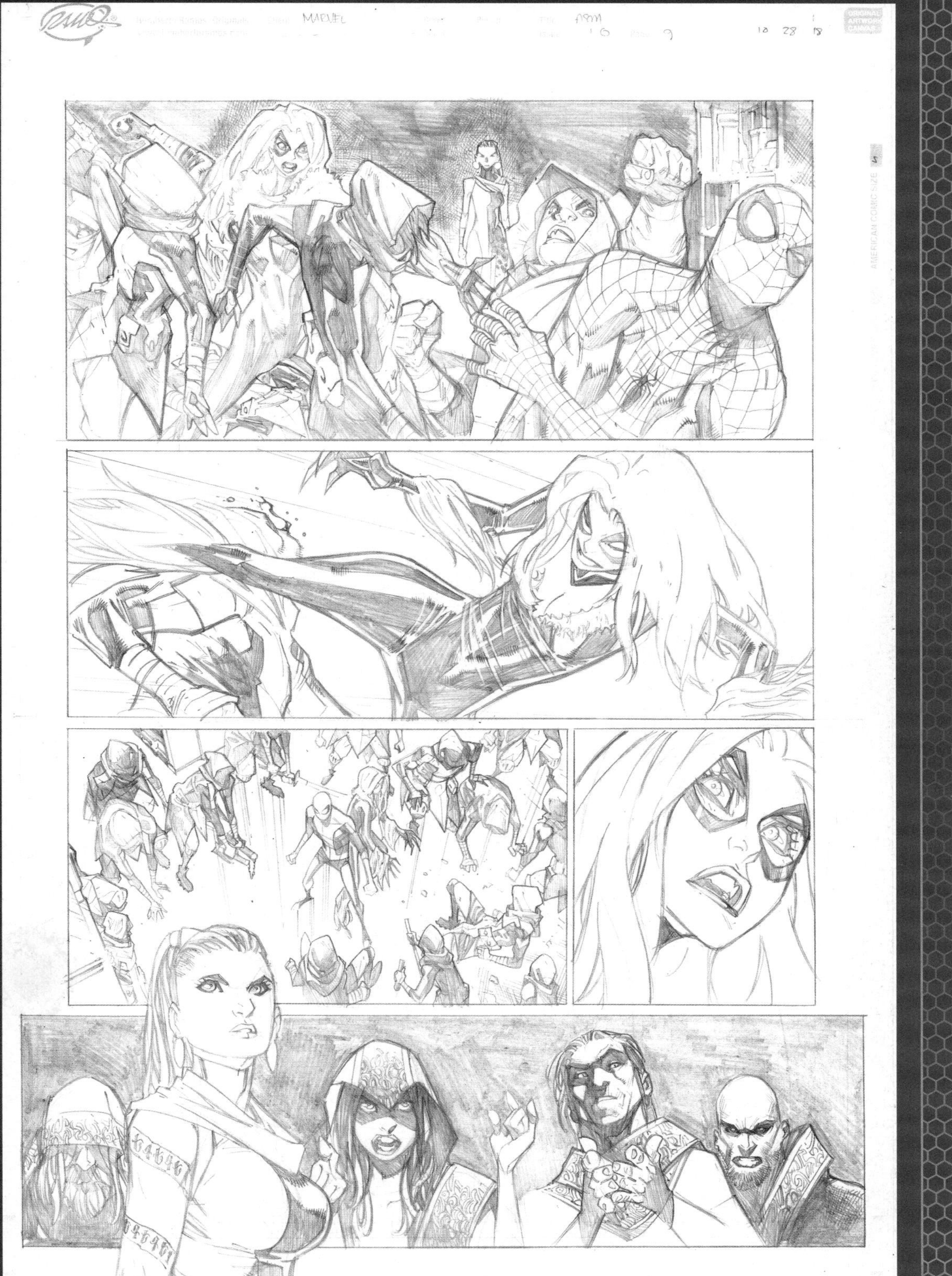
MARVEL
ASM
10
9
10 28 18
DOUBLE SPREAD PAGE CUT
ALL BLEED ART MUST EXTEND TO THIS LINE
DOUBLE SPREAD PAGE CUT

#10, PAGE 9 PENCILS BY HUMBERTO RAMOS

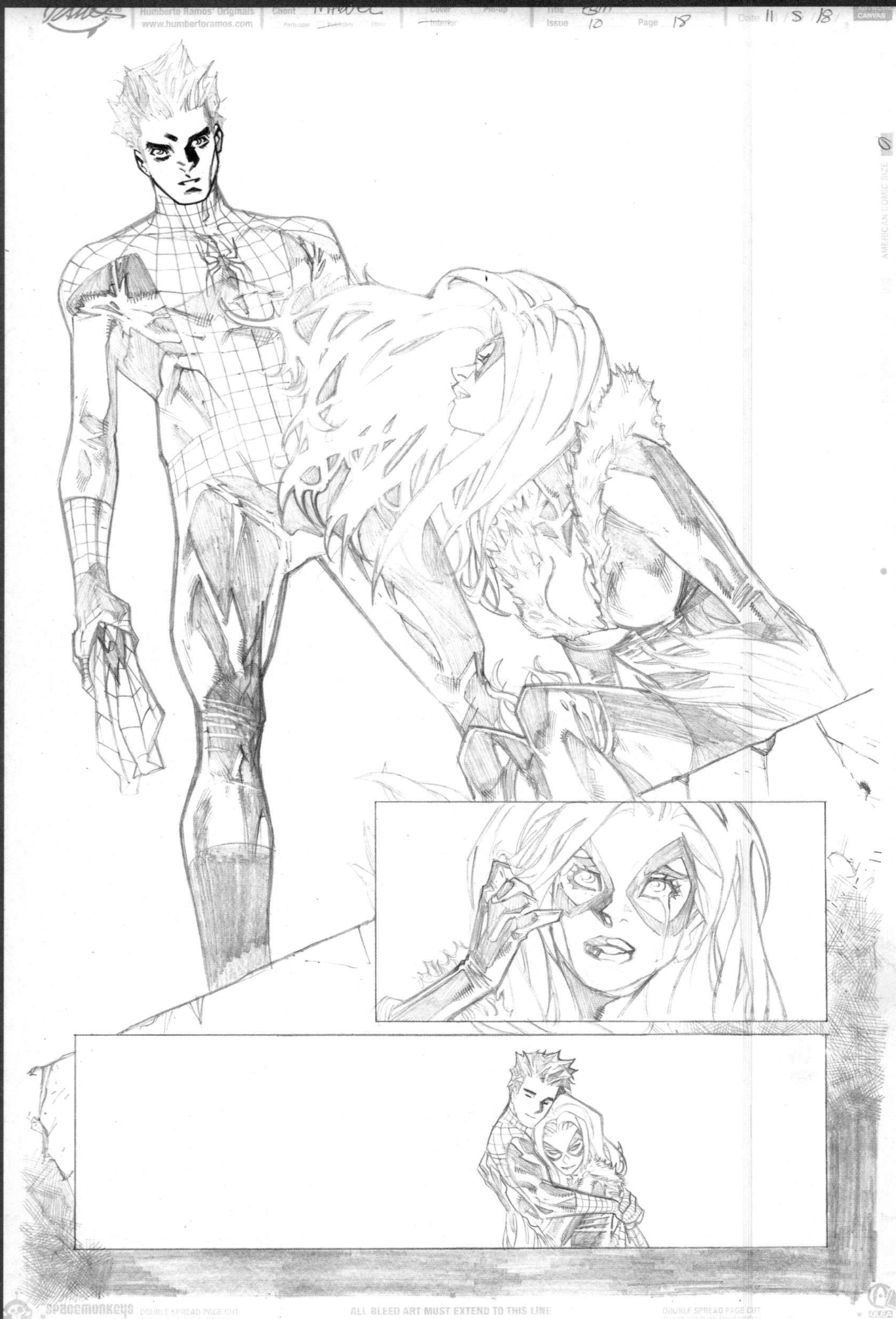
Humberto Ramos' Originals
www.humbertoramos.com
ALL BLEED ART MUST EXTEND TO THIS LINE
DOUBLE SPREAD PAGE CUT
DOUBLE SPREAD PAGE CUT

#10, PAGE 19 PENCILS BY HUMBERTO RAMOS